D1569143

IN THE
LION'S SHADOW

IN THE LION'S SHADOW

THE IRANIAN SCHINDLER AND HIS HOMELAND IN THE SECOND WORLD WAR

FARIBORZ MOKHTARI

The History Press

For my Father and all men of honour

First published 2011

The History Press
The Mill, Brimscombe Port
Stroud, Gloucestershire, GL5 2QG
www.thehistorypress.co.uk

© Fariborz Mokhtari, 2011

The right of Fariborz Mokhtari to be identified as the Author
of this work has been asserted in accordance with the
Copyrights, Designs and Patents Act 1988.

British Library Cataloguing in Publication Data.
A catalogue record for this book is available from the British Library.

ISBN 978 0 7524 6370 4

Typesetting and origination by The History Press
Printed in Great Britain
Manufacturing managed by Jellyfish Print Solutions Ltd

CONTENTS

PROLOGUE

This is a true story, a story of compassion and human connection. Arthur Schopenhauer (1788–1860) believed that in moments of crisis, humans had the capacity to share others' pains to the point of risking their own lives, for they would spontaneously realise the unity of all life. He reasoned in the nineteenth century – as the Iranian poet Sa'di (1194–1292) had done in the thirteenth – that all humans were united in life as if parts of a single living organism.[1] This recognition is what triggers selfless and instinctive acts of compassion. This story validates Schopenhauer's conclusion, best considered within its own historical context. The narrative centres on the lives of a number of Jewish families trapped in German-occupied Paris, saved by an Iranian Muslim diplomat. That diplomat – Abdol Hossein Sardari – represented a nation, a culture and a government. This is therefore a story within a story, for it also reflects a national sentiment.

Iran, one may argue, has certain uncommon characteristics. Its national history goes back 3000 years or more, and therefore its only rival in that respect may be China, with which Iran once shared borders. Iranians may have been the first to build a vast federated state with governing standards of justice, tolerance, liberty and cooperation. To ignore the culture is to miss much of the story, as if to watch an opera from afar on a stage barren of scenery amidst a chattering crowd.[2]

Robert Satloff set off on a journey in search of an Arab Wallenberg or Schindler and wrote about it in his book *Among The Righteous* in 2006.[3] Iranians, as they would sternly point out, are not Arab, but are mostly Muslim. They also have a culture of tolerance irrespective of the Islamic Republic's pretensions, exemplified by Cyrus the Great and manifested in his Charter of Human Rights.

I had heard stories of Iranians assisting Jewish refugees entering Iran from Iraq, Afghanistan and the former Soviet Union. I had heard persistent rumours of Iranian diplomats having helped Jews abroad for decades. When I saw a reference to one such diplomat stationed in France during the Second World War in a book by Professor Abbas Milani, I wanted to know more.[4] After contacting the publisher and the author, I was referred to three sources: Dr Fereydoun Hoveyda (former Iranian ambassador to the United Nations), Mr Ahmad Tavakoli (retired diplomat and former first secretary at Iran's consulate in Milan, Italy), and Dr Ahmad Mahrad (Professor, University of Hanover, Germany). Initial contacts resulted in my determination to dig deeper. To substantiate the testimonials, I searched through captured German documents at the National Archives in Washington DC. Although decades had passed, I had to find Second World War survivors to prove to myself that the story was indeed true. My appeals for information, thanks to the internet, spread worldwide. As fate would have it, the vital contact was closer than I had anticipated. Speaking to an old high school friend and his wife about my search, she suggested contacting a fellow high school mate of ours whose wife's family may have had relatives in France during the war. That conversation – much to my delight and surprise – resulted in contacts that made meeting and interviewing several survivors possible.[5] Other interviews followed and more survivors were found in Venezuela, France and Israel. Similarly, another casual conversation with an old friend from my conscription-basic-training days resulted in locating another survivor, a relative of his living in Paris.[6] Having established the story's essence, learning about the diplomat and his motivation became my next objective. Fortunately, several members of his family, particularly Ambassador Farhad Sepahbody, Mrs Angela Sepahbody, Mrs Firouzeh Ensha, and the late Ambassador Fereydoun Hoveyda were extremely helpful. I am grateful to Mr Manuchehr Omidvar and Ms Behnaaz Dilmanian of the weekly *Payam* magazine, Mr George Haroonian of the Council of the Iranian American Jewish Organization, Rabbi Mr David Shofet of the Nessah Educational & Cultural Center in Los Angeles, Dr Houman Sarshar of the Center for Iranian Jewish Oral History in New York, the Petrossian family, and many others who generously called or responded to my inquiries with their information. My gratitude to Mrs Eliane Senehi Cohanim, Mr Nasser Cohanim and the late Mr Ibrahim Morady is more than could be expressed in words. This story, I am convinced, had to be told. I hope that the readers, particularly young Iranians, find it as inspiring as I have. I hope that they renew their pride in their heritage of liberty and tolerance, and rededicate themselves to preserving it, for it is indeed a most precious national inheritance.

Iran has fallen upon hard times more than once, but has managed to rise up time and again. What has assured the nation's survival has been its profound cultural consciousness, which is expressed in its literature and the frequently

recited poetry. That is the essence of Iranian identity and the fountainhead of
Iranian national pride. *New York Times* Reporter Elaine Sciolino has observed,

> As I have encountered Iran over the years, I have found two important
> components of the Iranian soul: love of poetry and love of country. No other
> people I know takes its poetry so seriously. And few countries have such a
> deep-rooted and long-lasting sense of national pride. Even the revolution and
> the creation of the Islamic Republic could not eradicate that unique sense of
> Persianness that goes hand in hand with the poets who extolled the virtues of
> beauty, love, and bravery.[7]

The current Islamic Republic regime in Iran is over 30 years old; but it does
not reflect Iran's culture in its entirety. Nor do the Republic's policies represent
the nation's collective sentiments. Undeniably, the regime has survived for a
few decades, but that tenure, even if ten times as long, would be no more than
a passing moment if viewed in the Iranian historical context. The Iranian
contemporary philosopher Abdolkarim Soroush, once the darling of Iran's
revolutionaries, is reported to have declared that Islam had sunk such deep
roots in Iran that 'only an Islamic revolution could uproot it.'[8] The Islamic
Republic may very well see to it that the philosopher's prediction comes
through – and fast. Three decades after a theocratic regime rode the crest of a
revolutionary wave to establish the Islamic Republic, the number of Iranians
regularly performing the Muslims' mandatory daily prayers has significantly
declined.[9] The outcome of the 2009 presidential election suggested a similar
simmering crisis of political legitimacy and widespread disenchantment. A
survey commissioned by the Islamic Republic in October 2002 had already
revealed a public opinion at variance with the regime's foreign policy as 70 per
cent of the respondents favoured renewing relations with the United States,
while 40 per cent considered US policy towards Iran defensible. The regime,
taken aback, lashed out; 70 per cent approval for re-establishing normal
relations with 'the Great Satan' was just beyond the pale. The polling directors
– amongst them Abbas Abdi with the credential of being one of the hostage-
takers at the US Embassy in Tehran in 1979 – were promptly arrested.[10]
The lives of Iranian revolutionaries reflect the tragedy they brought upon
the nation in the name of virtue and national independence. Dr Soroush, a
bespectacled, balding, middle aged man with a stern face, greying facial hair
– and in keeping with Iran's post-revolutionary elites' fashion – sartorially
rumpled, spoke unhappily on 'Morality, Politics and the Principles of Post-
Religious Government' at George Washington University in Washington DC
on 15 November 2009. A disciple of Ayatollah Ruhollah Khomaini whilst
still a high school student in the 1960s, he emerged on the scene to purge the
faculty, curricula and personnel of Iran's universities to mould them to serve
the Islamic Republic. As his intellectual journey continued towards maturity,

he gradually advocated a democratic government in which religion and liberty would have a complementary coexistence. Once a committed devotee of Khomaini's theocracy and his *velayat-e faqih*, he had at last discovered that 'there was nothing divine about the clerical monopoly of power.'[11] He was dismissed from his university teaching position in 1995 for having come to the conclusion that the Islamic dictatorship he had helped to build had to be replaced with nothing less than an 'Islamic democracy'. He once told the American journalist Sciolino, 'If you do not preach the official interpretation of Islam, you will not be allowed to go to a mosque to preach, you will not be allowed to teach at a high school or a university. This official interpretation is an achievement – a negative achievement – of the revolution.' Many former firebrand revolutionaries are openly remorseful when engaged in private conversation. Mehdi Bazargan, the revolution's first prime minister, confessed 'We should have known better. The evidence was there all along.' [12] A former university professor from a clerical family close to the Khomaini household, a devout Muslim and former anti-Shah revolutionary, confided to the author that he had 'visited the late king's tomb in Cairo to seek forgiveness'.

I must thank friends and colleagues Professors William J. Olson and Lawrence Chalmer at the National Defense University and Professor Alfred C. Mierzejewski at the University of North Texas for reading and commenting on the manuscript. I am particularly indebted to Dr Mierzejewski for his assistance in my search of German documents and help in their translation. I am grateful to Mr Sean McBride, a capable doctoral student, who volunteered to assist me in the search for and translation of documents at the US National Archives, and Mr Joshua Yaphe who also helped with sources. I am much obliged to my editor Mr Shaun Barrington of The History Press, my literary agent Ms Leslie Gardner of Artellus Ltd and to my good friend of four decades Mr Farhud Batmanglich, President of Xanthus Design in Washington DC, for help in making this book possible.

It must be said that I alone am responsible for any errors. I humbly offer my apologies for any shortcomings and welcome additional information from readers with interest and appreciation.

INTRODUCTION

THE DIPLOMAT IN THE LION'S SHADOW[13]

Anoshiravan Sepahbody, Iran's seasoned Minister Plenipotentiary in France, finally left Paris for the little spa-town of Vichy on Saturday 26 October 1940.[14] German troops had already occupied Paris on 14 June and the new French Chief of State, the aged Marshal Henri Philippe Benoni Omer Joseph Petain, a hero of the First World War, had sought and received an armistice agreement with the occupiers.[15] Not allowed to form his government in Paris, Petain had relocated to Vichy in the unoccupied zone. Overwhelmed by the unexpected German victory an estimated seven million French civilians had also fled south in panic, sullen and demoralised. The German victory had come so quickly that many found it hard to comprehend.[16] Yet France had decisively lost the war and embassies and legations accredited to the French government had been compelled to relocate from Paris to the provisional capital in central France. The German 'Occupation Security Administration' had granted Sepahbody, his wife, their teenage son, their Swiss nurse-au pair and the legation's Spanish chauffeur, a single official safe passage on 23 October. The safe passage document – the *Ausweis* – had been stamped valid until the end of the month, giving them less than a week to relocate. Despite the official travel permit, the trip proved difficult. Vichy is only 350 kilometres (220 miles) south of Paris, but getting there at the time was not an easy task. Security check points on the way frequently halted all civilian traffic and troop movements caused long delays. The road was crowded too, although a far cry from the panic-stricken days of June when the German Army had punched through France's defences towards Paris with unprecedented speed. Complete demoralisation had triggered a mass exodus south that had clogged roads for days. The endless stream of people fleeing on foot was gone by November but automobiles, slow moving trucks and horse drawn carts were still on the road swerving in all directions to avoid potholes and the occasional bomb crater.

As the Sepahbodys moved further away from Paris the number of vehicles on the road decreased and their official embassy automobile with fluttering little flags mounted on its fenders could at last pick up speed. Cruising on an empty stretch of road some 50 miles north of Maulins, the passengers finally relaxed. Maulins was a city just north of the demarcation line that separated the occupied and the unoccupied zones. Seeing a road sign pointing to the city raised the anticipation of reaching their destination in a couple of hours, and when the roar of an approaching aircraft suddenly filled the air the passengers had no reason for concern. The sound became louder as two Luftwaffe fighter planes appeared behind the vehicle. The fighters suddenly swept low, buzzed the car and roared upwards. The envoy dismissed the move as a possible security routine to comfort others riding in the car. Alarm set in only when the planes that had already soared high in the sky turned around. Alarm turned to panic as the planes closed in fast and dived towards the car with blazing machine guns. The realisation that they had been targeted was sudden and terrifying. The German aviators, whether by mistake or for their own amusement, had chosen to strafe the Iranian legation's massive American-made black Buick. The quick thinking Spanish driver – who had witnessed the recent civil war in his own country – managed to swerve the car sharply away from the fighters' line of fire at the very last moment, saving it from the four streams of fire.

Although the occupants were lucky to have dodged the bullets, the planes had run their car off the road. It came to a dead stop after several violent jolts as the fighters soared away to disappear into the autumn sky. Relieved that the planes had departed and that no one had been hurt, the Sepahbodys, their au-pair and the driver gradually unfolded themselves out of the vehicle. They instinctively thanked God for having survived the incident, but were overcome with indignation. Having regained their composure, they set out to resume their journey, for they had no other alternative. The car was stuck in a ditch stubbornly defying all exertions to dislodge it. The back wheels kicked up clouds of dust, spinning frantically without effect. It took hours to find enough help from the surrounding farms to extract the car, then push it back onto the road. Once on the road again, they all realised the extent of damage to the front axle. The once grand automobile had been reduced to a sorry looking heap.

The car, with its droopy front end and wobbly wheels, squeaked as it slowly limped forward. Everyone felt some relief upon arriving in Moulins, hoping to have the car repaired quickly. They were soon disappointed for they were told that the repairs would take several days at least. Reluctantly they sought lodging, but not a single vacant hotel room could be found in the entire town. The German Army, it turned out, had sequestered every available room in Maulins for its officers. The sun had already set when Sepahbody, frustrated, tired and angry, lodged a protest at the German Army headquarters in Moulins. He expressed outrage over the aerial attack in violation of diplomatic norms and the compounded inconveniences it had caused his family and himself. His diplomatic status, Iran's neutrality in the war and its good relations with Germany, prompted an immediate response. Iran's Minister Plenipotentiary and his entourage were assigned suitable lodging at a hotel reserved for officers and a message from the commandant expressed regret for the Luftwaffe's mistake.

The family, upset and tired, finally settled in at the hotel for the evening. They had already covered nearly 80 per cent of the journey to Vichy, yet remained stuck in the occupied zone. Repairing the car would take a minimum of three days.[17] The next morning as Minister Sepahbody and his family entered the dining hall for breakfast, the Swiss au-pair was the first to notice a derogatory caricature on their reserved table. The drawing depicted a grotesque nose with the caption 'No Longer a Place for Jews Here.' She gasped in disbelief and protested at the top of her voice in German. The intended insult was an additional affront to the envoy of a friendly nation that German warplanes had assaulted the previous day and nearly killed. Sepahbody, the consummate diplomat, expressed his dismay, addressing the commanding general who happened to be at his own table in the room. The General walked to the envoy's table, politely clicked his heels, apologised, then turned to face the officers present in the dining hall. He sternly demanded to know who had been responsible 'for the stupidity'. After a moment's hesitation a young officer stood up ramrod straight. The young junior officer confessed he had not known the gentleman had been an Iranian diplomat. He had assumed erroneously, he said, that he had been a Jew. The General called the junior officer to step forward, slapped him once, gave him a tongue-lashing and ordered him to apologise to the Iranian Minister.[18] He then addressed the officers in the dining hall. He made it clear that he would not tolerate such an embarrassment from anyone under his command. He turned to Sepahbody once more, apologised and clicked his heels smartly before retiring to his own table. He was red-faced, irritated and clearly embarrassed.

France had been politically polarised before the war. Her defeat facilitated an authoritarian regime headed by the conservative Marshal Petain who embarked upon a delicate balancing policy of collaboration. His aim was to transform France through a national revolution, but also preserve her sovereignty and autonomy despite the overwhelming power of Germany. He resisted pressure to enter the war on Germany's side even after the British killed 1300 French sailors when they sank the French fleet in the Algerian port of Mers-el-Kebir in July 1940, to prevent it being used by Germany. Petain would not be persuaded. He clearly disappointed Hitler at their meeting in October as he refused to join the war effort. Petain was extremely popular at first, judging by the number of streets and squares named for him in towns and villages throughout France, and the torrent of gifts that arrived daily at Hotel du Parc, his headquarters in Vichy. Collaboration did not mean trust. Each side orchestrated an extensive spy network against the other. Vichy counter-intelligence proved itself a match for the Germans'. The Vichy arrested some 2000 German agents and executed several dozen in two years. Yet Petain's popularity dwindled in 1941 and he was soon accused of having sold out to the enemy by all sides. Occupation of the entire country in November 1942 and increasing numbers of executions by the occupiers – eight French victims in 1940, to well over 500 in the following 18 months – completely sapped Petain's popularity.[19]

The Nazi propaganda machine had declared Iranians an Aryan nation and a racial kin of the Germans. Iran and Germany had enjoyed excellent relations in trade, industry and general construction and both countries wished to maintain their ties, for they were mutually beneficial. Iran's government, having declared its neutrality in the war, was keen to maintain the relations to avoid disrupting its fast-paced national development, begun in 1924. Germany cultivated the ties with Iran for both economic and political reasons. Bilateral trade was significant and checking the influences of Russia and Britain in the Middle East was a welcome aspiration for both Iran and Germany.

Before leaving Paris, Minister Sepahbody had entrusted Iran's legation, housed in a beautiful French mansion at 5 Rue Fortuny, to his brother-in-law Abdol-Hossein Sardari, a young diplomat with a 1936 law degree from the University of Geneva. His doctoral dissertation, an examination of the late nineteenth-century labour market in Switzerland, reflected his tolerant disposition.[20] Sardari, working at the consular section of the legation, found himself unexpectedly charged with the responsibility of protecting Iranian interests in occupied France. Amiable and gregarious, Sardari was a member of the Qajar Royal Family that had ruled Iran until 1925. He was a charming bachelor with an uncommon gift for socialising in general and entertaining guests in particular. Under his direction the Iranian legation became a hub of social activity. Soon the lavish diplomatic receptions were popular amongst high ranking German military officers and civilian officials. As the Iranian flag – the tri-coloured green white and red with the golden lion and sun at its centre – continued to fly high over the legation, Sardari cultivated personal friendship with both German and Vichy officials.[21] The friendships allowed him to solicit support in protecting the Iranian community in France, particularly the Iranian Jewish businessmen and their families.

To protect his Jewish fellow Iranians against German racial policies he contrived an argument credible enough to give the Nazis pause. The bitter reality was that the Nazis with their anti-Jewish ideology had gained control of France. If the Iranian Jews were to be saved, they had to be distinct from all others. Thus emerged the argument that Iranian Jews were not Semite but of Iranian Aryan racial stock. The Persian Emperor Cyrus had freed Jewish exiles in Babylon in 538 BC and they had naturally returned to their homes. It was after that event that some Iranians, whom Sardari termed 'Mousaique' or 'Djuguten,' had gradually found the teachings of the Prophet Moses attractive. That Iranian passports and official documents did not refer to race or religion supported his observation that Iranians were not divided by racial distinctions.[22] Reasonable people may not agree that the narrative was Sardari's own intellectual creation. He certainly had the general sympathy and support of his government and fellow Iranians, pointing to the possibility that he may not have been alone in developing the argument. His idea or not, what remains important is that he followed through with it, argued it skilfully, and proved persuasive enough. A lawyer by training, he fine-tuned his arguments to fit official German positions. The Nazi Party distinguished non-Muslim Iranians as people of '*nicht Judische Abstammung* and *Blutmassig nicht Juden*'. The first included Iranian Armenians, Christians and Zoroastrians. The second comprised Iranians whose religion was based on the teachings of Moses but their blood and race were not Jewish.[23] The Nazi leadership in Berlin, perhaps in response to Sardari's arguments, initiated a number of inquiries in 1942 to determine the blood classification of the followers of Moses in Iran, Georgia and Afghanistan. The Racial Policy Department – *Rassenpolitisches Amt Berlin* – in a number of inquiries dated 15 October 1942, solicited expert opinion on the issue of blood classification from the New History Research Institute – *Institut fur die Erforschung der Geschichte des neuen Deutschland* – in Berlin, World Services – *Weltdienst* – in Munich and the Institute for Jewish Research – *Institut fur Erforschung der Judenfrage* – in Frankfurt/Main. More inquiries were addressed to a number of academic institutions.[24] The responses of the academics were frequently non-committal, accompanied by suggestions of further research that necessarily required funding. Some influential Nazis objected to the proposition that Iranian Jews were different as inappropriate nonsense. Adolf Eichmann, head of the racial policy department of the SS, in a letter dated 12 December 1942 to the German Ministry of Foreign Affairs, flatly rejected the distinction between Iranian and non-Iranian Jews.[25] There was of course tremendous confusion with regards to the very notion of precise 'biological' race. Otmar von Verschuer, the geneticist wartime director of the Kaiser Wilhelm Institute of Anthropology, Human Heredity and Eugenics – the immdiate superior of the infamous Dr Josef Mengele – doubted that Jews were a race at all. Verschuer considered them a 'mongrel breed, basically indistinguishable in terms of blood from the Germans,' although they could become a separate race through inbreeding. 'By committing itself to a policy based on biological racism, the [Nazi] regime was thus in fact condemning itself to extreme uncertainty, and this gave discretion to the policy-makers and permitted wide variation in nationalities policy from place to place.'[26]

Sardari exploited the internal ideological differences skilfully. He also utilised the Nazi propaganda that identified Iranians as a nation of Aryans.

With the assistance of his German, French and Iranian friends he succeeded in saving the Iranian Jewish families and their friends in France from certain harassment and possible annihilation. By 1940 the families had grown to over 100 in Paris alone. The de facto governor of occupied France, German Ambassador Otto Abetz, had assured Sardari that Iranian Djuguten would not be subjected to 'the special Nazi laws'.[27] Sardari was undeniably helped by some German diplomats. The German diplomatic corps had not been thoroughly 'Nazified' and some old aristocrats who had traditionally served in the German Foreign Ministry had remained. The old diplomats did not hold much respect for the new upstarts such as Foreign Minister Joachim von Ribbentrop and Otto Abetz, who had been late-comers to the German diplomatic service.[28] The opportunists who had jumped on the Nazi bandwagon to advance their own ambitions were the ones who carried out the Party's racial policies, but their motivations may not have been ideological. The so called 'Jewish Experts' of the Foreign Ministry's *Abteilung Deutschland, Referat D-III*, illustrate the point. These men had sought a civil service career and entered the Party between March and May 1933, just as the direction of the political wind became clear. It may have been opportunistic careerists who carried out the most inhumane of Nazi policies as civil servants.[29]

When inquiries regarding Iranian Jews finally reached the highest levels of the Foreign Ministry, they were referred to Friedrich-Werner Graf von der Schulenburg, the recognised old hand in Iranian affairs who had served as Germany's Minister in Tehran from 1924 to 1929. In a note dated 14 April 1943, he cautiously confirmed Sardari's thesis.[30]

> As I recall the Djuguten constitute a Muslim sect that essentially follows Mohammedan principles. The scope of the theology of Moses that they have adopted is very limited. On the basis of blood they are Iranian, not Semite. Therefore, applying the German Jewish laws to them seems unjustified. We are trying, despite all the difficulties facing us, to maintain our good relations with Iran. Prejudice against Djuguten will defeat our efforts and will give our enemies propaganda ammunition to use against us. The Political Bureau XIII [of the Ministry of Foreign Affairs] recommends not applying the laws of German Jews to Djuguten, or at the very least, postponing their implementation.[31]

Schulenberg, Professor Ahmad Mahrad has argued, must have tried as skilfully as he could to undermine Nazi racial policies. He was executed on 10 November 1944 for involvement in the Stauffenberg conspiracy to assassinate Hitler.[32]

Iranian Jews, having been assured of their own safety, implored Sardari to help their non-Iranian friends. Sardari faced a serious problem in September 1941 when Russian and British armies simultaneously invaded Iran from the north, south and west. Matters took a turn for the worse when Iran's Foreign Minister Mohammad Sa'ed Maraghei first persuaded his colleagues in Prime Minister Ali Sohaily's Cabinet and then the members of the Iranian Parliament to declare war on Germany. Sa'ed reasoned correctly that since Iran had already been occupied by the Allies and its neutrality nullified, joining the Allies would be advantageous to Iran after the war. The subsequent signing of the Treaty of Alliance by Iran, Britain, the US and the Soviet Union in Tehran on 29 January 1942 made Sardari's position horribly precarious. His government ordered him to join Mohsen Ra'iss, the Minister to Vichy (who had replaced Anoshiravan Sepahbody), and the legation staff there to leave France as soon as possible.

Sardari was committed to helping his fellow Iranians trapped in France, but was also aware of the potential consequences if he refused to leave. Remaining in France meant defying his own government, risking hostile relations with the Germans, jeopardising his diplomatic career and possibly endangering his life. After considerable soul-searching he determined to accept the risks. A friend's urging may very well have influenced his decision; Ibrahim Morady, a prominent Iranian carpet and textile merchant in Paris visited Sardari upon hearing rumours of his imminent return to Tehran. Morady implored him to stay. Sardari explained his dilemma, but Morady was relentless, and his sincerity moved Sardari. He finally looked into his friend's eyes and gave Morady his word. As Morady stood up to take his leave Sardari took his friend's arms with both hands, promising him he would stay no matter what happened.[33]

Sardari had the key to the legation's safe where some 500–1000 blank passports were commonly stored.[34] After having secured the safety of fellow Iranians, he issued documents for others, often recommended by his trusted Iranian Jewish friends. German archival documents suggest that Sardari managed to exempt 2400 Jews from Nazi racial laws, a number considerably greater than the entire Iranian Jewish population residing in France at the time.[35] Sardari's nephew, Fereydoun Hoveyda, recalled a chance meeting at Sardari's Paris apartment in 1947 at which he 'witnessed the leaders of the recently expanded Iranian Jewish community present Sardari with a carved silver plate in gratitude for his efforts during the occupation.'[36] Mrs Mehri Ra'iss-Farmanfarma, widow of the late Minister Mohsen Ra'iss, recalled in 2004 that Sardari's humanitarian efforts had been well known to her husband while serving in Vichy. 'We all knew well that Mr Sardari was being very very helpful in Paris.'[37]

When the Allies' armed forces assaulted Iran on 25 August 1941 despite Iran's repeatedly declared neutrality, they ended Sardari's privileges as a diplomat representing a neutral state on friendly terms with both the Allies and the Axis. With the subsequent occupation of the country, Iran's citizens in German-occupied territories had to secure the protection of a third state acceptable to Berlin. Switzerland proved acceptable to both Iran and Germany, and willing to allow Sardari to continue his efforts under Swiss protection. Under the new circumstances, Sardari had to rely on his own resources, his diplomatic skill and his personal relations. In a note illustrative of his effectiveness dated 11 November 1942, fourteen months after Iran's occupation by the Allies, Iran's Deputy Foreign Minister Mohammad-Ali Homayoonjah informed the Iranian Cabinet that:

> According to a telegram from the Iranian legation in Bern [Switzerland] efforts undertaken [in Paris] have resulted in convincing relevant authorities to have the designation of 'Juif' removed from identity documents and clothing of Iranian Jews in occupied territories. They [Iranian Jews] have been called to Paris for that purpose.[38]

Sardari's effectiveness can be measured against a blanket directive of 7 January 1943 that was to supersede previous orders. It declared that all Jews residing legally in France were to have the designation 'Jew' stamped on their identification and ration cards no later than 12 January. The directive warned that violators would be punished severely and concluded with the ominous statement that 'this is a general measure from which no Jew, regardless of category, will be exempt.'[39] Yet despite increased and widespread harassment of all Jewish residents, Iranian Jews remained generally unaffected.

Sardari avoided publicity, and to the end of his life in 1981 persistently shunned accolades for his efforts during the war years. He repeatedly dismissed references to his accomplishments, claiming that he had only performed his duty. He was finally recognised for his humanitarian work posthumously on 19 April 2004. The occasion was the Yom Hashoah, Holocaust Remembrance Day, at the Simon Wiesenthal Center in Los Angeles, California. The late Ambassador Fereydoun Hoveyda who attended the ceremony on behalf of his uncle's family, repeated for the audience his recollection of the chance meeting at Sardari's apartment in 1947.

> I happened to walk in as the city's Jewish representatives were presenting to him an inscribed silver plate, with an emotional statement of gratitude. When I realised what had just happened I excitedly volunteered to inform the media. My uncle sternly admonished me not to do anything of the sort. He said there was no reason for the fuss for he had only done his duty. They had been Iranian and protecting their interests had been his obligation. I reminded him that the gathering had shown that there had been non-Iranians among them too. That too was my duty, to God and to humanity, he told me.[40]

Abdol-Hossein Sardari was born in Tehran in 1914 into a wealthy aristocratic family. His mother, Afsar-Saltaneh, was King Naser al-Din Shah Qajar's niece and extremely conscious of her royal lineage. Afsar-Saltaneh's mother Ezat-Dowleh had married first in 1849 at her crowned brother's wish to the 50-year-old Prime Minister Amir Kabir, Sadr A'zam, while only sixteen years old.[41] Amir Kabir's reforms and modernisation policies threatened the influence of courtiers, including the King's mother. A court conspiracy, possibly unbeknownst to the King, saw him killed at the famous Fin Garden in Kashan in 1852, while he was reportedly on vacation.[42] Ezat-Dowleh remarried to Yahya-Khan Moshir al-Dowleh, a one-time foreign minister who too might have been killed by orders from the Royal Palace.[43] She had three daughters from the second marriage. One of the three, Afsar-Saltaneh, married the eccentric Solayman Khan Adib al-Saltaneh, bore three daughters and four sons but clearly favoured two of the children, her eldest son Yahya and youngest daughter Malekeh-Qods.[44] The rest of her children were often kept out of sight in the care of servants and relegated to their quarters. Abdol-Hossein and his younger brother Mohammad-Hassan were particularly neglected to the point of cruelty. The second son, Nasser-Qoli, fared better. Yahya and Nasser-Qoli were sent to France where they studied criminal justice, and upon their return joined the Iranian National Police Force. Yahya became an officer, rose to the rank of colonel and directed the national homicide bureau. After Reza Shah's exile from Iran, Yahya was named National Police Chief and promoted to brigadier-general. Naser-Qoli is credited with having organised and directed Iran's first national forensic investigation department. Abdol-Hossein, the third son, so often ignored by his mother, was sent off to England to a boarding school at the age of eight. His alcoholic father was of little help and died when the children were very young. Abdol-Hossein's third and youngest sister, Malekeh-Qods, born in Tehran in 1911, took it upon herself to protect him. After her marriage to Anoshiravan Sepahbody, a Qajar cousin born in 1888, she took Abdol-Hossein, three years younger than herself, under her wing. Abdol-Hossein received a traditional English education and became Anoshiravan Sepahbody's trusted protégé in the Iranian Ministry of Foreign Affairs.

Sepahbody had served as a diplomat since 1907, well before the Pahlavi Dynasty replaced the Qajar monarchy in 1925. When appointed permanent representative to the League of Nations and Minister to Switzerland in 1929, Sepahbody took the young Abdol-Hossein to Bern with him. He was not disappointed. Sardari enrolled at the University of Geneva, received a doctorate in law, and proved masterful at getting things done. Sepahbody gave him a temporary post at the legation and recommended his official entry into the Iranian diplomatic service. A 1931 photograph taken in Bern shows Sepahbody and Abdollah Entezam (who would later head the National Iranian Oil Company) leaving a building in official diplomatic garb followed by Sardari in a suit. Sardari accompanied Sepahbody to his other diplomatic assignments whenever possible.[45] By the time the Second World War broke out, Sardari had become a competent diplomat with a natural talent for mastering languages. He is said to have spoken English with the fluency and air of an English gentleman, German with the refinement of a

Swiss litigator and French with the accent of a cultured Parisian. Although often away from Iran since early childhood, his associates attest to his fluency in Persian and his remarkable Persian handwriting. His command of Persian literature suggests that he might have been accompanied by a Persian tutor while attending boarding school in England. Assigning a tutor to teach and chaperon youngsters abroad was common amongst Iran's noble families and Sardari's family had certainly had the means for it.

Sardari's eldest sister, Malekeh-Saba, married Abol-Qassem Farbod, an Iranian physician who had graduated from the Paris School of Medicine around 1879.[46] His second sister, Afsar al-Moluk, married Habibollah Hoveyda, posted to Saudi Arabia and later Lebanon as Iran's diplomatic envoy.[47] Afsar al-Moluk and Habibollah Hoveyda had two sons, Amir Abbas and Fereydoun. The two young Hoveydas followed their father into the Iranian diplomatic service, and were close to Sardari, their maternal uncle. Fereydoun remained a diplomat and achieved the post of Ambassador to the United Nations, a position he held until the Iranian Revolution of 1978. Amir Abbas left the Ministry of Foreign Affairs in 1958 to join the National Iranian Oil Company. He was appointed Treasury Minister in 1964 in Hassan-Ali Mansur's Cabinet and became Prime Minister upon Mansur's assassination in 1965. He held the position for over thirteen years, a record unmatched in Iran's modern history. The revolutionary theologians executed Amir Abbas Hoveyda in 1979 following a scandalous trial on charges of 'warring against God and corruption on earth'.

Sardari's childhood and youth affected him deeply; he became detached and emotionally aloof. Yet he would go to great lengths to treat his relatives and friends with the utmost grace and generosity. The lack of parental affection he had received during his early years gave him boundless empathy for the victims of human cruelty. He compensated for the affection denied him with outbursts of gregarious friendship. Yet he also experienced an infrequent dark mood, particularly after bouts of heavy drinking. His childhood may explain his desire to avoid lasting family commitments; but there was one glaring exception. Ironically, the one person to whom he was romantically committed suddenly disappeared from his life without a trace. Women reportedly adored him. When pressed to explain this, the women who knew him describe his trust and empathy; 'Women invariably felt that he understood them.'[48] He was silver tongued and had numerous female companions, but one clearly stood out. The classically trained Chinese opera singer he affectionately called Tchin-Tchin was the only woman with whom he wished to share his life. Tchin-Tchin was beautiful, artistic and sociable, and photographs of her with Sardari's relatives imply mutual affection. But she was also alone and in the midst of the Second World War separated from her home and family. Her parents had sent her to Paris with her brother as company, but he died suddenly from a ruptured appendix, a devastating blow.[49]

Sardari avoided discussing his experiences of the war years. He might have wished to forget the horrors or was perhaps too modest. He had always had friends of various nationalities, French, German, Swiss, English, American and Iranian, and consistently rejected the urge to simplify relations into 'them and us'. He understood life's many complexities, and rejected ideologies so fashionable in the 1930s, 1940s and 1950s that sought to erase all ambiguity in human loyalties. Having struggled to blunt the sharp edges of intolerance and rejection he had faced, he would not be intolerant himself. He shunned accolades for his deeds, and was prosecuted after the war for having allegedly over-stepped his authority. Worse yet, the revolution of 1978 robbed him of his wealth and even his well-earned pension. He died alone, broken and destitute, in a rented room outside London, far away from the woman he had loved, the country he had served and the friends he had cherished.

Sardari had embraced his cultural values and been deeply affected by them. Iranian history and literature were lasting influences on his character. He represented a government and a nation conscious of Iran's past, struggling to regain respect and sovereignty. A new generation of Iranians filled with hope had emerged at the turn of the twentieth century.

Several Iranian streams flow from the mighty Zagros Mountains in western Iran to become tributaries to the 515 mile-long Karun river that passes through the city of Ahvaz and joins Arvand-Rud at the port of Khorramshahr before pouring into the Persian Gulf. Similarly, *In the Lion's Shadow* is a story in which several historical streams meet at a specific juncture in history. The tributaries have included Iranians' cultural sentiments, resilience and entrepreneurship, as represented by Abdol Hossein Sardari, Mouchegh Petrossian and Rayhan Morady, converging at a point of historical calamity. That the Moradys were Jewish, the Petrossians Christian and Reza Shah, Sepahbody and Sardari Muslim, did not matter nearly as much as that they were all Iranian. That remains as true today as it was then, despite the hollering of a vociferous few in a nation of 70 million. So this book is not simply the story of one man's heroic actions; his story is a reflection of historical realities that have been obfuscated or denied about an entire nation.

The Country

Rayhan the Entrepreneur

Colonel Reza Khan,[50] the man who would be king, was a military officer with an impressive appearance. He was tall, over 6 feet 3 inches, but seemed a foot taller in the boots and karakul hat of the Persian Cossacks' uniform. He was physically fit, had a thunderous voice when incensed, and the most unforgettable, piercing eyes. He was not given to oratory and disliked long-winded speeches. He usually spoke softly but always to the point, and was invariably brief. The British Minister in Iran, Sir Percy Lorraine, reported to the British Foreign Office that he had once complained to Reza Khan bitterly that communicating with Iranian officials had been difficult for he just 'could not make them understand!' Reza Khan listened patiently then responded with a Persian expression that according to Lorraine 'completely disarmed me'. Reza Khan told Lorraine 'when a wise man argues with a fool, the greater part of the blame lies with the wise man.'[51]

Reza Khan had earned a reputation for bravery and competence as a soldier. His unwavering nationalism had attracted like-minded officers' loyalty and the troops' admiration. Following his promotion to the rank of colonel, he had rented a house in Tehran's Sangelaj district near downtown's Lalehzar Avenue, then the city's most desirable business district.[52] As he passed through Lalehzar every day at dawn on his way to work, the businessmen increasingly took notice of him. He was reputedly so punctual that the shopkeepers could set their watches by his appearance. Rayhan, a store-owner displaying fine Kashan carpets, textiles, handicrafts and antiques, was one of them. One day Rayhan's newly acquired white horse tied up in front of his store caught the colonel's eyes. Standing on the sidewalk he called through the store's entrance, 'Rayhan, how much for the horse?' In typical Iranian merchant's solicitous tradition Rayhan rushed outside with greetings. 'How much do you want for the horse?' Reza Khan repeated. 'It is not worthy of you Your Excellency,' Rayhan replied. 'Well, is it for sale?' he asked. 'If it pleases Your Excellency, I wish for you to have it,' he answered. The colonel waved away the platitude impatiently, turning away to move on. 'Take it Excellency right now please, ride it for a few days. If you decide to keep it, then there will be occasion to discuss the price,' Rayhan said. Colonel Reza Khan turned around and muttered 'very well,' mounted the horse, thanked Rayhan, and rode off. Two days later a junior officer showed up at the store with an envelope for Rayhan with the colonel's compliments and a message. 'Please see if the amount is agreeable.' The cash in the envelope was indeed a fair price for the horse. Rayhan was impressed.[53]

Rayhan was an ambitious businessman, well known amongst Tehran's merchants for his network of commercial contacts. He was from Kashan, a historic city in central Iran, but had assiduously cultivated links to suppliers, dealers and retailers in every major city in the country and several locations in Europe. Born to a prominent Jewish family in 1872, his father Mordechay had already created a thriving enterprise primarily in carpets, textiles, crafts and excavated potteries known as 'zir-khaki'.[54] The family's home in Kashan had a room exclusively set aside for displaying excavated potteries, neatly stacked in rows along the walls, so that Mordechay could examine and admire his findings. When he resolved to expand his business horizons, he turned to the third of his four sons. The first two, Molla Aba and Agha Eshagh,[55] had chosen the path of scholarship and theology. The fourth, Mirza Davood seemed destined to share the same interests. The third son, Ruben, on the other hand, had his father's passion for carpets, artifacts and antiques, coupled with a remarkable interest in commerce. Ruben's boundless curiosity was enhanced by his daring ambition. He had an uncommon talent for grasping opportunities and embracing well-calculated risks. Although the audacity he projected was often beyond his contemporaries' comprehension, his father recognised the young man's enterprising talent. When Ruben moved to Tehran, he did so with his father's support and blessing. Characteristically, he selected a prime location in the most upscale part of the capital for his store. Rather than putting his own name on the shop he selected 'Rayhan', an interesting Persian name with several meanings. Rayhan is known to mean sweet basil or a collection of aromatic herbs. But it also means 'the support of life,' 'son' and 'handsome'.[56] The store's name became so popular that it overshadowed the owner's. Gradually even family members addressed Ruben as Rayhan, and the name stuck.

Rayhan was flamboyant, self-confident and friendly. He was sociable, helpful to fellow shopkeepers and meticulous in customer service. His fellow merchants envied and admired him at the same time. Riding a fine white horse to work was expected of the nobility but not of the shopkeepers who normally walked to work or rode donkeys. Rayhan, however, was not a common shopkeeper. He had gradually created a network of trusted and trusting business associates as well as satisfied customers in the country's major cities. He had access to numerous producers of Persian carpets, tribal rugs, tapestries and handicraft nationwide. Relying on his hardworking relatives, friends and partners, he had ventured into exports to Europe with the same diligence. Repeated visits of Iranian royals and nobility to Europe had generated renewed interest in Persian products in the European markets. The demand for Persian carpets became so great in the West that it prompted Rayhan, already 50 years old, to move his family and business to France. He opened a store on Rue Clichy in the 9th District of Paris in 1924. The store sign had his initial and family name proudly displayed as 'R. Morady, Tapis Persans, Objects d'Art'. Rayhan's extended family joined the business, began to open new stores, and gradually ventured into textiles, antiques and even real estate. The family prospered and its businesses expanded. Business had its problems of course; transportation in particular posed serious risks, as entire shipments of merchandise occasionally disappeared in transit. However, the profits were good enough to cover the losses, just as Rayhan had figured.

When Rayhan Morady moved to France, his wife Soltaneh was by his side. Born in Kashan in 1886 and married to Rayhan before her twentieth birthday, she bore him nine children. The first child was a girl, Rachel, followed by a boy, Yussef. The girl-boy order of birth continued as Malek, Habibollah, Showkat, Ibrahim and Tal'at were born in Tehran, and Jahangir and Rose were born in Paris.[57] The family built a fine home at 8 Rue Francois-Adam, Parc Saint Maur, Seine et Marne, where friends gathered frequently. French life was fine for the Moradys and they enjoyed sharing their good fortune with friends and relatives. Another Iranian Jewish family, headed by brothers George and Morteza Senehi, built an impressive home at 77 Boulevard de Montmorency, Montmorency Seine & Oise, not far from the Moradys' house. When George – one of the two Senehi brothers – married Rayhan's daughter Tal'at, the two families united their business interests. Tal'at's first child, a daughter named Eliane, and second child, a son named Claude, were born at the Montmorency home. The nearby waterfront Enghein-les bains and its famous casino added to the elegance of the area. Rayhan felt blessed, and indeed he was.

Rayhan's four sons, Yussef, Habib, Ibrahim and Jahangir, had their father's charm, business acumen, and drive. They also enjoyed the benefits of a French education, language fluency and the savoir-faire that the combination offered. When Yussef suddenly passed away before he was 30 years old, Habib became increasingly involved in his father's business. Ibrahim, affectionately called Ibby, opened his own store in 1932 and named it 'Palais d'Iran' on the same street as his father's. Jahangir, the youngest son, nicknamed Jean, contemplated opening a branch in South America, and he finally did so in Caracas, Venezuela, after the Second World War.

Rayhan's homeland had been in decline and dominated by Russia and Britain for a century, but a sense of optimism had gradually reappeared in Iran in the 1920s. Visitors could detect a new feeling of pride among Iranian professionals and the expanding middle class. The feeling was particularly strong among military officers and those involved in business, public service and education. The country was gradually succeeding in asserting its own national interest in defiance of foreign imperial claims, beginning to break free from the internal discord that had plagued it continuously for 200 years and paved the way for imperialist interventions. Despite limited resources, Iranians of all walks of life began to rebuild their country. Rayhan had invested his energy and talent in commerce, whilst Reza Khan – whom Rayhan had met and admired whilst a storekeeper in Tehran – had wrestled with the nation's security and governance.

Iran's experiences with the West had not been easy. Encounters with Russia and Britain brought Iranians exploitation and insult. Three decades before Nazi Germany and the USSR shamelessly divide Poland, Russia and Britain in a display of imperial audacity had conspired on 13 August 1907 to divide Iran into three 'zones of influence'.[58] Policymakers in London and Moscow split the country into the Russian zone in the north, the British zone in the southeast and the neutral zone. A year earlier, on 5 August 1906, following months of widespread protests and strikes, Iranians had pressured King Mozaffar al-Din Shah Qajar to accede to a Constitution and a Parliament.[59] The gate to the Baharestan Garden where the Parliament, the Majles, was housed, commemorates the event with an ornate circular design crowning the wrought-iron arch over the entrance with the words '*Adl-e Mozzafar*' – 'Mozzafar's Justice'. The King did not live long enough to see the fruits of his decision. He died of kidney failure on 7 January 1907, leaving the throne to his son, Crown Prince Mohamad Ali.[60] Upon ascending the throne, Mohammad-Ali Shah, backed by Britain and Russia, opposed the Constitution and the limitations it imposed on royal absolutism. During the turmoil that followed, Russia and Britain divided Iran into the three parts mentioned. The ink on Iran's Russo-British-issued death certificate had hardly dried when the discovery of oil in Masjed-Solayman in the Neutral Zone complicated the imperial accommodations. The Neutral Zone suddenly become too attractive for the competing imperial powers to leave alone. Concerned that one might grab the spoils, both scrambled to shut the other out. The rivalry that ensued unsettled the 1907 concord.

Mohammad-Ali Shah's opposition to the Majles reached its peak when he staged a royal coup to abolish Iran's newly won Constitution. To assert the King's absolute power, the Persian Cossacks commanded by Russian officers – nominally in the service of Iran's monarch but reporting to Russian masters in St Petersburg and Moscow – shelled the Parliament building and the adjacent Sepahsalar Mosque on 23 June 1908. Their objective was to put an end to Iran's representative governance and the popular aspirations awakened by the Constitution. An English witness described the attack:

> In spite of the shrapnel poured in on the defenders, however, the resistance was continued for seven or eight hours, until finally the two buildings which had for the best part of two years been the centre of the Nation's hopes and the focus of the new spirit which had stirred the dry bones of a seemingly dead people to new life, the Baharistan and the Sipahsalar Mosque were reduced to ruins and the defenders either slain, taken captive, or put to flight.[61]

Tabriz, the provincial capital of Iranian Azarbaijan, the second largest city of the kingdom and traditional seat of the Crown Prince as governor, rose in armed resistance on the same day.[62] The uprising was significant, for the city's residents were familiar with the former Prince Governor's temperament. Other provinces followed Azarbaijan's example in support of the Constitution. The Bakhtiyari tribe in Esfahan rose on 2 January 1909 followed by uprisings in Rasht on 8 February, Torbat-Haydarieh on 14 March, Bandar-Abbas and Bushehr on 17 March, Hamadan and Shiraz on 25 March, Kermanshah on 27 March and Mash-had (Mashed) on 6 April.[63] In Kermanshah the uprising degenerated into lawlessness and looting of the property of vulnerable minorities. The nation's historical spirit of generosity toward the minority nevertheless asserted itself. The English observer wrote:

> Captain Haworth, the British Consul, was much astonished by the practical sympathy shewn by the Muhammadans in sending food and covering to the Jews. He adds that many Jews owe their lives to Muhammadans, who, in some cases actually stood armed in front of their Jewish friends until they could take them to their own houses.[64]

The constitutionalists were Iranians of every ethnic background, and even included some non-Iranian allies. Yephrem-khan, a Christian Iranian-Armenian, and Haji-Davoud Ebraham Ya'goub and Aziz-Asher Rabi-Rahamim, two young Iranian Jews, were representative of many amongst the Constitutionalists who fought bravely shoulder to shoulder with their Muslim brethren.[65] The most noted among the non-Iranian constitutionalists was Howard C. Baskerville, an American English and Science teacher, a 1907 Princeton University graduate. Baskerville lost his life leading a sortie of pro-Constitution defenders out of Tabriz on 21 April 1909. Baskerville's objective had been to elude the city's besiegers to acquire food for its starving residents. To reach the surrounding villages to find food, he had resolved to break through the royal forces that surrounded Tabriz.[66]

Military confrontation between the King's Persian Cossacks and the Constitutionalist Volunteers, who included a 5000-man Bakhtiyari tribal militia, finally resulted in the Monarch's defeat. The deposed King fled to Russia and his eleven-year-old son Prince Ahmad was proclaimed king in July 1909. The nationalists were euphoric. They strove to rid the country of foreign domination, reunify the nation, modernise government administration and reform the economy. The challenge, already great, became insurmountable through a combination of people's high expectations and impatience. Parliamentary disagreements and foreign intrigue made matters worse, and political rivalries between local notables and tribal chiefs added to the weak central government's burden.[67]

The crisis prompted the Russian government to persuade the exiled former king to attempt a comeback in 1911. The attempt failed and it actually reunited the country, but it also illustrated the state's vulnerability. Iran turned to the United States to hire advisors to speed up the intended reforms. Iran's leaders considered the United States, a rising power without vested interests in their country, a likely candidate to counter Russo-British incursions on Iran's sovereignty. With high hopes they hired a group of US advisors headed by William Morgan Shuster. Shuster was granted the office of 'State Treasurer General' upon arrival in Iran to reform the state's finances, revenue collection and taxation.

The Treasurer General began his work by instituting substantial financial reforms almost immediately. Highly popular with Iranians and supported by the Majles, Russia and Britain opposed Shuster from the outset; the Russian ambassador to Washington had been specifically instructed to abort Shuster's employment by the Iranian government. The ambassador had implored the US Department of State to recognise 'the predominance of Russian and British interests' in Iran. The State Department had responded that it did not interfere in US private citizens' employment or travel. That reply would not curb Russia's imperial appetite. Less than a year after Shuster's arrival in Iran, Russia issued an ultimatum demanding his immediate dismissal, with the added injunction that no foreign subject would ever be employed by an Iranian government without the consent of Russian and British legations in Tehran. Defending the nation's sovereignty, Majles representatives stood firm. Russia responded by invading the country – then demanding payment from Iran for the cost of the invasion! Russian troops moved south to Qazvin, west of Tehran, and to Mash-had in the east. As they advanced, they executed scores of constitutionalists and nationalists. Oblivious to public and world opinion and to show their disregard for Iranians, they even shelled the country's holiest sanctuary, the Imam Reza Shrine in Mash-had. The British lent their support to the Russian invasion with reference to their 1907 agreement to divide the country. In a remarkable statement that dismissed Iran's sovereignty, Lord Edward Grey, the British Foreign Minister, addressed the House of Commons on 14 December 1911 with these words:

Russia played fair ... [Shuster] should not have appointed treasury officials at Esfahan and Tabriz which are in the Russian Zone ... That won't do ... Russia is entitled to demand indemnity ...[68]

Iran's leaders, overcome by despair, requested assistance from the United States Government and the US Congress. The response was heartbreaking. The US State Department replied, 'In view of the circumstances ... the Secretary of State does not find it appropriate to offer any suggestions.' The US Congress proved equally dismissive. Although the Majles did not withdraw its support for Shuster's employment, Iran's cabinet was compelled to yield. Shuster was forced to leave Iran but the Russian troops remained.[69]

Wary of Britain and Russia and disappointed with the United States, Iran turned to Germany. Favouring close ties with Germany was a nationalist policy move to check, if not to shake off, the Russo-British stranglehold. When the First World War broke out, most Iranians hoped for a German victory as they wished to free themselves from the Allies' influence. Despite national sympathy for Germany, Iran's government cautiously declared its neutrality to safeguard the country against foreign incursions.[70] The pragmatism of the weak, however, was trumped by the obliviousness of the strong. Both Russia and Britain invaded Iran despite the declared neutrality. Ottoman troops too entered the country, occupied Iran's northwest, and engaged Russian forces to the north. When Iran's legation in Washington appealed to the US State Department it received a general pledge of 'support for Persian neutrality'.[71]

An orgy of fighting, property confiscation, killing, destruction and espionage then ensued on Iranian soil. Britain's Major Sir Percy Sykes arrived from India, organised a 5000-man force named 'the South Persia Rifles' and controlled much of the country's south. Germany tried to mobilise local tribes and militias to join her cause. Iran had become a battleground for belligerent foreign powers. The nation suffered not only materially, but psychologically. Grain expropriation, food shortages, starvation and bloodshed had become common. In parts of the west such as Hamadan and Kermanshah, people were reduced to seeking refuge in caves. Over 100,000 died of starvation and 10,000 villages were abandoned as a result.[72] Insult was added to injury when the British government and its Anglo-Persian Oil Company (APOC) demanded £700,000 indemnity from the Iranian government for the losses the Company had incurred during the war. Even a British diplomat observed, 'Persia had been exposed to violations and suffering not endured by any other neutral country.'[73] Such disregard for national dignity, human rights and international law, carved a permanent scar on the Iranian collective soul.

The Russian Revolution brought a respite, as most Russian occupiers finally left Iran in 1917. Their departure however, much to Iranians' chagrin, gave the British a free hand. Britain barred Iran's delegation from attending the Paris Peace Conference and prevented its attempt to address the Convention. The Iranians were handed a treaty in 1919 to bring their country under total British control. Britain wanted a mandate to rule Iran, but settled for *de facto* control to allay anticipated French and US opposition.[74] To further isolate Iran, the British government prepared a list of 'undesirables' to be expelled from the country – a demand it would repeat again in 1941. These included foreign technicians, archaeologists and scholars working in the country. When the Iranian delegation tried to meet with the Peace Conference leadership privately, Britain insisted on preventing any contact between the Iranian delegates and the Allied leaders. The treatment Iran received was known to all governments represented at the Conference. John L. Caldwell, the US Minister in Tehran, reported to the State Department that although Iran's grievances were greater than any other neutral state, Britain objected to her demands being heard.[75] The British Foreign Office went even further to undermine Iran's national interest by ordering its Tehran legation to bribe Iranian officials. The bribes included 15,000 tomans per month (equal to £4913) to King Ahmad Shah Qajar, and the lump sum of 400,000 tomans (£131,000) to Prime Minister Hassan Vosouq and two of his cabinet ministers, Akbar Mas'oud and Firouz Firouz.[76] The objective was to obtain the treaty of 'Friendship and Assistance' presented to Iran in 1919 as expeditiously as possible.[77] Although unaware of the bribes, Iranians were outraged at the treaty being forced on them and at the treatment their delegation had received at the Peace Conference. Faced with popular objection and perhaps moved by nationalism, Ahmad Shah Qajar and his ministers vacillated. The Majles finally refused to ratify the British imposition.

A nationalist military officer of humble background had gained a favourable reputation in the same period, having distinguished himself on and off the battlefield. Reza Khan, the only son of Abbas-Ali and his second wife Noush-Afarin, had been born in Alasht in 1878. His father, a junior officer in the Savad-Kouh Regiment, had died a few months after his birth, and his mother had taken him to Tehran. Noush-Afarin's three brothers, Ali a physician, Abol Qasem a non-commissioned officer in the Cossack Brigade and Hossein, the youngest, who accompanied her to Alasht and later to Tehran, helped raise the infant. Reza joined the Cossacks in 1893–1894 while sixteen years old. He was promoted to First Lieutenant in 1911, Captain in 1912, Colonel in 1915 and Brigadier in 1918.[78] He impressed Major-General Sir Edmund Ironside (later Field Marshal and Chief of the Imperial General Staff), who reported to the War Office in London on 8 December 1920 that a competent Persian officer commanding the Cossacks would 'enable us to depart in peace and honour'. On leaving Tehran for Baghdad for the last time on 16 February 1921, Ironside named the officer he had had in mind: 'I have seen one man in the country ... capable of leading the nation, and that is Reza Khan.'[79]

General Ironside arranged the withdrawal of the British forces from Iran but the Tsarist Russians (who had left during the Russian Revolution) had been replaced by 1920 by the Bolsheviks. Flying a different banner, they had re-occupied the Iranian coast of the Caspian Sea and installed the 'Soviet Socialist Republic of Gilan'. Amongst the few Iranians who had gradually replaced Russian officers of the Persian Cossack Brigade, Reza Khan stood out. While fighting separatists in August 1920 in the northern provinces of Mazandaran and Gilan, his competence was impressive.[80] A few days after victoriously entering Rasht, Gilan's provincial capital, the Persian Cossacks commanded by a Russian officer chased the remaining Bolshevik separatist forces to the port of Anzali. At the port they were surprised to confront newly arrived Russian reinforcements. The Persians retreated but suspected treachery by their Russian officers. As their suspicion grew, they disarmed and detained the officers. Faced with the *fait accompli*, Prime Minister Fathollah-Akbar Sepahdar-e Rashti had no choice but to nod his approval. His hand having been forced, Ahmad Shah's royal affirmation followed.[81] Yet the state teetered on the verge of collapse as economic turmoil exacerbated the crisis. The Prime Minister resigned, but after all other notables invited to form a new government declined, Ahmad Shah asked Sepahdar to return to office. He struggled to form a new cabinet for a month but succeeded only in reintroducing the old one. In the meantime law and order deteriorated across the country.[82] The national mood became one of anxiety and despair. Five days after Sepahdar-Rashti reintroduced his old cabinet, Tehran witnessed a bloodless coup d'etat on 21 February 1921. The coup leader, Seyyed Zia-al-Din Tabatabaii, a journalist, became Prime Minister backed by the Persian Cossack Brigade. The Cossack's commander, Brigadier Reza Khan, immediately assumed the offices of Minister of War and Commander-in-Chief of the Army.

Large segments of Iran's population, tired of the chaos, supported the coup, and Britain, anxious to counter the Bolsheviks' influence, did not object.[83] Prime Minister Seyyed Zia promised extensive reforms and anti-corruption trials. Despite fiery declarations and mass detentions, Zia failed to deliver on his promises. He angered the British Foreign Minister, Lord George Curzon, by demanding unpaid royalties from the Anglo-Persian Oil Company for the previous three years, and attempting to hire American financial advisors. Zia also alienated Iran's elite, many of whom he had detained but failed to put on trial. His failure to collect the royalties disappointed the nation and ruined his credibility. Reza Khan finally forced him to resign and leave the country on 23 May 1921. What had caused Reza Khan's anger was Zia's decision under pressure from Curzon to employ a number of British officers without consulting him as the Minister of War and Commander of the Army.

Zia should have known better, for Brigadier Reza Khan had openly and consistently opposed granting executive or command positions to British or Russian officers in Iran's armed forces.[84]

Having forced Zia's resignation, Reza Khan assumed his responsibilities as Acting Prime Minister in addition to his other duties. He gained in both popularity and respect when he immediately freed the nobility Zia had held in jail for three months without trial. From May 1921 to October 1923 several prime ministers were appointed and failed. At last Ahmad Shah received Reza Khan at the Royal Palace on 28 October to be appointed the Prime Minister. The King, Ahmad Shah Qajar, left Iran for Europe on 2 November, never to return. His departure coincided with the abdication of the Ottoman Emperor Sultan Muhammed VI and the institution of a republic in Turkey. Prime Minister Reza Khan escorted the King to the border and returned to Tehran on 11 November. In a matter of months Reza Khan's national status had soared while Ahmad Shah's, already low, had sunk irreparably. Replacing the monarchy with a republic had by 1924 become a topic of popular conversation. Reza Khan supported a republican regime but kept himself out of the public debate. On 22 February when he met with the recently elected Majles representatives to consider the Fourth Parliament's legislative agenda, he expressed his views on the subject. A parliamentary majority favoured a republican government at the time, but Seyyed Hassan Moddares, a cleric with the gift of oratory, strongly opposed it. Moddares used a variety of parliamentary delaying tactics for weeks to postpone a vote to replace the Qajar monarchy with a republic. By 22 March, Moddares and other prominent clerics apprehensive about developments in Turkey – where abolishing the monarchy had dismantled clerical influence – had managed to shift public opinion against a republic.[85] Reza Khan then announced he would resign his office, for he no longer could work with either the King or the Crown Prince. He promptly retired to his country home. By April, a well orchestrated clerical campaign had completely defeated the attempt to institute a republic. On 7 April Reza Khan actually announced his resignation, stating that he would leave the country. Politicians performed a swift *volte face* as a delegation of notables, including the President (Speaker) of Parliament, Hossein Pirnia, visited him at his residence to change his mind. The next day the representatives voted (96 to 6) to re-install Reza Khan as Prime Minister.

On Monday 4 September 1922 an obscure cleric, Agha Shaikh Abdolnabi, ordered a general strike in Tehran to seek restitution of his honour following a perceived slight by a Jewish resident of the city. The cleric's male servant had been riding a donkey on a sidewalk the previous day as children attending a Jewish Alliance elementary school were exiting the schoolyard in single file to go home. A school attendant had stopped the donkey momentarily for the children to get on their way safely. The servant reported the halting of the donkey to his master; the cleric considered the stoppage an outrageous insult directed at him. The donkey, the cleric reasoned, was ridden by his servant, and the servant represented him. In two hours the bazaars and the shops had closed and people had gathered in mosques. The following day gangs assaulted a number of town residents whom they assumed to be Jewish, amongst them a Muslim clerk employed at the US Embassy. On Friday morning, groups armed with clubs and sticks appeared in marching formation in several locations in the city threatening Tehran's Jewish residents. An Iranian military officer on the scene who asked the reason for the procession was told that two 'sayyed children' (descendants of the Prophet) had been killed by Jews.[86] The crisis ended only after Reza Khan ordered mounted troops to intervene. The next day, a Saturday, a parliamentary leader took the podium at the Majles to read parts of the Constitution aloud with emphasis on the principles of equality of all citizens before the law and equal protection, to warn all potential trouble-makers, cleric or otherwise.[87] Some Iranians alleged that the incident had been part of a calculated campaign by the British legation to portray Iran as unstable, unpredictable and barbaric, to discourage potential US investments. They charged that the anti-Jewish incident had been engineered to incense the US envoy, Joseph Saul Kornfield (1876–1943) a Jewish rabbi, anticipating that he would react by calling for the rejection of an oil concession offer under consideration by US oil companies.[88] Whether the rumours were credible or not may never be known, but a concession to explore for oil in northern Iran was a matter of great interest to both Britain and Russia. Considering that one had invaded Iran to expel an American financial advisor and the other had bribed the King and his cabinet to agree to a treasonous treaty, the possibility of such undercover agitation cannot be dismissed out of hand. Indeed, the incident was one of many events in Iran at the time that suggest an atmosphere charged with intrigue.

Having been prevented from establishing a republican regime by religious leaders, Reza Khan did not bring it up again. Known by his new title, Sardar-Sepah (Army Commander), his popularity reached its peak in 1924 after reunifying Khuzestan with the rest of the country. Gondishapour, the city founded by the Sassanid King Shapour I in AD 271 and the site of the oldest known teaching hospital and university, with a major library, is in Khuzestan, the southwestern province on the Persian Gulf. The ancient Iranian city of Susa – Shush in Persian, Shushan in Hebrew, mentioned in the Bible as the city where Esther became Persia's Queen – is also in that province. Susa is thought to be the location of the oldest known human settlement in the world, dating back to between 7000 and 4200 BCE. In the eighteenth century, some Arab tribes settled in Khuzestan causing references to it as Arabistan–Arab province.[89] A tribal leader, Sheikh Khaz'al, who had murdered his brother Maz'al (their father's successor as chief) to become chief himself, had ruled the region under British protection since 1897. The British government had given Khaz'al written assurances 'similar to those given to the Sheikh of Kuwait ... to prevent any attempt by the Iranian government to curtail the Sheikh's autonomy.' It also gave him a gift of shares in the Anglo-Persian Oil Company, and in 1917 decorated him with the Order of Knight Grand Commander of the Indian Empire (GCIE) and the corresponding title 'Sir Sheikh Khaz'al'.[90] Of the taxes, port duties and import fees regularly collected, Khaz'al had not forwarded any to the Iranian government, nor had he paid any income tax since 1913. His relations with the British government had been such that he had been considered a potential candidate for the throne of Iraq when the Ottoman Empire collapsed during the First World War. After the throne went to the deposed Hashemite ruling family of Arabia, the British government comforted the disappointed Shaikh Khaz'al by sending him a gift of '2000 of the latest rifles and ammunition, four mountain guns, a river steamer and a ceremonial saluting gun' as consolation.[91] Foreign Secretary Lord George N. Curzon, in a note dated 10 May 1923 to Sir Percy Loraine whom he had appointed Minister to Tehran in 1921, warned 'we have no intention to abandon [Sheikh Khaz'al] as we are bound to him by special obligations.' Loraine responded on 17 May that '[Reza Khan] is too much of a patriot to be a subservient instrument.'[92]

After several unsuccessful attempts to collect the embezzled government taxes and despite British objections, Reza Khan ordered a 15,000-strong army to move towards Khuzestan. Finance Minister Mohammad-Ali Furuqi was named acting prime minister as Prime Minister General Reza Khan – Sardar-Sepah – left Tehran for the south on 5 November 1924. He arrived in Khuzestan on 27 November, a day after an advance column led by the army's youngest general, Brigadier Fazlollah Zahedi, had reached the province, two weeks ahead of the main body of his troops.[93] Sheikh Khaz'al, facing a regular army on the march, surrendered to Reza Khan in Ahvaz on 6 December and asked for forgiveness, committing to settling his debt. Reza Khan granted Khaz'al forgiveness but appointed Brigadier-General Zahedi Governor-General of Khuzestan to reassert the national government's authority.[94] On his return to Tehran on 1 January 1925 Sardar-Sepah entered the capital a national hero. He had disregarded London's warnings and achieved a tremendous national feat without bloodshed. The famed cleric Moddares, who had engineered successful parliamentary opposition to Reza Khan over a year earlier, had tried to do the same in support of Khaz'al. This time, his support for Khaz'al cost him much of his prestige.[95] The mood in the legislature reflected the national sentiment as Majles representatives responded favourably to the popular prime minister's numerous reform proposals and passed into law several significant bills in quick succession. On 5 November all titles were abolished and the Law of Identity and Personal Status required Iranians to adopt family names and register identities. On 22 November a state sugar monopoly was created to fund the construction of the planned

Trans-Iranian Railways. On 8 June the Law of National Conscription passed, strongly supported by Iranian Christians, Jews and Zoroastrians, but opposed by Muslim clerics who sought exemption for their theology students.[96] On 31 October 1925, the Majles considered a bill to end the reign of the Qajar Dynasty. Only four members – Seyyed Hassan Taqizadeh, Hosein Ala, Mohammad Mosaddeq and Yahya Dowlatabadi – spoke against. All four praised Reza Khan, but Taqizadeh (1878–1969) called for the appointment of a commission to assure adherence to the Constitution, as he feared the resolution had been hastily drafted. Ala (1882–1964) spoke briefly to state that the resolution was unconstitutional. Mosaddeq (1881–1967) praised the Prime Minister for the valuable services rendered, but argued that while his retention as the country's chief executive would benefit the nation, granting him executive power as king would violate the Constitution. Dowlatabadi (1862–1939) argued that the resolution included unrelated matters that should be addressed separately. He favoured abolishing the Qajar Dynasty and although he had the highest respect for the Prime Minister and the Commander of the Armed Forces, he was opposed to hereditary monarchy in principle and could not support the resolution.[97] Despite the four speakers' eloquence the Parliament voted overwhelmingly to end the Qajars' reign.

Adhering to the new Law of Identity and Personal Status of 5 May 1925 that had abolished all titles of nobility, Reza Khan chose for his family name that of an ancient Iranian language, Pahlavi. The choice was to reflect Iran's glorious past rather than the previous Qajar dynasty's tribal affiliation or the Safavid's fourteenth-century religious heritage.[98] He was declared the first King of the new Pahlavi Dynasty on 13 December 1925 with the right of succession for his heirs. On 15 December he took the oath of office and was publicly proclaimed Reza Shah Pahlavi, Iran's king, the following day. The formal coronation ceremony took place on 25 April 1926 and Reza Shah's eldest son Mohammad-Reza was officially recognised as the Crown Prince on 26 April.

Reza Shah initiated a wide range of policies to foster national unity and restore the nation's pride. He modernised the institutions of the state, promoted industrialisation and encouraged commerce. Persian words replaced foreign words that had crept into usage and the nation's pre-Islamic culture, architecture and heritage was glorified. The wearing of the veil (chador) was forbidden and women's employment was encouraged. To promote national cohesion, a national dress law discouraged the wearing of local costumes as they signified tribal and regional differences.[99] The country's military units were reformed into one national army, supported by the new conscription law that drafted recruits from all provinces for a well equipped, well trained 40,000-man national army. Foreign influence was curtailed, the contract with the Anglo-Persian Oil Company (APOC) renegotiated, the much hated capitulation system abandoned and the foreign banks' authorisation to issue Iranian currency withdrawn.[100] A European-modelled Ministry of Justice and a judicial system equipped with an extensive legal code removed clerical judicial prerogatives. The influence of local notables and tribal chiefs as unchallenged arbiters of disputes was significantly diminished. A Ministry of Education instituted public schools throughout the country for the first time. Although reforms were laudatory and necessary, resistance was strong. As one modern scholar observed:

> One of the reformer's difficulties in Iran is the heritage of civilization with which he must either contend or which he must try and harness to contemporary purposes. Reza Shah was aware of this problem ... The Shah also emphasised Iran's past splendour. He had public buildings designed on the lines of Persepolis and encouraged archaeological investigations ... These were held up as examples to a people who suspected these externals and know from experience better than almost any other nation on earth how transient are material achievements and pomp and glory ... The Iranian people also see in those ruins a monument to the vanity of human success.[101]

In the light of the problems, real and perceived, of eduction in the madrassas of Afghanistan, Pakistan, Saudi Arabia and elsewhere today, it is important to remember the Iranian emphasis on educational reform in the 1920s. Introduction of the Ministry of Education and standardised schooling in effect removed the clerics' educational monopoly. In 1900 some 95 per cent of the population was illiterate. The country had 21 elementary schools and only one secondary school aside from a few religious and missionary classes. By 1923, religious classes (maktab), numbered 83 with 53 teacher-operators (maktabdar) and 2081 students. There were 40 seminaries (madraseh qadimeh), with 21 theologians (moddares) and 626 theology students (talabeh).[102] Reza Shah's regime increased the annual education budget twenty-fold, from less than 8000 rials in 1925 to 154,900 by 1940. The massive extra funding increased the number of primary schools to 2331 and secondary schools to 321, and established 32 vocational schools. To satisfy the pressing need for qualified teachers, a Teacher Training Law passed in March 1934 resulted in 25 training colleges in five years. By the time of Reza Shah's abdication in 1941, 36 teacher training colleges were in full operation and the number of female students in elementary and secondary schools had increased ten-fold.[103] Tehran University, Iran's first modern university, had instituted seven colleges by 1934 and was rapidly expanding.[104] To secure the professorial requirement, a programme to send at least 100 talented students abroad on government scholarship each year funded 2395 university students, 452 of whom had completed their studies and returned home by 1941.[105]

Distrustful of the Soviet Union and the British Empire, Reza Shah's government again approached the US in 1922 to hire a group of financial experts. The American advisors were headed by Dr Arthur C. Millspaugh, who set out to reorganise the state's financial system to enhance efficiency where Shuster had left off. The underlying reasons for approaching the United States, as in the case of William Morgan Shuster in 1911, were four-fold. The US – unlike Russia and Britain – did not harbour imperialist designs on Iran. American assistance to Iran could check Russo-British interferences and thus help the country to assert its independence. The country's financial reorganisation would enable the government to rely on a rational fiscal policy with dependable national revenues. Finally, a healthy financial system designed and implemented by American experts, it was thought, would attract American investment to free the country from predatory British and Russian loans. Millspaugh and his team's initial successes were encouraging. A National Bank was established, the country's finances were put on a sound footing and American engineers began to survey, construct and maintain transport infrastructure, including the impressive Trans-Iranian Railways. Numerous railroad tunnels and bridges were to cut through and cross over mountains to make the national rail connection possible. The final decision to build the railroad had been reached by May 1925. To finance the project the Majles passed a bill in February–March 1926 to tax tea and sugar. The construction of the railway connecting the Persian Gulf in the south to Iran's northern regions finally began in October 1927, supervised by American consultants. Yet Millspaugh seemed to test Reza Shah's patience.

Tension between the Shah and Millspaugh had been growing for some time, as Millspaugh demanded increased powers and criticised expenditure on the armed forces. More importantly he failed to attract American investment.[106] Reza Shah was determined to the point of obsession to rid Iran of foreign dictates of any sort. At a testy confrontation at which Millspaugh repeated his demands and criticism, Reza Shah reportedly warned him that there could not be two kings in Iran and that he – Reza Shah – was the one.[107] Millspaugh's influence declined and he finally left Iran in 1927.

Milspaugh's departure did not affect the railroad construction; a syndicate of international companies including the American Ulen and the German firms Philip Holzmann, Julius Berger and Siemen Bau, took over the project in 1928. Numerous others from the United Kingdom, Italy, Belgium, Sweden, Czechoslovakia and Switzerland also received construction contracts for different sections of the project. The Scandinavian Kampsax Consortium took over as the project consultant in 1933, and Reza Shah who had repeatedly walked several miles at a time along the tracks on his frequent inspection tours, finally laid the last rail between Arak and Khorramabad on 24 August 1938. The railroad traversed 2100 bridges, ran through 224 tunnels and took eleven years to build at a cost of £30 million ($146,700,000), and had been completed without a cent of foreign debt.[108]

Disappointed at US lack of interest in investing in Iran's development, the government turned to Germany for trade, technical assistance and investment. Iran and Germany had been trading for many years, as the former sought relations with a state capable of checking Russo-British imperialist intentions. Trade with Germany increased steadily, with a startling forty-fold growth between 1903 and 1912 and the trend had continued.[109] German technicians and engineers had moved to Iran after the First World War to construct buildings, roads, bridges and railways, and German firms took the lead to supply technology, heavy machinery and manufacturing equipment. German economic advisors were in Iran by 1925 and Junkers Airlines had secured permission to provide air service in the country by 1928. A most favoured nation treaty followed in 1929 and a German banker, Dr Kurt Jungblatt, was hired to head Iran's National Bank in 1930. Trade between the two countries continued to increase after 1933, particularly after the German Economic Minister, Dr Hjalmar Schacht, visited Tehran in 1935. More Germans moved to Iran, often with family members, to implement bilateral import, export, education, manufacturing, training and construction agreements. With Germany's assistance, factories were built, a national radio network established and higher education expanded. German professors were recruited to teach at the newly established Tehran University to provide the country with the expertise its development required. As a result the number of manufacturing plants increased from two, employing 462 workers in 1926, to 92, employing 40,000 in 1941. In the years 1934–38 alone, 58 new factories were constructed, employing 27,750 workers.[110] Rapid development, expanded commerce and industrialisation had truly transformed the country by 1940.

One indicator of the change was increased electrification; by 1940 nearly all Iranian towns had access to electricity.[111] There was also a shift in employment patterns; in 1920 90 per cent of the country's 12 million people were employed in agriculture and related services, which accounted for 80–90 per cent of the gross national product. Their standard of living, although higher than in some neighbouring countries, was close to the breadline. By 1945 however, agriculture employed 75 per cent of the workforce and contributed 50 per cent of the GNP.[112] Roads were also improved, as prior to 1920, with the exception of four short roads totalling no more than 800 miles, most roads were mule tracks. Road construction had begun in 1923 and by 1938, 14,000 miles of new roads, 3000 miles of which were first class highways, were in use. The country's topography required spectacular engineering feats to construct these roads; the Chalus Pass at 9384 feet above sea level, for instance, was carved onto the Alborz Mountain side to connect Tehran to the Caspian Sea. The number of Iranian vehicles soon increased in response to these improved transport links. There were only 632 motorised vehicles in 1925, but this had increased to 25,000 by 1942.[113] Both producers and consumers benefited from greater market accessibility and lower freight costs. Domestic commerce, agriculture, industries and services such as transportation realised substantial growth.

Reza Shah took a personal interest in nearly all the development projects. The governor of Kermanshah Province in the country's northwest had been asked by the Minister of the Interior to fund a new project in the village of Kerend. The proposal was an unfunded add-on to the projects already underway in the province, and the governor, his development funds fully committed, could not grant the minister's request. In frustration he travelled to Tehran to seek relief. As it turned out, the new project was favoured by the King. The governor requested and was granted a royal audience at which he named the projects under his jurisdiction and the ones already done. 'Have all those projects been completed?' Reza Shah asked for emphasis. The governor confirmed that they had. 'I will visit the area shortly for inspection to see the results myself,' the King said. 'What areas are being irrigated as the result of the newly constructed dam at Ravaansar? Will the reservoir irrigate Maahi-Shahr's farmlands?' The governor, startled at the King's command of details in his province, answered the inquiries to the Shah's satisfaction. He then reported that in order to complete all projects, including the newly ordered one in Kerend, he would require the equivalent of an additional 500,000 US dollars. 'Very well; visit the minister of treasury and get your funding,' Reza Shah instructed. The governor, E'zaz Nikpay, stated in his memoirs that 'the incident proved that reporting to Reza Shah with honesty and courage was not to be feared, for doing so would result in His Majesty's affection.'[114]

It is hard to imagine how far Iran's development could have gone had the pace of improvements been allowed to continue, but as the storm clouds of the Second World War gathered, Iranians became increasingly apprehensive. Greater international tension, intrigue and propaganda persuaded Reza Shah to clamp down on political opponents. The restrictions, based on his experiences of the First World War, were in part to safeguard the nation's hard-won unity and to protect it from foreign-instigated sabotage. Groups of Nazi sympathisers, Anglophiles, Francophiles and Russophiles emerged, giving the King and the government cause for concern. The pro-Russian elements had organised the Communist Tudeh (masses) Party that many nationalists saw as a Soviet fifth column. As far as Reza Shah was concerned, Russia and Britain were imperialist states, the US was either unreliable or unwilling to check Russo-British ambitions, and Germany had become preoccupied with its own expansion and ideological agenda. None could be trusted, for none had Iran's interests in mind.

Determined to stay clear of any potential European conflict, Iran re-established relations with the United States in October 1938 and declared its neutrality on 4 September 1939. Many Iranians – who thought there was much to admire about the West – were baffled at the madness that seemed to have taken over Europe. The ideology that had taken over parts of the continent, one that condemned to extinction entire ethnic groups and socio-economic classes, was incompatible with Iranian cultural values.

As the situation in Europe worsened, the Shah repeatedly expressed to confidants a sentiment widely shared by Iranians, that Iran was alone and weak. Her neighbours, friends and allies had repeatedly turned against her or let her down in her moments of need. The only way out was genuine national strength. Only national strength would make the state independent, without need of alliances on which she had learned she could not depend.[115] Iran had fallen upon hard times since the beginning of the nineteenth century. Inadequate military power had had a lot to do with the failure of course, but Iranians could always count on other sources of strength. William H. Forbis, who took the time to live among Iranians before writing about them, made this observation:

> In the days of Cyrus and Darius, nothing, it seemed could stop the powerful and confident Persians. In most of the centuries since Alexander, the Iranians have had to accept military defeat and try to turn it into cultural victory, usually with remarkable success. A few years after Genghis Khan conquered and razed Iran, for example, his descendants had converted into thoroughly Persian poets and calligraphers ... A wry Persian proverb says: 'Defeat makes us invincible.'[116]

To be an Iranian is first and foremost a state of mind.

2

THE PEOPLE

FROM KASHAN TO PARIS

Kashan is a city of contrasts.[117] It is a historic town located on the edge of the Iranian plateau's central desert, yet is known for its lush gardens. The most of famous of these is the Fin Garden, where a noted Iranian prime minister, the visionary moderniser Mirza Taqi Khan Farahani, was executed in 1852. Mirza Taqi Khan, born in Farahan north of Kashan in 1807, had risen from a very humble background to the post of Amir Nezam (military commander). He was popularly known as Amir Kabir (the great commander), for he had championed westernisation of the country with tangible results.[118] Kashan has produced scores of influential scholars, artists and theologians, and been home to a significant Iranian Jewish community. It was the birthplace of the famed poet known by the pen name 'Amina', who wrote in both Persian and Hebrew in the late seventeenth and early eighteenth centuries. Amina enjoyed a rich cultural mix of Iranian Muslim and Jewish heritage.[119] The well known writers and scholars Moshe Halevy, Babai Ben Lutf, Shmuel Ben Pir Ahmad and his son Elisha, Rabbi Yehuda Ben El'azar and Babi Ben Farhad are among Kashan's Jewish poets. Kashan was once known as the 'Little Jerusalem' with a thriving economic life, enriched by lively spiritual values and rituals. According to Ben Farhad, Kashan had thirteen synagogues and thousands of Jewish families as far back as 1730.[120]

Kashan is known for its craftsmen, artists and especially its weavers; their carpets have for centuries adorned opulent halls and modest homes around the world. Each Kashan carpet reflects intricate designs in vivid colours, tightly knotted by women's delicate hands. It is said that the weavers put a bit of their souls in each knot they tie and the designers do likewise in the patterns they create. The hundreds of stylised patterns and the millions of knots that make a Persian carpet reflect both the perplexing wonder of life and the intensity of human aspirations. The designs are almost always metaphors for spiritual aesthetics, in keeping with the notion that to seek perfection is to pray.[121]

Kashan has produced artists such as Mohammad Ghaffari, ennobled by the title Kamal al-Molk,[122] a court painter during the reigns of four kings. Mohammad and his brother Abu-Torab were both accomplished illustrators as their father Mirza Bozorg-e Naqqash-e Kashi had been and their uncle Mirza Abolhassan Khan Sani'al-Molk Naqqash-Bashi, both Nasser Al-Din Shah's court painters. That position was in turn granted to Kamal al-Molk after his uncle passed away. Kamal al-Molk died in 1939 at the age of 90, having left behind a collection of remarkable works. His family, by the time of his passing, had produced an unbroken chain of excellent painters for several generations.[123] The family also produced a diplomat in the person of Hassan-Ali Ghaffari (1888–1980) who moved from the Ministry of Foreign Affairs to the Imperial Court as Grand Master of Ceremonies when Reza Shah ascended the throne. The family's mastery of the arts was thus not limited to illustration.

Kashan's geography may have encouraged its residents to defy their isolation through intellectual and artistic inquiry, unhindered by physical barriers. The Kashi gardener dreams of an oasis and builds one within a walled enclosure, keeping harsh and barren reality out.[124] The artisan dreams of paradise and weaves its imagined similitude to spread over the parched desert soil. The artist confined in the city's isolation creates a tableau to open a window onto a world of beauty. Whether strolling in a walled garden, sitting on a carpet or contemplating the beauty of a painting, the Kashi's aim is to seek perfection, to uplift the spirit and to discover the mystery that is a life well lived.

Rayhan Morady came from a Jewish family of art dealers in Kashan with ambitious dreams unbound by political or geographic limitations. His interest in the arts brought him ever closer to the town's artisans, calligraphers and weavers. His personal curiosity influenced his interest to seek markets beyond his home town. His first great adventure was to set up shop in the capital Tehran at the turn of the twentieth century. Iranians like to promenade in the evenings along tree-lined, shaded streets, and every Iranian city has them for the purpose. The most attractive business districts, if not the covered bazaars, are along tree-lined promenades. Lalehzar Avenue, a few blocks north of the Golestan Royal Place and the Baharestan Garden, the site of the newly constituted parliament, was then not only the place to shop, but the place to stroll and be seen.[125]

In preparation for the crowds, shopkeepers would sprinkle water on the sidewalks every afternoon following sunset to cool off the area. Pedestrians would often appear in groups, talking, shopping and meeting friends, while perambulating back and forth from one end of Lalehzar to the other. Some would stop at favourite cafés as their daily meeting places to discuss politics or literature. The well-to-do would arrive in their horse drawn carriages to commence leisurely walks. Women also frequented the sidewalks, strolling gracefully with measured, unhurried steps, always accompanied by female companions and often followed by male attendants who walked a respectful few paces behind. Although covered by chador and neqab, the ladies attracted considerable attention.[126] The height and figure, manner of gait, patterns embroidered on the veil and the style of shoes worn, all commanded attention. Young men would spend hours in pursuit of an unseen beloved, hoping to steal a discreet, 'accidental' look. If inclined to favour the suitor, she would lift her neqab briefly to pretend to glance at a piece of merchandise. Such a momentary glance was a victory worthy of celebration. The women themselves could see the suitors clearly. They would convey their interest to their confidantes, who would discreetly pass on the information to the man's female relatives.[127] A prospective groom's mother would then initiate a request for a visit to the potential bride's mother to commence discussions of possible marriage. With the parents consent, the eligible bachelor accompanied by his family would be invited to visit the girl's home. During the visit, the prospective bride would enter the room briefly to serve tea. The ritual would allow each to see and hear the other, to charm, and to be charmed. Lalehzar was thus more than a shopping district; it was the throbbing heart of the nation's capital. Rayhan had selected his store's location judiciously and with ambition. That same ambition drove him to expand his business to Europe and eventually to move to Paris.

Iran was about to leap out of a long period of stagnation. The country had declined over a period of half a millennium, but suddenly awakened. The elite and the middle classes were the first to anticipate the tremors of imminent change. Iranians had begun travelling and studying abroad and European ideas had attracted eager adherents. Rayhan had foreseen the changes and his store had kept pace with the public taste. He kept his Tehran showroom attractive, well appointed and always well stocked. Rayhan made a point of visiting nearby shops every morning to greet his fellow shopkeepers. At times he would bring his children to work to teach them customer relations and the many intricacies of good business. Rayhan's shop gradually evolved into a centre of Kashis' network in Tehran. He welcomed that development and cultivated contacts with different circles, including the aristocracy and the newly emerging European-influenced nationalist middle class. Rayhan had thus established not only a successful business, but a web of relationships close to the centres of power, commerce and information. His third son, when a mere six-year-old, had already manifested his talent for business.

Ibby (Ibrahim) Morady had accompanied his father to the store one day, and Rayhan instructed his son to mind the store as he extended his customary morning greetings to the neighbouring merchants. A European couple walked into Rayhan's shop while he was out. As they looked around they admired a fine silk rug hung on the wall behind the counter. Ibby knew that his father would accept 250 tomans (2500 rials) for it as his bottom line. When the couple asked the price, he invited them to examine the exceptional workmanship closely first, before quoting the price at 300. The couple remained interested. The little boy ran outside to call for his father, and when the latter entered the shop, Ibby announced 'They like the rug you couldn't possibly sell for less than 300 tomans.' Rayhan took the hint that the deal was already done. The rug was sold for 300.

Some twenty years later the family was in Paris and Ibby was a dashing bachelor businessman. His store was on the same street as his father's and the proximity helped sales at both. Ibby had intuitively felt the two showrooms would attract comparison-shoppers, increase traffic, enhance customer confidence and in turn lead to greater sales at both locations. He had been right. Ibby was successful in business and popular with a wide circle of friends. He was handsome, articulate and always well dressed, preferably in well tailored double-breasted suits and fashionable designer ties. Although living in the family's spacious house, he also maintained an apartment of his own and was reputed to have never had fewer than five girlfriends. Ibby appreciated the good life and enjoyed cultivating friendships. Proud of his Iranian heritage, he never missed an opportunity to participate in Iranian cultural events or to represent his country at exhibitions.

Ibby's personality mirrored in many ways that of a fellow Iranian bachelor, Abdol-Hossein Sardari, also residing in Paris. Sardari worked at the Iranian legation's consular office and was a charming hedonist. The two had numerous occasions to meet and ample reason to become good friends. Until his marriage in 1952 to Bahie, Ibby remained a popular bachelor in Paris.[128] Sardari owned a cottage outside Paris but lived in a spacious atelier in the city. The atelier, a one-bedroom artist's studio, was located in a fashionable district within walking distance of Iran's legation.

By the time the Second World War broke out, Ibby's sociability, charm and trustworthiness had gradually seen him take the lead in the family business. As Paris was threatened, the Morady family moved to the relative safety of the large riverside family compound with its expansive garden. Ibby remained in Paris and prepared for the worst.

The news of Nazi atrocities seemed at first too outrageous to believe. When the Germans marched into Paris in June 1940, the Gestapo did not find it difficult to recruit collaborators to identify Jewish families, rewarding anyone from building attendants, doormen, rubbish collectors, hospital orderlies to mailmen for giving them pertinent information. A racial affairs office was soon established, registration of Jews began, and the degrading yellow patches that were to be worn on outer garments were given out.

A few months after the Iranian Minister Anoshiravan Sepahbody had left Paris for Vichy, Ibby heard a rumour that Iran's legation in Paris, already reduced to an interest section, was to close altogether. He visited Sardari to ascertain the truth. His heart sank when Sardari revealed that he had been ordered to depart for Tehran. Ibby implored him to stay. 'You cannot leave!' Ibby told him. 'Your fellow Iranian folk need your help. It will be a sin if you leave us,' he pleaded passionately. Sardari was a moral man and an informed diplomat. He understood the threats that his fellow Iranians who happened to be Jewish faced. As it turned out, he did not need much persuasion. He had thought about the Iranian Foreign Ministry's orders – to close the legation and to depart for Tehran – for a number of anxious days and sleepless nights. He knew his career was on the line and the consequences of insubordination would be severe. Yet he also knew what his superiors may not have known that leaving his post in Paris could result in disastrous consequences for many of his fellow Iranians. He determined to stay. Yet, remaining in Paris would make sense only if he could counteract the Nazi racial policies.[129] Sardari and Morady would confer a couple of days later but find the challenge ahead overwhelming. They clearly needed further deliberation with trusted friends before making a move.

Ibby called his close associates that day, the moment he reached his showroom. To avoid suspicion, they were to meet at his store. When all arrived, one was holding a large book tightly pressed against his chest to hide the yellow patch he had been ordered to wear. The doorman of his apartment building had identified him to the Gestapo. What could they do, he asked? Everyone was overwhelmed by a million mundane crises of daily life, monstrously magnified under the German occupation. They discussed the problems they faced, the threats against their families, the difficulties of residing in areas infested with informants and the impossibility of liquidating assets to leave German-occupied territories. One suggested hiding their children at home, another proposed bribing informers to buy their cooperation, and a third advised laying low until the storm blew over. The meeting ended inconclusively but Ibby remained in deep and anxious contemplation. Pacing back and forth, it suddenly occurred to him that the answer he had been seeking may have been there under his feet all along. He was standing on a fine Kashan carpet with a grand intricate design, woven methodically by tying thousands of colourfully dyed yarns into millions of little knots. He and his friends would weave an intricate design of a different kind.

Carpet as metaphor is a common theme in Iranian stories. Iranian nobility, including royal families, had traditionally required their children to learn a trade regardless of education or wealth, as prudent insurance against a change of fortune. The fable of a captured prince whose life was spared by the enemy for his mastery of weaving exquisite rugs is a popular story learned by many Iranian children. The captors, so the fable goes, wanted as many precious rugs as the prince could produce. Gradually some ended up in market places and one found its way to the prince's capital city and the royal palace. The royal household soon recognised the patterns and deciphered the intricate designs that guided them to the prince's captors and secured his subsequent freedom. Ibby called four trusted friends to a second meeting. The group included two French carpet dealers and two Iranian businessmen. They agreed that the problem they had to confront was first and foremost the Nazi ideology. If they could neutralise the ideology, they could overcome the other difficulties. Being realistic, they recognised that any systematic approach required funds. One suggested asking Iranian Jewish families to contribute. Ibby was incensed. 'Why ask struggling families for money at this stressful time? The five of us here are all well to do and we know it. I say that we, the five of us, could manage the cost.' None of his friends objected. The first crucial decision had been made.[130]

Ibby did not dislike Germans; he had met many before the war and his parents had had a close German family friend for years. Numerous German military officers visited his store after France's defeat, nearly all amateur Persian carpet aficionados. It was remarkable, he thought, that German officers always paid cash for their purchases. They were mostly direct but correct, often with disciplined, courteous manners. Such people could not be all bad, he thought.

When he met Sardari again it appeared that both had thought along the same lines. The Germans could be cultivated, decent officials befriended, hard-line ideologues neutralised – and some petty officials bribed. The objective was to save Iranian Jews residing in France from certain harassment and possibly much worse. But achieving this objective required a well designed plan with dedicated and persistent implementation. Sardari's legal education and diplomatic experience would help craft the grand design. It would all be carried out under the auspices of Iran's legation, supported by an integrated network of friends.

Ibby and his four friends had to commit themselves and their fortunes to the cause and they did so, voluntarily assuming financial responsibility for their community's safety. The war's outcome was far from certain in 1941 and under the circumstances such commitment was nothing short of heroic. The five chivalrous men who embraced the awesome responsibility were David Dorra, 40 years old, Sami Dorra, 21, Morure Lazarian, 32, Rahim Papahn, 38 and Ibrahim Morady, 26.

The Dorras were not related. Both were French, although they were to claim Iranian nationality during the German occupation. Morady, Lazarian and Papahn on the other hand, were Iranian, born in Tehran. Papahn's name was at first a joke, then a humorous nickname before becoming his surname. Rahim's original name had been Haji Rahim Nakhi-Musa, but his friends called him Rahim Pawpahn for he had big wide feet. ('Foot' is 'paw' and wide is 'pahn' in the Persian language.) As familiar Jewish names became dangerous under the Nazis' watchful eyes, Rahim recognised the nickname's utility and welcomed being widely known by the French-sounding pronunciation, 'Papan.'[131] A sixth person, a man named Solayman or Solaymani, joined the previous five later on and become fully involved. He may have been Solayman-Khan Nasseri, who in the 1950s owned a carpet store on Haussmann Boulevard.[132]

Having created a fund, the next task was to identify the community members at risk. An initial list of families was drawn up by the group of six. One evening in autumn while walking home alone and deep in thought, Ibby contemplated the task ahead. It was getting dark and the streets were almost deserted. Trees were shedding their yellowed leaves. There was a chill in the air, so Ibby raised the collar of his overcoat to keep warm and quickened his pace. Suddenly a violent gust of wind blew behind him, the thrust of it pushing him forward.

Still on his feet but off-balance, he heard a loud crash right behind him. As he twisted around he saw a large storm window shattered on the pavement. The window had clearly just fallen from the multi-storey building above. Had the blast of the wind not shoved him forward, the heavy window would have surely smashed his skull, killing him instantly. He took that as a sign and resolved to redouble his efforts. Over 60 years later he still recalled the event with considerable awe, as if it had just occurred.

3

THE UNLIKELY SAVIOUR

SARDARI AND HIS FRIENDS

The building on 112 Boulevard Malesherbes in Paris, Arrondissement XVII, pulsated with excitement nearly every day. A classically ornate building about a mile from the La Madeleine Palace, it housed several art studios, each with an unending stream of attractive models and visiting clients. There was a photo studio on the ground floor, frequented by aspiring starlets. Guy-Charles Revol, the famed Parisian sculptor, had an atelier on the same floor often visited by celebrities who modelled for his work.[133] The noted painter Jean Denis Maillart worked in an atelier on the second floor with his models and patrons.

Most models and aspiring starlets in Paris were devoted customers of Alexandre's hair salon, located in Pigalle, the city's nightclub district. Alexandre styled his favourites' hair free of charge and accompanied them to the photo studio on 112 Boulevard Malesherbes to ensure they were photographed in the most photogenic way. Sardari lived on the third floor of the same building in a charming one-bedroom studio that he had leased from the Paris municipality in 1939. The location was conveniently close to the Iranian legation located on 5 Fortuny Avenue, where Sardari worked at the consular's office. He often walked the one-third of a mile there, a pleasant stroll that took only minutes.

Everyone at 112 Boulevard Malesherbes knew Sardari well, for he always received his neighbours with open arms. Alexandre was an especially close friend who would often march his charges up to Sardari's studio apartment for photo shoots in surroundings more exotic than the studio downstairs. An Iranian friend of Sardari – an artist and former student of the Iranian court painter Kamal al-Molk – also used Sardari's studio. Eskandar was a competent painter but could not find enough work in Paris at the time. To make ends meet, he supplemented his income through photography, freely using

Sardari's equipment and apartment. Photography had been one of Sardari's many hobbies for years; he was particularly fond of the German-made Leica cameras, of which he had a collection.[134]

To visit Sardari's two-storey apartment one entered through a tall walnut double door that opened into the foyer, filled with professional photography equipment and several antique cameras. There was also a book-binding press, another of Sardari's hobbies. There was a powder room to the right of the entrance and a narrow service hallway leading to a hidden staircase to the kitchen on the second floor. The foyer opened to the main hallway leading to another double door that opened into a sunny living room. A master bedroom was on the opposite side. The main room was huge, with a sixteen-foot-high ceiling, two large cathedral windows and two skylights. The windows were about three feet off the floor and continued all the way to the ceiling. Naturally well lit and spacious, the room projected a romantic yet palatial atmosphere. At one end of the room and on a raised platform stood a Steinway concert piano. A built-in marble fireplace shimmered behind the grand piano creating an atmosphere of subdued elegance. At the opposite end of the room an attractive spiral staircase unfolded, rising gracefully towards a dramatic loft with a balcony overlooking the room. The balcony led to two small rooms and a kitchen, which was equipped with a large wooden table and a professional-grade gas stove. A refrigerator and a cabinet were placed under a large horizontal window that provided the space with ample natural light. In the master bedroom downstairs a French double door opened onto an ornate outdoor terrace, which overlooked a formal manicured garden. A small sunken alcove at the foot of the bed provided a cosy place to sit, to carry on an intimate conversation, or to read. A bathroom was built into the side of the alcove.

Visitors were awed by Sardari's tasteful decoration: the Persian carpets, two classic hand-carved teak chairs, several antique hardwood doors adorned with inlaid Persian calligraphy on built-in wall cabinets and an assortment of paintings and sculptures. One pair of the antique inlaid doors opened to reveal a well-stocked liquor cabinet. There was an original sculpture by Auguste Rodin that Sardari favoured, but the focal point of the room was a beautiful bust of an attractive young woman with oriental features, created by Revol at Sardari's request. The apartment appeared spacious but intimate, elegant but informal, beautiful but functional. Sardari was a marvellous host and could entertain more than 100 guests at a time.[135] When he entertained – and he did so frequently – he served only the very best. He was charming as an entertainer, gracious as a host and superb as a chef. He spoke French, German, English and Persian with flair, and showered his guests with compliments. He loved good food and drink, good friends, and was a genuine admirer of beauty. He adored women and enjoyed their company. Socialising and entertaining were central to his character, perhaps to the point of necessity. He filled his life with friendship, beauty and excitement. His family inheritance helped him maintain the lifestyle he so deeply enjoyed.

Sardari was a man of many talents. He was a linguist, a lawyer and a diplomat, but also a competent self-taught photographer and an excellent bookbinder. Bookbinding had been a part of his traditional aristocratic education, for as previously mentioned, an Iranian nobleman was expected to learn a trade in youth.[136] He was also a well regarded cook, recognised by chefs at several Parisian restaurants. Alcohol would occasionally awaken his taste for practical jokes. Once, after an evening of drinking, he managed to talk a French policeman into lending him his uniform, and wearing it, he called on a visiting Iranian diplomat at his hotel room. Pretending to be there to arrest him at that late hour, he scared the poor diplomat – Abdollah Entezam – out of his wits before Entezam recognised him in the borrowed uniform. Entezam had known Sardari from earlier days at the Iranian legation in Bern, Switzerland in the 1930s. He would become the chairman of National Iranian Oil Company (NIOC) in 1957 and Sardari would join the company the following year.

Sardari was fascinated by gadgets of all sorts and was often among the first to acquire them. As soon as tape recorders became commercially available he bought one. After a great dinner and several glasses of fine wine at his apartment one evening, a French diplomat began criticising his own government. Sardari, once again in the mood for a practical joke, placed a microphone behind the diplomat's chair and using the still uncommon machine, recorded the spirited political oration. Later in the evening and at a suitable moment of quiet he turned the machine on. The diplomat turned ashen faced until he realised that it had all been a joke.[137]

Sardari enjoyed fast cars and motorcycles. He once had a 1938 Peugeot motorcycle that he gave to his cousin Amir Mansur Sardari, then a medical student in Paris. Later he purchased a state-of-the-art shaft-driven BMW, then later a powerful Norton. When the BMW arrived, he hired two labourers to carry it up to his third floor studio apartment. He would ride it on holidays and weekends but would not leave it outside unprotected. He owned a riverfront cottage in the suburb of Moulineuf where he enjoyed fishing. He invited his nephew Fereydoun Hoveyda to ride with him to the cottage once on the newly acquired BMW motorcycle. Hoveyda recalled he was absolutely terrified by the time they reached the cottage. Another nephew, Farhad Sepahbody, remembers Sardari occasionally riding the Norton to the legation. Sardari owned a convertible Citroen sports car before the Second World War and an early Jaguar roadster after it. The roadster reportedly could do 200 kilometres (120 miles) per hour, remarkable for a car at the time. Women loved to ride with him and he loved to thrill them with speed. When on official business he would use one of the legation's two black sedans, a Citroen and a Peugeot, with diplomatic licence plates. As well as high quality vehices, he was also particular about his clothes and often acquired his wardrobe from Sulka of Paris before and after the war, often custom tailored at significant cost.[138]

Sardari had numerous female friends, but only one true love. He was enchanted by a beautiful Chinese student of opera, a singer he affectionately called Tchin-Tchin. A stunning beauty, she was tall, and accentuated her height wearing pompadour hair and high heels.[139] Studying at the Paris Conservatoire, Tchin-Tchin was an accomplished singer. She was interested in Iranian history and culture and would not miss an exhibition if it had anything to do with Iran. Mrs Irene Petrossian, wife of the famed caviar importer, usually joined her on the museum tours and cultural events.[140] Tchin-Tchin accompanied Sardari to the various official receptions and diplomatic functions so regularly that many assumed they were married. The truth was that Sardari wanted to marry her but Tchin-Tchin was not ready for the commitment.[141] Tchin-Tchin's father, an industrialist in China, had sent his daughter and younger son to France together. The parents obviously valued a European education for their children, but did not want them to be separate and alone so far away from home. When war broke out, the two were stranded in Paris unable to return to China or receive funds from home. Sardari simply assumed responsibility for them both. Greater tragedy struck in 1941 when the brother fell ill unexpectedly and died of a ruptured appendix. The pain of the loss was compounded, for the body could not be sent home for proper burial as required by Chinese tradition. To ease Tchin-Tchin's anxiety, Sardari promised to have the body preserved for the eventual return home after the war. The body was kept in a freezer at the Paris morgue at Sardari's expense.

Sardari had fallen in love with Tchin-Tchin by the time war broke out. Having lost her brother and being stranded in Paris, she finally moved in with him but declined to marry him. Nevertheless, they were inseparable and lived together as a married couple. She was frequently addressed as Mrs Sardari, an error she seemingly did not care to correct. Some of Sardari's friends and relatives thought they had quietly married, while others suspected the relationship not entirely reciprocal. There is no doubt that Tchin-Tchin was fond of Sardari but it is not clear whether she loved him as much as he loved her. That is a point on which Sardari's surviving relatives do not seem to be in agreement.

Soon after he had taken charge of Iran's legation, Sardari called his Iranian-Armenian friend Mouchegh Petrossian to meet him. They met at the Lido, the famous nightclub, one evening in early November 1940. Mr and Mrs Petrossian were already there waiting when Sardari and Tchin-Tchin arrived. Both Petrossian and Sardari were well enough known at the nightclub to get one of the better tables in the house. This was not the first time the couples had met there but Sardari and Petrossian both seemed particularly preoccupied that evening. Over the first bottle of champagne Sardari broached the possibility of hosting a reception at the Iranian legation. As Iran's highest-ranking diplomat in Paris after Minister Anoshiravan Sepahbody's departure for Vichy, Sardari wanted to keep the legation in the limelight. Petrossian, a keen businessman and patriot with political acumen, was ready to help without hesitation. He knew Sardari would not settle for anything less than the best and offered a number of suggestions accordingly. The two thus began to plan the first of several lavish banquets.

Mouchegh Petrossian (1895–1981) and his younger brother Melkom had established themselves as the sole importers of Russian caviar in Paris.[142] Born in Tabriz, Iran, and holding Iranian passports, the brothers had studied in Russia, where Mouchegh had married Irene, born in Kislowodsk. Back home in Iran the brothers had enjoyed the Caspian Sea sturgeon eggs and noted the Russian fondness for 'the black pearls'. Following the Russian Revolution of 1917, a flood of the displaced Russian nobility arrived in Paris, with an already cultivated taste for the prized delicacy. They thus created a European market for caviar, but all commercial links with Russia had been severed and Iranian caviar was not being directly exported. Detecting Bolshevik Russia's need for foreign trade, the brothers contacted the commissars with a proposal to purchase caviar for the European market. Moscow expressed interest and offered an exclusive export deal, but in return demanded hard currency, credit was not an option. The brothers risked everything, liquidated all their assets, stuffed the money in a suitcase and met the communists' demands. The suitcase was delivered by hand to a Bolshevik representative and the exclusive deal was sealed. Remarkably perhaps, the Bolsheviks honoured their contract and the Petrossian brothers became the sole importers of Russian caviar.

At first the chefs of Paris were slow to serve caviar at their restaurants, so the brothers had to devise creative marketing plans. They offered free supplies of caviar to selected restaurants if the chefs would simply agree to test the market for it. Cajoled to add caviar to their menus and to invite cosmopolitan customers to taste the delicacy, the chefs gave the Petrossians a chance. Much to their surprise, their customers acquired a taste for it and the market exploded. The brothers made a name for themselves and their business expanded quickly.

By the time the Petrossians, Sardari and Tchin-Tchin left the Lido in the early hours of the morning, the essentials for the first banquet at the Iranian legation had been planned. Mouchegh Petrossian would cater the food, the caviar and the drinks. Sardari would invite the diplomatic corps, the military leadership and the German and Vichy officialdom. His friends and neighbours would invite an attractive group of stars, starlets, artists and intellectuals. Tchin-Tchin would arrange and oversee the musical entertainment. The banquet would be the talk of the town and a reception to be remembered.

The next day Sardari consulted with his friend Alexandre about how to enhance his guests' entertainment. The Germans, particularly the educated aristocrats, admired French art and literature. Paris had its seductive artistic-intellectual attractions and the German occupiers wished, particularly in the early days, to reassure the French intellectual community. Parisians witnessed a boom in publishing, fashion shows, movie premieres, concerts and gallery exhibitions. The Germans even protected painters, sculptors and poets from the threat of censorship, engulfed in battles over modernist versus classic interpretations of French culture. Ambassador Abetz, who had championed Franco-German friendship as far back as the 1920s, was instrumental in the diplomatic effort towards reconciliation. His 'Groupe Collaboration' was in effect the old 'Cercle France-Allemagne' that attracted artists, writers, journalists and publishers during the occupation. Aside from receptions at the German Embassy, he organised major public exhibitions, the first of which, 'La France Européenne' in the summer of 1941 in Paris, attracted 653,000 visitors. The popularity of the events diminished after 1942, but the exhibition series still attracted three million people. The Berlin Philharmonic performances and lectures by noted intellectuals on a variety of topics such as democracy's failings and the idea of the Volk, added to the excitement.[143] France's painful defeat was to be portrayed not as a reflection of national weakness but a manifestation of outdated ideologies professed by misguided leaders.[144]

At Sardari's request, Alexandre recommended a group of beautiful starlets to amuse the guests at the banquet. Tchin-Tchin arranged the musical entertainment, and Sardari's friends – artists, sculptors, writers, philosophers, actors and actresses – joined in to provide the desired intellectual atmosphere. A number of businessmen, government officials, diplomats, physicians and additional socialites completed the guest list.

The Iranian legation was an old, gracefully ornate mansion, elegantly furnished. Although opulently decorated, Iranian merchants dealing in carpets, antiques and tapestries were called upon to lend additional objects of interest to enhance the building's already attractive interior. The point was to make the reception impressive enough to ensure that attending future events at the legation became irresistible. Nothing was to be left to chance.

The banquet was a tremendous success. The highest ranking officials in Paris had been invited and nearly all of them appeared. Sardari dazzled his guests with his charm, command of several languages, disarming friendship and generous compliments. The guests were treated to an uncommonly lavish feast. The alluring entertainment, highlighted by the presence of beautiful aspiring stars, added to the enjoyment. The intent had been to give the legation an unprecedented status in the new political environment in Paris, and soon an invitation from the Iranian legation became prized currency. Iran was a neutral country, in war with none and friendly to all. Yet it had played along with the German propaganda overtures that had declared Iranians to be of the same Aryan stock as the Germans. The distinction had resonated with the German occupiers and created grounds for their good will towards the Iranians.

The banquet was of course the means to an ambitious end: to cultivate relations with France's new rulers to influence their decisions. Sardari was determined to repeat the exercise as often as necessary. He made contacts, forged friendships and strengthened personal bonds. As a result, he could conduct numerous tasks through unofficial means. The banquets were also gateways to more exclusive receptions. Selected guests would be invited to intimate parties at Sardari's atelier where he was chef, bartender and host. On occasion he would take his guests to fashionable restaurants with private guestrooms where his chef friends would supply the ingredients from their kitchens and he would prepare the meal in full view of his guests, with consummate showmanship. His dishes were orchestrations of heavenly aromas, a pageantry of colours and mouth-watering ingredients, and every meal was complemented by the finest wines and spirits available. The relations he so carefully cultivated were constantly reaffirmed by repeated contacts, visits and offers of assistance.

Sardari would never ask for favours from authorities during his frequent official visits. To do so would have jeopardised the trust and brought into question the motivation for the personal friendships he sought. Favours would be asked only during private, unofficial gatherings, always after a good meal. The subject would be approached in total confidence as a private personal inquiry between friends, unburdened – at least for the moment – by official responsibilities and policies. Trust in Sardari's assurances of confidentiality was the key and he carefully cultivated that trust. He would steer a conversation artfully to entice a German or Vichy official to make the first suggestion in resolving an implied concern. Usually willing to reciprocate Sardari's friendship, the officials were also afforded the cover of deniability that drinking at a private reception made plausible. Any information exchanged or any assistance promised was understood to be non-attributable and strictly private.

The flexibility inherent in the German occupation policy was very helpful. Hitler's governing preference was to rely on individuals rather than what Martin Bormann characterised as 'desolate centralism'.[145] Sardari was not interested in political ideology, nor was he interested in supporting one political party over another. His first priority was a life well lived, which implied decency towards others whom he saw as individuals, not as nameless members of races or classes.

Sardari knew an Iranian physician in Paris who had practised medicine for a decade. Dr Mansur Badie had a good reputation, with numerous influential friends, acquaintances and patients. Sardari persuaded him to join the legation as a cultural attaché to help maintain, if not elevate, its influence. It might have been through Badie that Sardari met another physician, Dr Asaf Atchildi, an émigré from Soviet Russia's Central Asia.[146] Atchildi was a Russian-educated physician born to a Jewish family in Samarkand, Uzbekistan, that had been under Russian occupation since 1886. He was born in the 1890s, had attended a gymnasium, and after the October Revolution was permitted to enrol in medical school in Russia. He had practised medicine in Moscow upon graduation until his departure for France, apparently for political reasons. In France he had been compelled to re-enrol in medical school to receive his French medical licence in 1935. He was conscripted into the French Army as a reserve medical officer in 1939 but returned to his practice when released from duty in 1940. He was generally known as a Russian immigrant, but his Jewish heritage remained a secret. He set up a health spa offering hydrotherapy for a variety of pains and ailments, and some influential French and German officials and military officers had found Atchildi's unusual treatments highly effective and had spread the word. Subsequently, an increasing number of high-ranking Germans became his patients. Both Badie and Atchildi would, when necessary, solicit their patients' assistance on behalf of their Jewish friends and clients. Atchildi confirmed his involvement in rescuing Jewish residents of Paris in 1940–1944 in an article published in 1967. Although his account includes some inconsistencies and is sometimes at odds with the recollections of others, it confirms that Sardari and Atchildi were instrumental in saving Jewish lives.[147]

Although he did not register himself as a Jew under German occupation, Atchildi claimed to have presided over a community of 150 Jews of Central Asian background. A friend at the Afghan Embassy and a few former officials of the defunct Georgian Democratic Republic had reportedly given him the inspiration.[148] According to Atchildi's account, the Afghan diplomat offered to testify that Atchildi and his wife were of Afghan, rather than Jewish, origin. Atchildi claimed that the Georgians, one of whom was Georgia's former Prime Minister M. Eugene Gueguechkori, came up with the idea of exempting 'Jugutis' from the application of German anti-Jewish racial laws. Atchildi's 1967 article suggests that he had initiated the effort to save Afghan, Georgian, Bukharan and Iranian Jews by himself and that his first encounter with 'the Iranian diplomat Sardari' had been after 11 February 1942. He asserts that he received a letter from the Iranian Consul General (Sardari) on 11 February 1942 in which Sardari invited Atchildi to meet him. When they met, Atchildi reports, Sardari asked 'My dear Doctor, president of the Jugutis, how does it come about that you have left the Iranians out of your list of Jugutis?' Yet, Atchildi's published article includes a facsimile of an official letter on Iranian consulate stationery signed by Sardari and dated 29 October 1940 – some sixteen months earlier – that contradicts this. Sardari had attested in that letter that 'Djougouts' of the ancient khanates of Bukhara, Khiva, etc., within the Soviet Republics of Uzbekistan and Tajikistan, were not of Jewish race. Furthermore, Sardari's letter was written in response to an inquiry by the French Ministry of Foreign Affairs dated 28 October 1940, indicating an ongoing bureaucratic haggling on the subject between the Ministry and the Iranian envoy. In the article Atchildi mentions a Jacob Issachar Zadeh [sic], his childhood friend and neighbour in Samarkand, married to a Nadia Yablanski.[149] Their son Sova appealed to Atchildi in Paris for assistance.

> I went with Sova to the Iranian Consulate to request that the Consul conduct a [birth registration] search in the archives. But the following day a surprise awaited us at the Iranian Consulate, when we saw in the registration book of 1923 the name of Jacob Zadeh-Yablanski with the note: Jew born in Jerusalem.[150]

Why the Iranian Consulate would have the Issacher-Zadeh (Asqarzadeh is a Persian last name) birth registration record, if he was not an Iranian citizen, Atchildi did not explain. If the family members were Soviet citizens, why would they seek their birth and marriage records at the Iranian consulate? That Atchildi may have tried to minimise Sardari's role in their mutual endeavour and hide his own partnership with him, is indeed puzzling. Yet, the survivors remember 'Dr Atchildi' as Sardari's close friend and collaborator during France's 52 months of German occupation.[151]

As the war dragged on, the circumstances became increasingly dreadful. The Sephardic Cultural Association – *Association Culturelle Sephardite de Paris* – for instance, requested the German Embassy in January 1942 to exempt the Sephardic from anti-Jewish measures, as they were racially different from the European Jewry. The request included several supporting documents. One claimed that the Sephardic Israelites in Saloniki, Greece, had been already recognised by occupation authorities as Aryan. Another referred to the Sephardic colony in Hamburg-Altona, members of which had been allowed to retain their German citizenship. The embassy's request for clarification from Berlin generated numerous inquiries. The final reply from the Foreign Ministry, dated 13 February 1942, was a sharp denial of the Association's request. Signed by Franz Rademacher of the Foreign Ministry's department Referat DIII in charge of the Jewish question, racial policy, German refugees and national policies abroad, the statement was categorical:

> A special treatment of the Sephardim is out of the question. They are Jews just like the others. The Sephardim in Hamburg are treated as Jews. The claim of special treatment in Saloniki appears unbelievable. The question will be verified by the German representative in Athens, who has received a directive to ensure that any possible special treatment be repealed.

On 20 February 1942, the German Consulate in Saloniki reported the claim of the Association – that the Sephardim had been recognised as Aryans of the Mosaic faith – had been a lie. An 'expert opinion' solicited by the Foreign Ministry was more ominous as it foresaw the Nazi effort to come.

> The claim of the 'Association Culturelle Sephardite de Paris' that they are 'Aryans of Mosaic faith' due to differences between the Sephardic and Ashkenazi Jews is completely untenable. That is simply a Jewish attempt to use this thesis to save the European Jewry from complete destruction.[152]

Sardari knew Otto Abetz (1903–1958) who had followed the German Army into France and been named ambassador in November 1940 – a position he held until June 1944. Abetz had been posted to Paris as a German diplomat before the war but been expelled as *persona non grata* in 1939 for having allegedly bribed French journalists. His return with the conquering army may have been to humiliate the French. Yet as a Francophile, the former art teacher interested in French culture and married to the French Susanne de Bruyker since 1932, was also an ardent supporter of Franco-German national collaboration. Diplomatic prudence dictated that Iran's only envoy in Paris pay the new ambassador a visit, and Abetz received Sardari in his grand office with expressions of warmth and friendship. Abetz spoke of German-Iranian racial fraternity and all the glory that their future promised. Germany had had allies, he said, but many had been allies of convenience influenced by Germany's ascendance. Iran was different, for Iranians were the Germans' blood kin and as such genuine allies, soon to renew their ancient glory. As Abetz spoke, Sardari's mind raced.[153] He examined the possible moves ahead, as a chess master would anticipate an opponent's. Next he visited another German diplomat, First Secretary Krafft von Dellmensingen. Dellmensingen was a career diplomat from an old and respected aristocratic Bavarian family. He, as was the case with many career diplomats in the German Foreign Ministry, had not bought into the Nazi propaganda or Hitler's exhortations. He had been one of Sardari's genuine friends and that amity would deepen over time, lasting well beyond the war years.

Sardari stopped to visit several Iranian business owners on the way back to his office. He was, as always, greeted warmly. He asked about their businesses, their employees, their families – and problems with the occupying Germans. One of the stores he visited was Ibrahim Morady's *Palais d'Iran*. After exchanging pleasantries and admiring some of his newly displayed carpets, he asked Morady in confidence to prepare a list of all Iranian Jewish families in Paris. To deflect Nazi harassment, he would need their names, addresses, occupations and dates and places of birth. The required information may have been suggested by Sardari's German friend Dellmensingen earlier that day.

As Sardari arrived at the Iranian legation through the large gate that opened into a courtyard, an idea that had entered his mind earlier had begun taking shape. He parked the Citroen sedan with the *Corps Diplomatique* plates and climbed the marble steps to the main floor. That he had to drive himself since the legation's chauffeur had gone to Vichy with Minister Sepahbody actually suited him. He collected his messages from the two secretaries and rushed to his office. He responded to telephone messages, urgent telegrams and other inquiries from Tehran and Vichy before attending to an assortment of other diplomatic and consular matters. Hours had passed by the time he had completed his routine tasks. Finally he left his office for the building's library. As he passed through the hallway decorated with framed posters depicting Iran's cultural heritage, perhaps he glanced at a particular one picturing a clay cylinder with its cuneiform inscription. The inscription was Cyrus's Charter of Human Rights, read by the great King at his coronation held on the first day of spring marking the Iranian New Year's Day in 539 BC in Babylon. Sardari had read Cyrus's Charter before, but he may have stopped to read it again for inspiration.

> Now that with the blessings of Ahura Mazda [God] I put the crown of Iran, Babylon and the nations of the four directions on my head, I announce that I will respect the traditions, customs and religions of the peoples of my empire and never let any of my governors and subordinates to look down upon or to insult them as long as I live. I will impose my monarchy on no nation. Each is free to accept it, and if any one of them rejects it, I will not resort to war to reign [over them]. For as long as I am the King of Iran, Babylon and the nations of the four directions, I will never let anyone oppress any other, and if such occurs, I will return the rights [of the oppressed] and penalise the oppressor. I will never let anyone take possession of properties of others by force or without compensation. I ban unpaid forced labour. Today I announce that everyone is free to live and work in any region, provided he/she does not violate the rights of others. No one could be penalised for his or her relatives' faults. I ban slavery and my governors and subordinates are obliged to prohibit exchanging men and women as slaves within their administrative domains. Such traditions [as slavery] should be eradicated in the entire world. I implore Ahura Mazda to help me succeed in fulfilling my obligations to the nations of Iran, Babylon and the ones of the four directions.[154]

The legation's library was indeed a comfortable sanctuary with a rich collection of books on law, diplomacy, international relations, philosophy, literature, geography and history. Deeply upholstered chairs invited visitors to sit down. A section was devoted entirely to Iran's history, culture, arts and literature. Sardari would often visit the room to immerse himself. A bookbinder himself, he treated books gently, almost with loving care. He was particularly enchanted by the beauty and thoughtfulness of Persian poetry, and would often lose track of time, lingering in the library for hours.

He took his precious fountain pen out of his pocket – his loving youngest sister's gift upon defending his doctoral dissertation in Geneva – and began jotting down a series of notes. By the time he stood up to leave for home, everyone in the building had already left for the weekend. As he bade goodbye to the legation's gardener who doubled as doorman and strolled towards his apartment, he continued to refine his thoughts. He would often spend his weekends at his cottage away from Paris to relax. He would do the same that weekend. If he was to protect his fellow Iranians, he had to set the stage for a grand plan as soon as possible. It was a risky undertaking and he knew it, but Cyrus would have approved and so would his country's current king.

Was his beloved Tchin-Tchin at home that evening? Probably. Perhaps she was at the the grand piano he had purchased for her, practising. Maybe he cooked her favourite Iranian dish, *fesenjan*, chicken slowly cooked in a concentrated pomegranate sauce with peeled crushed walnuts and aromatic seasoning.[155] He must have wanted such moments to last. Life could be so wonderful, yet some were doing their utmost to turn the joy of life into abject misery; barbarity that was being propagated in the name of science, progress, racial superiority. Was moral idiocy modernity's gift?

4

HUBRIS AND HYPOCRISY

'SMALL NATIONS MUST NOT TIE OUR HANDS'[156]

Two big black cars, an English Rolls-Royce and a Russian ZIS, little pennants fluttering, glided through the empty streets of northern Tehran at 4:00am on 25 August 1941.[157] Both coasted to a stop at their destination, the Iranian Prime Minister's home. Sir Reader Bullard, the Russian-speaking British Minister, and Andrei Smirnov, the French-speaking Soviet Ambassador, emerged from their automobiles, looked at their watches, nodded, shook hands, exchanged pleasantries in Russian and proceeded towards the iron gate of Prime Minister Ali Mansur's residence. They rang the bell at exactly 4:15am. The unexpected guests were ushered into the guest room as a servant rushed to wake up the head of government.[158] Prime Minister Mansur dressed in haste and rushed in dishevelled. The two envoys told the Prime Minister in well rehearsed words that British and Soviet forces were crossing Iran's borders as they spoke.[159] They then presented the stunned man with two official notes and departed as abruptly as they had arrived.

Iran had declared its neutrality on 3 September 1939, two days after Germany had attacked Poland. Russia and Britain, in contravention of International Law, had invaded Iran despite the neutrality, as they had done during the First World War. The Sa'dabad Pact signed at Reza Shah's personal residence on 8 July 1937 by representatives of the governments of Afghanistan, Iraq, Turkey and Iran proved worthless. Article V of the treaty stated that no signatory would allow a third party to use its territory from which to attack a pact member by air, sea or land forces.[160] The British had nevertheless used Iraq as a springboard to invade Iran.

Reluctant to wake up Reza Shah at 4:30am, Mansur prepared to present the news to the King in person at 6:30am when the monarch began his daily work schedule. As Mansur was getting ready to meet the Shah, 120,000 Soviet and 35,000 British, Indian and Gurkha troops were invading the country.[161] The moment the Prime Minister, pale and visibly shaken, stepped out of his car in the grounds of the Sa'dabad Palace, Reza Shah, who was standing under a tree, was the first to notice his sad state. 'What is the matter?' the King inquired, alarmed at Mansur's distressed appearance. After a moment's hesitation the Prime Minister relayed the news. Regional military commands had direct wireless links to the royal palace and the commander-in-chief may have already received cryptic reports of activities at several border crossings. Whether he had received reports or not, the Shah was taken aback. He reflected for a moment, lit up a cigarette, and thought aloud. 'That is incredible. Our friends, England and Russia, are giving us the same treatment that Hitler gave to Belgium and Mussolini to Greece. I cannot understand how, while we were prepared to give England peacefully whatever she wanted, they [the Allies] should so foolishly invade a small, peaceful country.'[162] The Allies had in effect orchestrated the kind of attack on a non-belligerent country that the President of the United States was to characterise as 'the day that will live in infamy' after the attack on Pearl Harbor three months later.

Already the war and particularly the British blockade of all German sea commerce had dealt a serious blow to Iran's economy, despite the country's neutrality. Iran depended on exports of agricultural commodities, carpets, petroleum and raw materials and imports of industrial equipment, spare parts, machinery and steel.[163] Desperate to maintain its trade, on 6 September Iran asked Germany to secure an overland transit agreement with Russia. A Russo-German agreement to that effect was concluded on 28 September, but unreasonable Soviet demands by late October precluded a Russo-Iranian accord.[164] Although similar Soviet demands had already driven Turkey to seek a defensive alliance with Britain and France on 19 October, Russia insisted to the German Ambassador in Moscow, Count Graf von der Schulenburg, that Germany press Iran to yield to its demands. The Soviet Union had also begun reinforcing troops in the Caucasus on the Iranian border at the same time.[165]

In response, in January Tehran instructed its envoy in London to seek military assistance from the Allies. Iran's Minister of War also personally approached the British military attaché in Tehran with a proposal to coordinate war plans against Russia.[166] The British military chiefs of staff informed the war cabinet on 6 October 1939 that the Soviets had indeed been reinforcing positions along their Turkish-Iranian borders with aircraft and armoured units.[167] On 3 January the British War Office ordered the Indian Army to prepare one division for possible deployment at Anglo-Iranian oilfields. On 15 January the British War Cabinet altered the order to have three divisions prepared instead.[168] Having asked the chiefs of staff on 7 February to review Iran's requests for military assistance and force coordination, they then agreed with the chiefs' assessment presented on 23 February that no forces or equipment could be spared to help Iran. They suggested that there was no reason to coordinate plans nor to earmark forces to 'help the Shah' in defence of northern Iran against a Soviet attack. The chiefs' recommendation was to 'preserve Iranian neutrality until such time as we need Iranian cooperation'.[169]

The French had planned to cripple both Soviet and Nazi war machines by destroying Russian oilfields. The French general staff reported its assessment on 22 February 1940, in response to Prime Minister Edouard Daladier's request. The report stated that six to eight bomber groups based in Syria, Turkey, Iran and Iraq could destroy Soviet oilfields and refineries in the Caucasus.[170] The French prepared to launch their attacks by late June or early July 1940,[171] but on 10 May the Germans preempted the French plans as Wehrmacht panzers spearheaded into Belgium and then France, as German paratroopers landed in the Netherlands. Emboldened by France's collapse, the Red Army occupied Lithuania, Latvia, Estonia and Eastern Romania in June, and informed Germany of its intention to seek rail transit rights from Iran, as well as free zones in the Persian Gulf.[172]. Iran quickly declared its neutrality in the Russo-German War on 26 June 1941, reiterating the previous declaration of 3 September 1939.[173]

London seized the opportunity to join forces with its former foe, sacrificing Iran in the process. The Russo-British alliance was not unlike the Russo-German partnership that had sacrificed Poland. On 11 July the British War Cabinet directed the chiefs of staff to consider a joint British-Soviet attack on Iran.[174] The British Minister in Tehran reminded London of his previous assurances to Iran's Prime Minister of His Majesty's Government's policy of respect for neutral states. A demand to expel all Germans residing in Iran to be used as a pretext, as the British Foreign Office had suggested, would not be in compliance with that policy. 'We can produce surprisingly little proof of fifth column activities here although we are sure they must be going on,' he confessed.[175] The German Minister in Tehran, Erwin C. Ettel, in a secret telegram transmitted to Berlin on 2 June 1941, had confirmed that 'The Shah has pursued through his foreign policy during the war strict neutrality consistent with his country's interests.' He also reported that German Jewish immigrants were trying everything possible to remain in Iran and that the rumour of a coup d'etat in Iran was baseless.[176] On 18 July, despite lacking evidence, the British minister and the Soviet ambassador in Tehran presented a note to Iran's Acting Foreign Minister demanding the expulsion of Germans residing in Iran. The British and Soviet nationals residing in Iran at the time outnumbered the Germans four to one. The minister replied that complying with the demand would be contrary to his country's declared neutrality and would enrage Germany.[177] The numbers of expatriates working in Iran at the time were approximately 2590 British, 390 Soviet, 690 German, 310 Italian, 190 Czechoslovak, 70 Swiss, 260 Greek and 140 Yugoslav citizens and their families.[178]

Undeterred, the British Foreign Minister Anthony Eden and Soviet Ambassador to London Ivan Maisky prepared a final note to be delivered to Iran's Foreign Minister on 16 August, in which they demanded that four-fifths of the Germans be expelled by 31 August. The US government was aware of the scheme as the US ambassador in London had been consulted on 8 August, and given a copy of the Eden-Maisky ultimatum.[179] On 9 August, the British Minister Bullard informed London that the Iranian surveillance was such that even if the Germans wanted to stage a coup they could not succeed. British intelligence, having decrypted Italian diplomatic communications, confirmed Bullard's assessment.[180] Eden shamelessly instructed Bullard on 12 August to assure Iranians of 'the difference between British expatriates residing in their country and the German Nazi agents who disguised as technicians undermined neutral states.' At the very same time that the proposed distinction was to be made, British agents and military officers masquerading as employees of Iran's oil industry were preparing maps to facilitate the movement of invading British forces and seizing oilfields and refineries in and around Abadan in the south and Kermanshah in the west. The US Minister in Tehran, Louis G. Dreyfus Jr., cabled Washington on 16 August reporting the Anglo-Soviet ultimatum. He predicted that the Soviets would occupy northern Iran, the British the rest, and that the Shah would lose his throne.[181] Bullard and Smirnov visited Prime Minister Ali Mansur separately that day to present their jointly prepared notes, demanding a reply within three days.

Several Iranian diplomats had warned their government of Anglo-Soviet intentions. Iran's Ambassador to Turkey, Anoshiravan Sepahbody – who had been posted to France before Istanbul – sent an urgent report to that effect to Tehran. Turkey's President Ismat Inonu had personally informed Sepahbody that he had been notified of an imminent attack.[182] Particularly well informed, Sepahbody had been a friend and confidant of Mustafa Kemal Ataturk, and had shared the same affinity with Ismat Inonu after Ataturk's passing. He was also on very good terms with his German and British counterparts in Turkey, Ambassadors Franz von Papen and Sir Hugh Knatchbull-Hugessen. Von Papen and Knotchbull-Hugessen, two old schoolmates, enjoyed Sepahbody's regularly scheduled embassy receptions. Since Iran had declared its neutrality, the receptions were scheduled from four to six in the evening for the Allied diplomatic representatives, and from six to eight for the Axis. Sir Hugh, a former Minister to Tehran, would not depart early and von Papen would never arrive late so that the two old friends could meet briefly, despite representing warring governments.[183] Reza Shah was aware of Sepahbody's connections and trusted him implicitly. He knew also that Ankara was, as were Bern and Lisbon, hives of espionage. It is inconceivable that the monarch would have ignored a top-secret warning from the president of Turkey conveyed through his own trusted envoy. Yet, much to Sepahbody's consternation, the warning was not even acknowledged.

Foreign Minister Javad Ameri requested an urgent royal audience on 16 August to report on the second 'note' from the Soviet and British envoys. 'Apparently they did not like our answer,' Reza Shah said calmly. 'They have designs for us. Don't you know what they really want?' 'I am not certain, Your Majesty, but could only guess that what they want is access to roads to ship arms to Russia,' Ameri replied. 'That is it, but why don't they say so?' Reza Shah inquired. That night the Shah attended the cabinet meeting. The government prepared a reply similar to the first one that emphasised Iran's neutrality and gave assurances that the Germans residing in Iran could not possibly pose a threat to the interests of the Allies. The Shah asked Prime Minister Mansur, 'If those gentlemen want the right of way, why don't they discuss it with us? Besides, do they know the sacrifices we have made to construct the railways and the roads? Are they willing to pay for the use to compensate for our nation's sacrifice?' Ali Mansur replied he did not have the answer, but proposed to discuss the matter with the British and the Soviet envoys. The Shah then suggested that Foreign Minister Ameri talk to them and report back.[184] Ameri met with the British Minister Bullard a day before the invasion to assure him that 'Iran would do whatever the Allies wanted.'[185] The US Minister Louis Dreyfus had cabled Washington three days earlier on 21 August that Bullard had informed him whatever Iran's reply might be, it would be unacceptable. He added that the British propaganda campaign against Iran had reached a fever pitch, spreading falsehood such as broadcasts from New Delhi and Cairo reporting that a trainload of Germans had arrived in Iran and that a rebellion had broken out in the Iranian Army. The Iranian side of the story was never told and newspapers assisted the British campaign by accepting their propaganda as truth.[186] He concluded, 'The British and the Russians will occupy Iran because of overwhelming military necessity no matter what reply the Iranians make to their demands. I must add emphatically to avoid misunderstanding that I am in full agreement with the British action and believe it to be vitally necessary for the furtherance of our common cause.'[187]

On 22 August 1941 *The New York Times* ran the front-page headline: 'British and Russians Poised to Move into Iran.' Reporters asked President Franklin Roosevelt about the report at a press conference that afternoon at his residence in Hyde Park, New York. He denied knowing anything about it, then called his Secretary of State Cordell Hull to tell him to deny the accuracy of the report.[188] At 11:00am Iran's Minister to Washington, Mohammad Shayesteh, met with Secretary Hull to plead for help. 'If your Government would say but one word to the British, I believe they would not invade Iran,' he pleaded. The Secretary remained silent.[189] In the evening of 24 August, just hours before the attack, Bullard informed Dreyfus of the details. At 3:30am in

Moscow Iran's Ambassador Mohammad Sa'ed was awakened by a telephone call and summoned immediately to the Kremlin for an urgent meeting.[190]

At 4:13am on 25 August 1941, HMS *Shoreham* opened fire on the Iranian warship *Palang* ('Leopard'), which was tied up south of the Abadan refinery. *Palang*, unprepared and undefended, burst into a ball of fire and the crew were thrown from their bunks. The gunnery officer Lieutenant Kahnemooei 'rushed to a gun-mount but was mortally wounded when a secondary explosion severed his hand. Shouting orders, "Fire! Fire!" Kahnemooei collapsed and died. The captain, Lieutenant Commander Milanian, lay bleeding nearby from shrapnel lacerations.'[191]

Back in 1929 Reza Shah had lamented that British policy had continuously compromised Iranian sovereignty in the Persian Gulf while speaking to Ambassador Anoshiravan Sepahbody. Sepahbody had then suggested that unless Iran had its own navy, its territorial integrity in the Persian Gulf and the Gulf of Oman would remain at risk. Reza Shah had asked Sepahbody to look into all available options to create an Iranian Navy. Italy had proved willing to build ships for Iran and to train their Iranian crews. The first of the Iranian naval vessels, the small gunboat *Niroo* ('Power') was delivered in 1935 with Sepahbody, then Iran's ambassador to Italy, Mrs Sepahbody and Iran's Navy Commander Gholam-Ali Bayandor, present at the launch ceremony. The occasion was marked throughout Iran by a commemorative stamp, and celebrated as the birthday of Iran's modern navy.

The first shelling by HMS *Shoreham* surprised not only the Iranian warship *Palang*, but also *Babr* ('Tiger') that morning, with similar effect. On shore, the shelling awoke Rear Admiral Bayandor in the nearby port city of Khorramshahr. He hurriedly put on his uniform and rushed out to the navy yard, which was already under fire. By about 6:00am Bayandor was in his staff car visiting army posts to coordinate defence. He was on his way to contact Tehran by wireless radio when the car came under machine-gun fire from a British armoured vehicle. As the car stopped and Bayandor accompanied by another officer stepped out, they were gunned down.[192] The British Lieutenant-General E.P. Quinan noted afterwards that 'This officer had an English wife and, while giving full allegiance to the Shah, was very friendly disposed towards us.'[193] As the British, having achieved total surprise, invaded southern Iran and moved north, the Soviets bombarded northern cities, broke through northern frontiers and drove south.[194] Another British column crossed Iran's western border with Iraq and moved rapidly towards Kermanshah.

That afternoon Nasrollah Entezam, Chief of Protocol at the Royal Court, called Mohammad Ali Furuqi at home to invite him to the palace.[195] Furuqi was 64 years old, ill, running a fever and laid up in bed. He had an inkling he would be asked to form a new government after having heard of the invasion report. Furuqi did not own a car, so he asked his son to hire one and to accompany him to the Palace. When the two arrived on the palace grounds Entezam was waiting at the entrance. Dressed in a tailcoat and top hat, bowed by age and illness, Furuqi leaned on his cane and on his son's arm to climb the few steps leading up to the building's main entrance. He had been there as a cabinet minister and prime minister before, but had been out of royal favour in recent times.[196]

Mohammad Ali Furuqi (1873–1942), a scholar, educator and journal editor, was elected to the Second Parliament (1909–1911), appointed Minister of Justice (1911–1915), served on Iran's High Court of Appeal between ministerial appointments and was selected to represent Iran at the Paris Peace Conference in 1919. He served as Minister of Foreign Affairs, Minister of Finance, Prime Minister, Minister of War, Ambassador to Turkey, Minister of National Economy and Foreign Minister twice, through 1935. He was forced to resign his cabinet post on 3 December 1935 as his son's father-in-law was implicated in an alleged rebellion. Out of government service and out of royal favour, he had devoted his attention to literary pursuits since.[197]

The King greeted the ailing statesman upon arrival and thanked him for the visit. He then expressed his confidence in Furuqi's wisdom, ability and patriotism. Reza Shah told him their beloved country faced a national emergency that required supreme sacrifice from all nationalists. He was aware that taking charge of the government under the Allied onslaught was a tremendous burden, but in his opinion Furuqi was the one most qualified for the responsibility. Would he answer the call? Would he accept the post of prime minister, the King asked? Furuqi did not hesitate. His commitment to his country was total. Reza Shah knew that Furuqi would do everything possible to save the country.

5

THE SACRIFICE

'EVERYONE HAS A DESTINY'[198]

Sir Reader S. Bullard chose 11 September 1941 as the occasion to display his imperial power in Tehran. The British envoy, whose country's armed forces in concert with Russia's Red Army had invaded Iran two weeks earlier, was to visit the country's bedridden Prime Minister Mohammad-Ali Furuqi that morning. The choreography was classically British, designed to belittle and intimidate. Preceded by an advance military contingent, Bullard arrived at Furuqi's home with all the pageantry of a viceroy inspecting his colony. Escorted by some 30 Indian troops in their ceremonial uniforms and with colours flying, he intended to impress upon Iranians that the British masters were back and in charge. To enhance the theatrical effect, Bullard's advance contingent, having arrived earlier at the residence in the city's downtown, had positioned themselves visibly in the grounds, on the rooftops and in the surrounding buildings. Bullard had already demanded the immediate removal of Reza Shah, 'Otherwise' he had warned Furuqi, 'the Allied armed forces will enter the capital and treat the government of Iran the same way they have treated other governments in occupied territories.'[199] Prime Minister Furuqi had invited Bullard to his bedside to discuss the Allies' demands.

The ailing host and the overbearing guest talked for a long time, a discussion punctuated by Bullard's annoyingly frequent telephone calls to his Soviet counterpart, Andrei A. Smirnov. Finally the British minister acceded to giving the King five days to leave his country. As soon as Bullard and his entourage departed, Furuqi called Foreign Minister Ali Sohaily to discuss what had transpired, then called the royal palace to request an audience for that afternoon. Minutes later, Nasrollah Entezam, the Chief of Protocol at the Royal Court, returned the call.[200] 'His Majesty would meet you at the Marble Palace downtown if you are not well.' The Prime Minister replied in deference to the King that he would rather travel to the summer palace at Sa'dabad, north Tehran, for the audience. Furuqi, running a fever and taking medication every hour, asked his two sons to accompany him, the elder son to help him to walk, the younger to carry a medicine bag. As they entered the palace grounds in the afternoon, they saw the monarch pacing back and forth in the garden wearing his usual plain army uniform. Reza Shah invited Furuqi to remain in the garden under the cool shade of an old elm tree as the others were ushered inside the building.

Trying to convey the odious ultimatum delicately, Furuqi offered the observation that the monarch deserved a holiday. Reza Shah disliked beating around the bush. Looking at his Prime Minister with his piercing eyes, he spoke calmly but firmly. 'Mr Furuqi, you understand that I am a military man. I know they will determine my fate. Now tell me exactly what was said this morning. Tell me everything so I can figure out what to do.'[201] Furuqi reported his talk with Bullard in detail. He tried to sweeten the bitter pill by expressing his happiness that the Crown Prince would ascend the throne.

Reza Shah looked down for a while. Finally he spoke as if thinking aloud. Where would he live after abdication? Who would support the royal family? What would become of the country? At last he looked up. 'Very well; so the Crown Prince will be king. I had wished the same.' Then he took a deep breath and said, 'This has been my fate!' Furuqi, overcome by emotion and weakened by illness, began to fall. The king helped him into a garden chair. As if to comfort his loyal minister, Reza Shah observed, 'Everyone has a destiny; mine has been this!'[202]

Upon returning home Furuqi called Foreign Minister Sohaily again to report on his meeting with the King. Sohaily, who spoke French, Russian and English fluently, contacted Smirnov and Bullard to inform them of the King's decision. Bullard replied abrasively that Reza Shah had only four days left to abdicate and that a British ship was on the way to the Iranian port of Bandar-Abbas in the Persian Gulf to collect him and his family. He then proceeded to warn Sohaily that a delay under any circumstances would be unacceptable. Sohaily then visited Furuqi to report his conversations with Bullard and Smirnov. The following day the invading forces moved towards Tehran in battle formation. By 14 September Soviet forces had camped just outside the capital at Darvazeh Karaj – the Karaj Gate, an ancient entrance to the formerly walled city – poised to enter Tehran at any moment.

On 16 September at the Marble Palace Reza Shah, accompanied by his eldest son, signed the letter of abdication that Furuqi had already drafted. Addressing Furuqi while pointing to Crown Prince Mohammad-Reza Pahlavi, he said 'I spoke with His Majesty yesterday. Now I entrust him to you, and both of you to God.'[203] The father and son embraced for a few moments, then Reza Shah turned away from the Prime Minister to hide the tears that he quickly wiped away with a handkerchief. The royal father and son's farewell 'could have shattered a heart of stone,' Furuqi told his own son afterwards.[204] Reza Shah then said goodbye, looked at his son and his palace one last time, got into his black Rolls-Royce and ordered the chauffeur to drive south to Isfahan. The rest of the royal family, including the Egyptian Princess Fawzia who was married to the Crown Prince, had already left for Isfahan.

The new King, Mohammad Reza Shah, and Prime Minister Furuqi called Foreign Minister Sohaily from the Marble Palace as Reza Shah's car left the palace grounds at about 8:00am. Sohaily reported that Bullard had called him moments earlier to threaten that if Reza Shah did not leave the capital that day the Russo-British forces would occupy Tehran. Furthermore, the foreign minister had been told to meet Bullard at Smirnov's summer quarters in Zargandeh at nine that morning.[205] Furuqi told Sohaily to go ahead to the meeting and that he would join him at the Soviet Embassy's summer mansion as soon as he could. Furuqi then called the speaker of the Majles to request a special parliamentary meeting as soon as possible that very day. Within the hour Furuqi had joined Foreign Minister Sohaily at the Soviet summer compound. He informed the British and Soviet envoys in person that Reza Shah had abdicated and that the Majles would consider the abdication and the ascension of the legal heir to the throne at a special session that day. Bullard protested that he had 'not received direction from London. about Reza Shah's heir. Furuqi, unable to accept Bullard's attitude in silence a moment longer, had the last word. Cutting Bullard's objection short and mustering every ounce of energy he had left, the old patriot told Bullard and Smirnov 'My Government and I have legal and constitutional responsibilities that we will carry out,' before leaving the meeting.[206]

Furuqi's impression of Bullard, widely shared by other Iranians, was that of a man with prejudicial intent against Iran and its people. Dour, often insulting, he has been described as an envoy devoid of diplomatic skills. He discussed his intentions with his Soviet colleague openly and often succeeded in persuading him to support his wishes.[207] Furuqi had begun negotiating with the Allies on 27 August. Much to his surprise, he found the Soviet ambassador more accommodating than the British envoy.

Five days after the Allied invasion, on 30 August 1941, the British and Soviet envoys demanded the expulsion of all German citizens from Iran within a week. The only exceptions were 'genuine diplomats at the German Embassy and a few essential technicians employed at Iran's telecommunication and military bureaux,' who could remain, but only with the Allies' approval. The British and Soviet political representatives would review their residency permits upon receiving their names and requests.[208] The demand altered the following day. On 31 August, the Allies called for all German citizens to be turned over to the Soviet and British occupation forces, rather than expelled.[209]

Iran's reply to the first note (dated 30 August 1941) was submitted to the envoys at 11:00am on 1 September 1941. The government spelled out its case painstakingly. It pointed to Iran's neutrality, the Allies' invasion, Iran's cooperation with the Allies after the invasion, Iran's legal and contractual responsibility towards foreign nationals working in the country, as well as a moral obligation towards them. Finally, citing the difficulties of international travel in the midst of a global war, the practicality of immediate expulsions as demanded was questioned. Bullard responded caustically that he had instructions not to consider any proposal from the government of Iran before a change of regime. 'Your regime must change to a republic,' he demanded.[210] Every demand, it seemed, was a prelude to another insulting imposition.

Erwin Ettel, the German Minister in Tehran, met with Foreign Minister Sohaily the same day on 1 September 1941. Ettel wanted the Germans to evacuate to Turkey. Sohaily had no idea what the Allies had in store for the Germans. 'The English Government intends to intern the German colony in any event. If the Iranian government were to expel the Reich Germans, it would amount to delivering them into the hands of the enemy,' Ettel said. He warned Sohaily that expelling them without safe conduct would have very grave consequences for Iran.[211] From that day on, British radio broadcasts from London, Delhi and several other locations began a relentless campaign against Iran's King, demanding his removal. That evening the British radio broadcast announced that 'President Roosevelt had given Prime Minister Churchill approval for the plan to invade Iran at the Atlantic Conference.' The US Ambassador Louis Dreyfus denied it, but 'the friendship felt by many Iranians towards the United States turned immediately to bitterness and a feeling of betrayal' as Churchill boasted of the 'good results which have been so smoothly obtained in Persia.'[212] He proposed doubling the railroad capacity from the Persian Gulf to the Caspian Sea and requested ships to transport troops and supplies through the 'sure route by which long-term supplies could reach the Russian positions in the Volga basin.'[213] President Roosevelt finally responded to Reza Shah's urgent plea of 26 August on 2 September. The President was 'following the course of events in Iran with close attention' and the US government 'has noted the statements to the Iranian Government by the British and Soviet Governments that they have no designs on the independence and territorial integrity of Iran.'[214] As Roosevelt's reply was being delivered to Iran's monarch, the Russo-British envoys were trying to persuade Prime Minister Furuqi to abandon the monarchical regime by promising him Iran's presidency. He refused. They approached Mohammad Sa'ed, Iran's ambassador to Moscow, with the same proposition. He too turned them down. They then sought to end the Pahlavi monarchy by reinstating the Qajars. The former Qajar Crown Prince Mohammad-Hassan Mirza's three sons in England, Malek-Hossain, Hamid (a submarine officer in the Royal Navy) and Rokn al-Din, were potential candidates; but reinstating the Qajar dynasty proved impractical. Finally, they tried to put Reza Shah's third son, the 18-year-old Gholam-Reza on the throne, to bypass Crown

Prince Mohammad-Reza and the second son Prince Ali-Reza. Furuqi resisted the Russo-British attempts on constitutional grounds. He finally succeeded in frightening Bullard into having second thoughts. In an agitated outburst during which he must have lost patience with the imperious British envoy, Furuqi convincingly accused him of bullying Iran into the arms of the communists. Furuqi charged that Bullard was wilfully trampling on Iran's existence as well as working against the essential geopolitical interests of the West. It was then that Bullard reportedly backed off and dropped his objection to Crown Prince Mohammad-Reza's ascent to the throne.[215]

Uninterrupted radio propaganda from London and Delhi against the person of Reza Shah and the Pahlavi monarchy peaked in September. Sudden elimination of censorship had energised opportunist publishers, many of whom had sung the praises of the regime until the previous week. Most notable amongst them were a group of legislators, men such as Mr Ali Dashti who had never missed an opportunity to flatter Reza Shah. The same flatterers suddenly accused the King they had glorified for two decades of robbing the nation of its treasures.[216] To counter their accusations, Furuqi's government formed a committee, including legislators to inspect and catalogue the crown jewels and to report to Parliament. In the same vein, Dr Mohammad Sajjady, Minister of Roads, was sent to Isfahan to seize the abdicated monarch's property and a government commission was appointed to receive it.

On 4 September the British and Soviet envoys had appeared at the Iranian Foreign Ministry with a new demand: immediate closure of German, Italian, Hungarian and Romanian embassies and the surrender of their nationals to the occupation forces. Foreign Minister Sohaily reported the demand to the Parliament, which publicised it immediately through radio and newspapers nationwide.[217] The public's reaction was one of disbelief and revulsion. The Allies who had sung the praises of international law and the sanctity of diplomatic missions had violated Iran's neutrality and now demanded Axis embassies closed and their citizens working in Iran detained. Rounding up foreign nationals working for Iran in order to hand them over to their enemies was a despicable betrayal of the nation's guests, contrary to traditions of honour, hospitality and human decency.[218] Reza Shah was reportedly deeply saddened by the imposition.[219] Adding to the injustice was the reality – well known to Reza Shah and the new King Mohammad-Reza Shah – that many German expatriates in Iran were Jewish refugees.[220]

Systematic humiliation of Iranians continued. Bullard demanded Iranian currency from the Acting Treasury Minister to pay for the British occupying troops at the exchange rate of 168 rials per one British pound, disregarding the official exchange rate of 68–70 rials per pound. The minister, Abbasqoli Golshaiyan, was taken aback. He refused the demand as unreasonable and suggested the appropriate exchange rate could not be better than 90 rials per pound. Bullard protested that the minister's refusal to accede was proof of Iran's obstructiveness. Bullard finally had his way. He sought Golshaiyan's removal from the treasury and when Furuqi introduced a new cabinet after Reza Shah's abdication, Hassan Mosharraf Naficy had replaced Golshayan. The new minister and the cabinet revised the exchange rate on 28 September from 68 rials to one pound, to 140 rials. The exchange rate for the US dollar was also revised from 17 rials to the dollar to 35 rials.[221] The national economy deteriorated rapidly under occupation and the cost of living increased by 700 per cent over the next four years. There were acute shortages of necessities and finally a famine in 1942. Tribal leaders, with British backing particularly in the south, took advantage of the pressures applied to the central government to reclaim their lost influence. Newly formed British-sponsored political parties also sought to undo Reza Shah's accomplishments by supporting the clergy to further limit the national government's authority. Several dozen communists who had been detained in 1937 and freed under occupation joined forces to re-constitute the Tudeh Party with its own radio station that broadcast pro-Soviet propaganda nationwide.[222] An American Presbyterian minister noted in his diary a conversation he had had with a young Iranian on 17 September, a day after Reza Shah's abdication. The young man told him:

> The evil that [the Shah] did is only a fraction of the good he accomplished. He was a powerful man. No man like him can be found in the East, and [governments] might have accomplished much in his name. But now he is gone, and all the reactionary forces will break loose. He broke the power of the mullahs, but now they are all ready to take their revenge … Already women have appeared in their veils. I was much displeased by the speeches which members of parliament made about the Shah, for they showed a lack of appreciation for what he had accomplished. This just shows how very evil we are! It has been a great mistake.[223]

The Allied troops that Bullard had threatened would enter the capital unless Reza Shah abdicated and left Tehran by 16 September, entered the city two days after the King had departed. Once in Tehran, Major-General William Slim ordered several howitzers strategically positioned around the German legation to force out anyone who had sought sanctuary inside the compound. Some 130 people gave themselves up to the British. General Slim then turned over to the Russians about 30 men among the group wanted by Soviet agents. The Soviets expressed their gratitude to Slim by offering to provide him any information he wished, after the Russians had 'interrogated them severely'.[224] The German Minister Erwin Ettel and the legation staff including 58 men; 274 women and 136 children had departed earlier, reaching the Iran-Turkey border on the same day. The Soviets had arrested one of the diplomats on the way and plundered his party's belongings.[225]

The Minister of Roads Sajjady arrived in Isfahan on 25 September as the former King and his family prepared to depart for Kerman. Sajjady had been called to the Royal Palace in Tehran on the evening of 22 September for an audience. At the palace the new King Mohammad Reza Shah, with Prime Minister Furuqi present, asked Sajjady to travel to Isfahan as soon as possible to seek the transfer of the former King's property as Furuqi had recommended. Sajjady was given the delicate task for he had the respect of all concerned, including the former monarch. Mohammad Reza Shah wrote a personal letter addressed to 'My Crowned Father'. Writing the letter was difficult for he admired his father and felt intimidated by the challenge of living up to his legacy. The letter explained the difficulties that the government and the monarchy faced that had necessitated the transfer request.

Travelling, even for a cabinet minister, required authorisation from the occupiers. Sajjady, accompanied by Ibrahim Qavam Shirazi (Princess Ashraf's father-in-law), left for Isfahan on 24 September, but only after the British minister had finally granted them permission to travel at 1:00pm.[226] The 210 miles/350 kilometres took over six hours by car. Sajjady and Qavam reached Isfahan late at night and met Reza Shah the following morning at the Kazeroonis' mansion. He was about to depart for Kerman on the way to the port of Bandar Abbas when Sajjady and Qavam entered the residence.[227]

Sajjady told him he had an urgent message from His Majesty Mohammad Reza Shah to deliver in private. Reza Shah walked Sajjady to the guestroom, and the latter presented the letter to the abdicated King. He read it carefully, then looked up. 'Very well, I had planned to do the same. Give me a pen and a piece of paper so I turn over all I own.' Sajjady suggested that a legal transfer required proper registration of the document in the presence of a magistrate. 'Do as you think appropriate but quickly, as we must depart for Kerman as soon as possible.' Finding a magistrate on a Friday, the Muslim Sabbath, was difficult. Sajjady finally located the head of the Bureau of Document Registration in a bathhouse. He in turn found a magistrate at home. The two brought the magistrate and the public registration books to Governor Amir Nosrat Eskandary's residence. The transfer was recorded on two official declarations and in the official registration books. Sajjady and the magistrate then carried the huge registration books to the Kazerooni residence for Reza Shah's statement and signature, which was to be witnessed and notarised. Reza Shah offered the statement and signed the documents and the registration books immediately.

In the Name of God the Most Sublime

Since the founding of [the Pahlavi] Monarchy I have been consistently mindful of the country's development, which I placed at the forefront of national reform planning, envisioning that the improvements would encourage all farm and property owners to do the same. I had hoped to be able to benefit all citizens and residents of the country from the yields of the properties. Now that my beloved son His Majesty Mohammad Reza Shah has taken over the reins, the opportunity has presented itself for me to convey all my properties and belongings, whether fixed or movable, including manufacturing plants and other assets of any kind, to His Majesty for ten grams of rock candy, to be utilised for [the public] welfare and education in accordance with the national interest, in any manner His Majesty determines to be appropriate. Registration is an accurate representation of the document.

Signed: Reza Pahlavi

After the signing, as the magistrate and the head of the Document Registration Bureau were leaving, Reza Shah asked Sajjady to remain. He then summoned his personal valet, Mahmoud, who would accompany him throughout his entire time in exile, to fetch his briefcase from the bedroom. The valet returned with a well-worn black leather briefcase that Reza Shah opened in Sajjady's full view. The former King took out a chequebook and looked Sajjady in the eyes. 'My total cash holding amounts to 680 million rials deposited at the central branch of Bank Melli Iran [Iran National Bank] in Tehran. Doctor, I am certain that the moment I leave the country rumours will spread about my funds at foreign banks … but none of it is true. I tell you with certainty that I do not have any money in either foreign or domestic banks other than what is in this Bank Melli account.' He then took out a notebook from the briefcase and handed it to Sajjady in which every property he owned with its annual yield and expenses was listed in neat columns. The figures were pencilled in, in the former monarch's personal handwriting. 'No one to this moment has been aware of this notebook's existence. I wanted it so to assess the accuracy of annual accounting reports by comparing each year's figures with those of the previous years. I kept this notebook close to me through my reign, but now have no use for it any longer. Please give it to my dear son.'

Dr Mohammad Sajjady had met Reza Shah as a cabinet minister numerous times before, but this was different. Reza Shah spoke with heart-felt emotion, sincerity and sadness. Sajjady found him not angry, but profoundly worried for the country. The betrayals he and his country had suffered, the hypocrisy of the parliamentarians in Tehran and the lies and rumours that the British broadcasts spread to defame him, weighed heavily. 'Will there be a just person, a truly informed one, to ever discern my wishes for the common good?' he asked. 'No human is without shortcomings. Surely I have done things in my reign that some would consider inappropriate. Truthfully, what are the good and the bad that I have done?' Sajjady replied, 'With one exception Your Majesty's policies have served the people's interest.' Reza Shah asked him what that exception had been. 'Your Majesty, impositions by officials of the Special Properties Bureau (Royal Estates) had caused despair.' Reza Shah slapped his forehead with the palm of his right hand. He remained motionless, holding his forehead in his hand as if in deep thought for a while. Then animated again, he said, 'You are right. Curse on them who abused my good intentions pressuring poor farmers – my fellow Mazandaranis.' (Reza Shah was born in the Province of Mazandaran). 'Curse on those who did not keep me informed! Well said Doctor!' Then referring to a former official he added, 'Where did he get the million rials he had hidden in the ceiling of his room in Kiakola in Baabol? Had I not received a report, had I not walked into his room unannounced, had I not ordered the ceiling searched, he would have been still in charge; and as you put it causing people despair.' He thought for a while before speaking again. 'It is this point of weakness that foreign radios exploit, insulting me every night. Where is the media through which *I* could reveal the truth? How could I defend myself that I was not aware of the abuses? My true objective for buying properties was to improve cultivation, develop agriculture, increase crop yield and expand exports.'

The conversation continued for another hour before Sajjady requested permission to depart. Sajjady was to leave for Tehran as soon as possible and was aware that Reza Shah too had to depart for Kerman. 'I made my final decision last night. I must leave my beloved Iran to sail to South America.' As Sajjady was about to leave Reza Shah called him back. 'Two pieces of jewelry from the Crown Jewels borrowed for Princess Fawzia's wedding are with Princesses Shams and Ashraf. Take them with you to deliver to the National Bank.' Sajjady suggested he assign the responsibility to his travelling companion Ibrahim Qavam Shirazi. The princesses were called and the jewelry handed to Qavam. Once back in Tehran, Qavam returned the jewelry to the Crown Jewels Repository at the National Bank in the presence of the Treasury Minister Golshaiyan, Director-General of the National Bank Mohammad-Ali Farzin and the Parliament's inspector Moayyed Ahmadi, collected a receipt, and submitted it to the Imperial Court for record keeping on the same day. The former king's rumoured astronomical bank holdings, at the exchange rate of $1.00 to 35 rials, amounted to $19.5 million. The parliamentarians, assured that the crown jewels were intact and that Reza Shah's entire property had been seized, next demanded his holdings outside of Iran. When informed, Reza Shah signed over any funds he might have had to his name in foreign deposits before leaving the country. As it turned out, and just as he had stated to Sajjady and others, he had none.[228]

Sajjady's trip to Isfahan took two days. Once in Tehran, he drove to the royal palace to present the documents to the new King. Mohammad Reza Shah told Sajjady 'Don't leave until we complete the task,' and called Nasrollah Entezam, Director of Royal Protocol to join them. Mohammad Reza Shah wished to turn all his father's property over to the government, and the entire 680 million rials in deposits directly to the nation. Sajjady:

I remember well that Mr Entezam and I were with His Majesty until one past midnight on the second of Mehr, 1320 (24 September 1941) to allocate the entire 680 million rials to the construction of schools, hospitals and orphanages throughout the country. I regret that [as I later found] of the 50 million rials presented to Azerbaijan Province only six million was utilised and the rest embezzled. When I became the governor of Azerbaijan I was astonished to discover the scandal. I was overcome by sorrow for our country, where social thieves do not refrain from stealing even the king's property and his presents to the public. The gifts earmarked for cultural institutions and public welfare have been embezzled, and there is no one around to turn in the gang of thieves to [answer to] the courts of law![229]

The former monarch and his family drove to Kerman where on 25 September 1941 the British consulate issued a single group visa to enter India for Reza Shah and the eight persons accompanying the monarch. The group was comprised of Mrs Qamar Mobasher, attendants Mrs Behjat Moshar, Miss Moluk Zamaani, Mrs Fatemeh Mahesti, Mr Ja'far Tavakoli, Mr Hassan Maaleki, Mr Mahdi Safar Fashandi and chef Mr Nasrollah Naavaki.[230] Reza Shah wrote to his eldest son and heir on the same day expressing hope for his success but also concern for expenses in exile. The letter reflects Reza Shah's anxiety for he feared that promises made by the Allies would not be kept. His concern for a dignified life for his family and himself is palpable. Without funds, his destiny controlled by enemies who had forced him to leave his country, he wrote with a heavy heart. His worry about paying off his daughter's debt is compelling.

Kerman, 3 Mehr 1320 (25 September 1941)
Your Imperial Majesty:
My Dear; Apple of My Eye,

I received your kind letter of 29 Shahrivar (20 September) delivered by my dear Prince Ali Reza. I was very much touched by your affectionate and sorrowful feelings. You had wished a happy and carefree life for me and the family. I do not think I would be happy in a foreign country. My happiness, considering the events that have befallen, centres on the good health and success of Your Majesty in putting in order the affairs of the state. You had not mentioned the funding of this large family's journey abroad, nor the source, or the manner in which it is to reach us. You are aware that in a foreign land one cannot await a monthly stipend from Tehran. The funding source must be identified and credit arranged with an international bank to disburse to us the determined amount regularly, without requiring approval from Tehran every time. Otherwise, there is no confidence in the current confused situation. Determination of individual stipends for the princes and princesses is not necessary. You had not considered, or referred to the relatively large sum required for us to settle down. I expect we will not be treated as ordinary foreigners. Perhaps someone will be assigned to address these concerns systematically. In closing, I have heard that [Princess] Ashraf owes a sum of money to Ahmad Qavam. Please pay off her debt to put her mind at rest.

Reza Pahlavi[231]

The royal party arrived at Bandar Abbas at 7:30pm on 26 September and boarded a British ship on the morning of the 27th. The port city's residents had gathered at the harbour to see the deposed monarch. Before boarding the ship for the anticipated trip to South America he told the crowd, who appeared confused and frightened, 'I can no longer be of any help to you, nor can you be to me. But your King in Tehran needs you, and you need him. Help him, and seek his help.'[232] In a follow up letter written shortly before boarding the British steamer, Reza Shah expressed his anguish regarding his expenses in exile. Addressing his son he wrote:

At this time that I am leaving Iran, I bid farewell to my beloved son. I am hopeful to be able to see you again. I pray to God for your health, good fortune and success. I have sent you the documents of Bank Melli account totalling 600 million rials ... It is necessary to transfer travel expenses for 25 people from the funds the government is appropriating for our expenses. Also, the cost of residing in America is to be considered by Your Majesty in transferring adequate funds so that I won't be impoverished. A substantial sum will be needed upon arrival in America to secure a home, to pay the initial expenses.[233]

His worries were well founded; London denied a request to transfer £25,000 to Lloyd's Bank branch in Delhi. All transfers in pounds, the bank stated, required approval of foreign exchange officials in London.[234] Later, Lloyd's Bank, in a telegram addressed to 'His Majesty Reza Shah,' dated 11 November, requested permission to transfer the funds to Port Louis, Mauritius Island in the Indian Ocean, where the former king had been taken.[235] Reza Shah had been informed in Bombay that he would be taken to Mauritius instead of South America. His subsequent inquiries remained largely unanswered. Several months later mysterious rumours circulated that he would be moved to Canada. Reza Shah's letters to the island's governor seeking relocation to a place with a more favourable climate illustrate his distress.[236] The governor's response of 21 January 1942 referred to the difficulties of transportation because of the war but assured him that the British government was giving the matter its careful consideration.[237]

Iran, Britain and the Soviet Union signed a treaty of alliance at the end of January 1942 that precipitated a congratulatory note to Reza Shah from the island's governor.[238] In response, Reza Shah renewed his request to leave the island. The governor informed him on 2 February that the Canadian government would welcome him. The trip, however, would require a few days stop in South Africa, where he would be transferred to another ship. The note said that 'His Majesty's Government' had agreed to cover the cost of the journey to Canada but inquired if Reza Shah would assume the expenses of the stay in South Africa and residence in Canada.[239] In a note dated 5 November 1942, Reza Shah agreed.[240]

The British Colonial Office had deported 1760 Jewish refugees to Mauritius Island upon arrival in Palestine in November 1940 and prepared to send an additional 2240.[241] Germany prohibited Jewish migration from the European areas it controlled in August 1941 and blocked the previously available escape routes as the British government continued its policy of preventing Jewish flights to Palestine. Of the European Jewish refugees interned on Mauritius, one – a pianist – befriended Reza Shah. He would visit him daily, play for him and offer him piano lessons. He may have been his only friend on the island and his only companion other than his few family members and attendants.

The former King was finally moved to Johannesburg in South Africa, but the promised journey to Canada did not materialise. His son Mohammad Reza Shah had asked him repeatedly to write his memoirs but he had declined. Finally, after the young King persisted, Reza Shah replied that he could not write his memoirs for doing so would sap his nation's hopes and all optimism.[242] He died in Johannesburg on 26 July 1944, 40 months after he had boarded the British steamer at Bandar Abbas in 1941 for retirement in South America. A sad end for a King, a man who had inspired Sardari, Sepahbody, Rayhan, Furuqi and millions of other Iranian nationalists.[243] A leader who had turned his country around in less than two decades, implemented impressive reforms and asserted Iran's national independence, deserved better. His body was not returned to Iran but sent to Cairo for burial. Reza Shah's remains finally arrived home on 7 May 1950 (17 Ordibehesht 1329).[244]

The King's humiliation and removal had unleashed extremists, opportunists and charlatans. Years of political assassination and social discord followed. The two occupying powers became masters of Iran's political and economic life again, as they selected prime ministers, ministers, governors and members of parliament. The British sought to ingratiate themselves with and thereby exploit the tribes and the clerics, as the Russians organised communist parties in every province. Within three days of Reza Shah's abdication – before he had even left the country – the Soviets had founded separatist movements in Azerbaijan.[245]

Reza Shah's principal aims had been to re-establish Iran's political and economic independence and to rebuild the country. He sought international acknowledgement that Iran was no longer a pawn of the great powers and was to be treated with respect. He lived simply. There was no court life and no entertainment in his royal palaces. He was attentive to his family and took nearly all his meals with his children. The food was typically simple. His autocratic rule, a subject of much criticism, was not uncommon at the time, similar to the regimes in Italy, Germany, Spain, Portugal, Russia, most of Eastern Europe and the entire Asian continent. His glaring character flaw was in his desire to acquire land, but the Qajar kings had done worse before him. It is worthy of note that land acquisition had a political motivation. The vast landholdings by tribal chiefs had been the traditional sources of revenue and manpower for repeated challenges to the national government. It is undeniable that local administrators in some areas used coercive means to acquire land for his estate, yet the objective may have been more than mere self-enrichment. Cyrus Ghani writes:

> On the eve of the Russo-British invasion there was a strong central government such as Iran had not seen for 140 years, free of manipulation by foreign powers, nomadic uprisings and undue clerical influence. There was a viable financial structure and the beginning of industrialisation ... Reza Shah was far from a philosopher king, and undeniably a flawed individual. But he was unquestionably the father of modern Iran and the architect of the country's twentieth-century history.[246]

At an address given at Chatham House, London, on 15 October 1935, A. Cecil Edwards who had travelled and conducted business in Iran for decades stated:

> I think we may justly say that about the year 1921 an era was drawing to a close in Persia which began 1200 years ago with the Mohammadan conquest. Immediately after that event vital changes took place in the country ... But from that time on what really fundamental changes have occurred in Persia? Dynasties have come and gone; this conqueror or that has ravaged the country and for a brief period has held the stage; but when those adversities were over, the life of the common people continued, down the centuries, almost unchanged. And then – within the last few years – something quite different, the New Persia, appears ... I found [the middle class Persians] ... different. I found less deference, less of that disarming, ironical point of view, which used to be such a charming feature in the educated Persian. I found an awareness, an activity, where there had been apathy before. The Persian of today is independent, sure of himself, ready to meet you and to exchange ideas on a plane of perfect equality. He is proud of the achievements of his country; proud of the roads, the railway, the army, the factories, the schools and above all, proud of Tehran.[247]

Reza Shah's single most significant contribution was to change the nation's outlook. He gave it back its pride.

Prime Minister Furuqi, overwhelmed by the occupation of his country, served as Iran's head of government for about five months. Faced with constant pressure from the Allies and political posturing by obstructive members of parliament, he resigned in favour of his capable Foreign Minister, Ali Sohaily.[248] Prime Minister Sohaily, as educated, dedicated, accomplished and energetic as he was, would not last for more than three months. Ahmad Qavam, known by his pre-Pahlavi title of nobility Qavam al-Saltaneh, formed the next cabinet, but resigned after bread riots broke out the following year.[249]

The Iranian government requested that the Allied forces leave as soon as the war ended in Europe on 19 May 1945, as specified in the Tripartite Agreement signed by Britain, the Soviet Union and Iran in January 1942. The Allied forces, according to the Agreement, were to leave Iran within six months following the end of hostilities with Germany. The Tripartite Agreement had been further confirmed by the Tehran declaration signed by the leaders of the United States, the United Kingdom and the Union of Soviet Socialist Republics on 2 December 1943.[250] Both Britain and the United States questioned Iran's interpretation of the treaty, but began to withdraw. The Soviets however remained and promoted separatist soviet republics in Iran's northern provinces.[251] When Ahmad Qavam became prime minister again in 1946 the Soviet occupation had already turned into an international crisis.[252] The courageous performance of Iran's Ambassador to the United States, Hossein Ala at the UN Security Council, and President Harry Truman's warning to Stalin, helped to force the Red Army to leave Iran.[253]

The impact of the withdrawal was immediate and dramatic. Soviet-sponsored secessionist 'republics' previously protected by the Red Army collapsed in quick succession in the face of popular uprisings. Christopher Sykes, a British correspondent in Tabriz (Azerbaijan's provincial capital) at the time reported that 'Except in France in 1944 I have never seen such violent and spontaneous enthusiasm.'[254] Qavam selected Anoshiravan Sepahbody, Iran's Ambassador to Turkey and formerly Minister to the League of Nations, Switzerland, France and Italy, as his Foreign Minister. Sepahbody, who had entrusted Iran's legation in Paris to Abdol-Hossein Sardari before departing for Vichy in October 1940, displeased the Allies in 1946. Foreign Minister Sepahbody rejected attempts at charging the Iranian treasury for the heavily used military equipment, locomotives and other surplus items that the US had imported into Iran and used to deliver over five million tons of munitions and other war supplies to the Soviet Union. President Franklin D. Roosevelt had stated in a memorandum to the State Department after the Tehran Conference of December 1943 'I was rather thrilled with the idea of using Iran as an example of what we could do by unselfish American policy.'[255] Earlier, John Jernegan of the Division of Near Eastern Affairs had proposed to the Assistant Secretary of State Dean Acheson in January 1943 that the United States had an obligation to fulfil the principles of the Atlantic Charter and to assist Iran to become self-reliant and prosperous. 'If railroads, ports, highways, public utilities, industries, are to be built, we can build them and turn them over to the Iranian people free of any strings.'[256] Despite the good will, the new US Ambassador, George V. Allen, who had replaced Ambassador Leland Morris in the spring of 1946, insisted on charging Iran for the used surplus equipment. Sepahbody would not give in. Considering the hardship imposed on the nation and the premature degradation of transportation infrastructure caused by the war, Sepahbody demanded that the used machinery be either left behind at no cost, or removed from Iranian soil at the owner's expense. The US ambassador requested the foreign minister's removal. Prime Minister Qavam, interested in maintaining good relations with the US to counter Soviet ambitions, was pressed not to offend the United States. The outcome was a face-saving cabinet reshuffle. Sepahbody lost the post of Foreign Minister, and the US ambassador returned home.[257] The United States eventually presented a cheque to the Prime Minister on the fourth of Khordad 1326 (26 May 1947) for a mere 14,231,970 rials ($406,623) as compensation for the use of Iran's railways during the war.[258]

In the decade that followed Iran's occupation in 1941, Iranian governments lasted on average only seven months. Seventeen successive governments struggled to deal with the country's crises but failed as parliamentarians proved more effective at forcing governments to fall than helping them to govern. Clerical influence that had subsided before the occupation exploded after the foreign armies departed. The most notable of the activist clerics was Ayatollah Abol-Qasem Kashani, who had anti-British and anti-communist credentials. Although the Tudeh Party was better organised to field street demonstrators at will, Kashani had the 'Fedaiyan-e Islam' (Devotees of Islam) as his foot soldiers. Fadaiyan members assassinated Ahmad Kasravi – a noted journalist, publisher and critic of the clerics – inside a courtroom at the Ministry of Justice on 11 March 1946. Kashani attacked Prime Minister Ibrahim Hakimi's government for a bill introduced by his Minister of Education Abdol-Majid Zangeneh to seek authorisation to ban journals that denigrate the principles of Islam, insult the institution of monarchy, or cause public unrest. The attacks incited growing demonstrations that forced Hakimi's government – the seventh since the country's occupation – to collapse on 6 June 1946. Kashani then opposed the next government headed by Ahmad Qavam for establishing a Senate, as prescribed by the Constitution. Forming a government required four procedural stages: nomination of candidate for premiership by a simple majority of the lower House (the Majlis); royal appointment of the nominee as prime minister; introduction of the cabinet to the Majlis and the Senate where the prime minister would present the government's plans and priorities; and finally a parliamentary confirmation by a vote of confidence. In 1948 Prime

Minister Abdol-Hossein Hazhir faced Kashani's opposition. He sought and received the parliament's vote of confidence on 29 June and again on 23 August. Yet daily demonstrations forced him to resign on 6 November 1948. The 1949 parliamentary elections were hotly contested but Kashani's supporters did not win. The Tudeh Party, the National Front and the Fedaiyan joined Kashani's supporters to successfully press the King to dismiss the election results and call for new elections. On 4 February 1949 the young monarch, attending a celebration at Tehran University's College of Law, survived an assassination attempt with several minor bullet wounds. The gunman, reportedly a journalist, was shot dead after he had discharged his weapon several times. The government and the King reacted by seeking more assertive roles to deal with the turmoil. The government thus called a Constitutional Convention to consider additional powers for the executive branch.

Iran elevated its informal relations with Israel to diplomatic representation in March 1949. Eight months later a Fedaiyan-e Islam assassin fatally shot the former Prime Minister Hashir in a mosque adjacent to the parliament building. New elections were held in the same month. The results announced in May 1950 showed all National Front candidates (a coalition headed by Mohammad Mosaddeq) victorious, and Ayatollah Kashani – who had been exiled to Lebanon after the attempt on the Shah's life – elected to the Majles as one of Tehran's representatives. Foreign intrigue fanned the fires of domestic turmoil. The Soviet Union, for instance, refused to return the 20 tons of Iranian gold bullion reserve that it had removed to Moscow during the occupation and subjected the nation to daily threatening demands by radio.[259] Kashani returned to Tehran on 10 June to welcoming crowds of clerics, trade associations, bazaar merchants and National Front supporters. The newly forged political alliance was manifest on 18 June when Dr Mosaddeq read a statement by Ayatollah Kashani in a parliamentary session. The statement demanded punishment for those responsible for his exile, called for the nationalisation of Iran's oil industry, declared that dictatorship would not be tolerated and that the Constitutional Convention convened following the attempt on the Shah's life was invalid. It also charged that the King's assailant had been killed by security guards in order to to cover up a conspiracy.

On 26 June 1950, Major-General Haj-Ali Razmara was named prime minister. Razmara had distinguished himself as a professional soldier and gained a high reputation during the liberation of Azerbaijan in 1946. He was known to be close to his brother-in-law Sadeq Hedayat, Iran's leading man of letters at the time, and Hedayat's circle of literary friends. In keeping with parliamentary procedures, Razmara attempted to introduce his cabinet to the Majles on 27 June but was heckled relentlessly by a well orchestrated group of deputies led by Mosaddeq and six of his associates.[260] Razmara received a vote of confidence from the Majles on 4 July 1950 – 93 of the 107 representatives present voted for him – followed by a vote of confidence from the Senate on 10 July. Daily demonstrations against the government and demand for oil nationalisation came to a head on 7 March 1951 when a Fedaiyan-e Islam member assassinated Prime Minister Razmara at an ayatollah's funeral.[261] On 15 March another Fadaiyan member killed Dr Majid Zangeneh, Dean of Tehran University College of Law and former Minister of Education in the Hakimi Cabinet. Hossein Ala, the elder statesman and former Ambassador to the United States, was named prime minister on 20 March, but facing unreasonable demands for nationalisation of the oil industry resigned only two weeks after introducing his cabinet. The day after Ala's resignation, Representative Jamaal Emami nominated Mosaddeq for the post and 79 Majles members offered their support. Mosaddeq received his royal appointment as prime minister on 30 April 1951.[262]

6

THE TERROR

THE SOUND OF POLISHED BOOTS

Habib Morady could not have been happier. His wife, Victoria Cohan (an English woman from Manchester), had just delivered a baby boy in the early hours of 8 December 1941. They had been married since November 1936 and the Morady family had celebrated their wedding in Paris by hosting a large reception. Victoria's pregnancy had greatly pleased Habib's parents, Rayhan and Soltaneh, but Habib had taken Victoria to hospital the previous evening without calling them, or for that matter his brothers or sisters. Getting around in occupied Paris at the time, particularly at night, was difficult and Habib did not wish to cause them undue anxiety. Having spent the night at the hospital he stopped at his brother's apartment in the morning on his way home for a quick wash and change of clothes. Ibby was going through his morning routine when Habib rang the doorbell. Ibby grabbed his robe and rushed to the door with trepidation. The occupation had created fears previously unknown, and an unexpected visitor was cause for alarm. He expected only bad news as he hesitantly unlocked and opened the door. Much to his delight what he saw was his brother's smiling face staring right at him. 'I have a son,' he whispered as he squeezed himself in before Ibby had opened the door completely. As Habib shut the door gently the brothers embraced for a long, joyous moment. Ibby murmured: '*Khoda-ra sadhezar martabeh shokr*,' 'a hundred thousand thanks to God!'

Ibby hurriedly poured some tea into a couple of teaglasses, placed some cheese, bread, butter and jam on the kitchen table and invited his brother to sit down.[263] By the time the brothers had had some tea and a little to eat, it was time to call their parents at the family home at 8 Rue Francois-Adam, Parc Saint Maur, Seine et Marne. It was a joyous occasion and the grandparents were elated. Rayhan answered the phone and shouted the good news to his wife. Habib could hear his mother screaming with joy and stamping on the floor, as if jumping up and down, running or dancing. The extended family would surely want to visit the hospital later in the day. After the call Habib rushed home to wash, shave, change his clothes and return to his wife and son. Ibby left for his store nearby but would join his parents at the hospital later on. The grandparents arrived in Victoria's room – as is the Iranian custom – with pastries and sweets for everyone in the maternity ward to enjoy. Ibby showed up in the afternoon with flowers and a beautiful little needlework pouch containing scripture – a Safer Torah – to be pinned to the baby's clothes, to protect him from the evil eye. Victoria had already named the baby Robert. Little Robert and the new mother would leave the hospital for home in three days.

Habib's mother and his five sisters pitched in to prepare the couple's apartment for Victoria and the baby. The excitement of Robert's birth had energised everyone, but by the third day both Victoria and Habib were exhausted. The day after Robert and Victoria had arrived home Habib had left for his father's store, back to his normal working schedule. The Morady family relied on Habib for the business, and the transactions he handled had remained unattended for a week. Victoria, alone with the baby and sleep-deprived, had planned to rest at home all day. She had fallen asleep while breastfeeding Robert when the doorbell rang. She woke up in a daze with the baby still in her arms. Disoriented, she heard the bell ring again. She eased her newborn in his crib, rushed out of the room and closed the door so he would not wake up, but the doorbell rang again and he did. As she rushed back to pick up her crying baby, the ringing continued. She reached the door as fast as she could, carrying the baby, upset, frustrated.

She was stunned as she opened the door. Bewildered, gripped by fear, she stood there paralysed. The visitor was an impatient, bespectacled Gestapo officer. In his heavily accented French, he told her that the Gestapo had been informed of her newborn son's circumcision at the hospital. She was therefore required to report to the General Office for Jewish Affairs, at 1, Place des Petits-Freres in Paris the following day. The tone of his voice, his uniform, his polished jackboots, brought the life she had known to a halt. Victoria remained standing in the doorway long after the Gestapo officer had gone. She kept hearing the march of the departing boots and imagining their return. Finally Robert's cry jolted her out of her daze. She regained her senses and locked and bolted the door before returning to the bedroom. She closed and locked the bedroom door too, desperate to feel safe again. She clutched her baby and sobbed quietly.

Hours passed before Habib returned home. Habib was alarmed the moment he saw her. It took Victoria a long time to explain the experience through uncontrollable sobbing. By then Habib was angry and scared, yet he tried to comfort his wife as best as he could. He prayed and cursed.

He thought a million thoughts but none could ease the pain he felt in his heart. He recalled the Persian proverb: 'Beware of a mother's burning heart, for it could set the world on fire!'

The following day Habib, Victoria and their newborn son reported to the Jewish Affairs Bureau as ordered. Habib was instructed to wait with the baby outside; Victoria was to be questioned alone. Based on the report of her son's circumcision the Gestapo had already determined that she was Jewish. Yet she was still asked if she was. She could not or would not lie; she replied in the affirmative. She was issued the customary yellow patches to be sewn on her outer garment and on her son's, and told to report any change of address to the Gestapo until further notice. She was ordered to wear the patch immediately before being dismissed. She was convinced at that moment that she would be 'sent away'.[264] Her expression as she walked out worried Habib. They exchanged few words; neither was in a talking mood. The experience was unreal, disorientating.

Habib rushed to the Iranian legation as soon as he had returned Robert and Victoria home. Madam Daruvar, the legation's kindly and sympathetic French secretary, ushered him into Sardari's office right away. After hearing the story Sardari tried to calm him down. 'Does she have an Iranian passport?' he asked calmly. She did not. Applying for a non-British passport had not crossed her mind.[265] Sardari pulled an application form out of his desk drawer and asked Habib to fill out the form and return it with the required passport photos. 'She and Robert will have an Iranian passport as soon as you return with the documents and she and you won't have to worry again. You have my word,' Sardari told him. He spoke soothingly, with confidence. Sardari assured him that Iranians would not be harassed by German or Vichy officials. Victoria Morady and her son had an Iranian passport the next day. Sixty years later and residing in Caracas, Venezuela, she recalled that she did not wear the yellow patch ever again and was never subjected to Nazi harassment after receiving that Iranian passport.[266]

Robert's circumcision had been reported to the Gestapo by one of the many willing informants the Nazis had recruited in hospitals, apartment buildings and places of employment. Informants received rewards for every Jewish family they found, and soon many Jewish families decided to abandon their homes and businesses in search of safe havens. Others sent their family members away to locations they hoped would be unassailable. The Senehis were one such family. Tal'at, one of the Morady sisters, had married George Senehi in 1929. By all accounts it was a happy union. George and Tal'at were both educated and well-to-do. George was a businessman, successful and handsome, while Tal'at was a charming young woman, fashion-conscious, tall and beautiful. In 1940 they had a seven-year-old daughter, Eliane and a four-year-old son, Claude. When the war broke out, George, disturbed by a cousin's arrest and detention on a visit to Germany in 1934, determined that

Europe had become too dangerous. The cousin in question, Rahim, was a jovial hair stylist and amateur musician. He loved Iranian music and seemed almost inseparable from his beloved 'tar', a string instrument with two joined but unequal sound boxes.[267] With his tar, Rahim was the life of every party in the Iranian community in Paris. Before returning to Iran and on the way home, in keeping with his adventurous character, he travelled to Germany to see as much of Europe as he could.[268] The visit, judging by his happy photographs, must have been very pleasant at first; but the Nazis arrested him. George hired a lawyer from Paris to free him, but it took almost two years of relentless struggle to get him out.[269] The ordeal persuaded George to leave his property behind and move his family to Iran after Germany occupied France. The Moradys supported George's decision, for they too feared the consequences of the war in Europe. Indeed, they were so concerned that they asked George and Tal'at to take the youngest of the Morady sisters, Rose, with them.

Any movement or transaction at the time required multiple papers. German officials and inspectors were never satisfied with a single permit, document, or identification form. To be caught without the proper papers was at the very least troublesome, if not dangerous. Issuing identification was thus a complicated, time-consuming process that necessitated several supporting documents with citations for cross referencing with existing official files.[270] Yet despite all this Nazi bureaucracy, a visit to the Iranian Legation secured the documents required for safe passage through Europe in a matter of days. George, Tal'at and their two children finally left Paris for Tehran accompanied by Tal'at's younger sister Rose in the spring of 1941. Some family members relocated at the same time to the Senehis' large home in Montmorency to be together, feel more secure, protect the property and save on necessities. Heating fuel, including firewood and charcoal, had become extremely scarce. Eliane, then only seven years old, recalls:

> Leaving our beautiful house at Montmorency and my own room with all my dolls and books, my little pillows that my grandmother had made for me with special Persian fabrics she had brought from Iran, was very sad. Those memories are still very vivid in my mind and in my heart. Our separation from the family, particularly my mother's separation from her parents, brothers and sisters, was so painful. Everyone was crying. My mother's anxiety was profound and lasted for years. Fear of the war and its consequences raged within us and we knew that communication between Iran and France was virtually impossible. Thanks to the Red Cross, a letter would arrive once in a while.[271]

The trip was long and difficult. Eliane, an inquisitive little girl, recalls the repeated stops at Nazi-controlled checkpoints. The checkpoints appeared to her to be 'one every five minutes'. At every one of those stops the guards would ask for papers and passports. Although they had all the required documents, and therefore were allowed to pass through the checkpoints without incident, George, Tal'at and Rose were terrified every time. Eliane remembers her parents and her aunt shaking with fear as they handed their passports to the officers manning the checkpoints. She still cringes when recalling the tone and mannerisms of the German officers demanding passports, and the sound of their boots walking towards her and her family. Recalling travel by train through German-occupied territories reawakens her childhood terror. Whenever inspectors checked tickets and travel papers on board trains 'the sound of their boots coming closer and closer' to their compartment terrified her and her family. Her parents would ask Eliane and Claude to sleep, or at least pretend to be asleep whenever the sound of boots came close. 'The compartment door would suddenly slide open with a Nazi official demanding passports in the usual harsh accent and tone.' Eliane's parents would silently gesture towards the sleeping children to solicit the inspectors' consideration. The inspectors would often respond by lowering their voices and moving on quickly. The routine helped to shorten the family's recurrent torment by seconds, but even a moment of relief was precious.

Although travel permits, safe passage and transportation tickets were strictly controlled and rationed, everyone wanted to travel. Even if lucky enough to get the required permits, one could not always choose the shortest way or the most desirable transport. The family's month-long journey to Iran began with a train ride from Paris to Switzerland. Then it was to Vienna, Austria. From there they travelled to Hungary, Romania and Bulgaria before reaching Turkey. Crossing the border into Turkey was a memorable moment. The relief was overwhelming for they had not felt safe until then. There had been numerous stops, checkpoint inspections, changes of trains and long, anxious stretches of waiting. The family had travelled light. Eliane had her favorite doll in her arms during the entire trip. Her brother Claude had carried his most precious possession, an electric locomotive. In Turkey they could finally relax and were immeasurably grateful for that. After a brief but restful stay in Istanbul they travelled to Erzurum, their last stop before crossing into their beloved homeland.

Accommodations in Erzurum, unlike Istanbul, were spartan. They checked into the only hotel in town, but found it wanting. 'Everything was dusty, but we were alive and safe – nothing comparable to the horror in Europe,' Eliane recalls.[272] Several days later they were on the road again. They were overwhelmed with joy when at last they crossed the border into Iranian territory. They were free from fear. Time passed quickly as they pressed on through picturesque mountains, valleys, towns and villages. Hours later they were at their destination in Tehran. The exhilaration was beyond measure as their relatives, uncles, aunts and cousins welcomed them. Some relatives had come all the way from Kashan for the occasion. They met a fellow refugee,

George's cousin Rahim Senehi, who had arrived in Tehran after detention in Germany, had already fulfilled his conscription duty and met his future wife Qodrat while in the Iranian Army.[273] George, Tal'at, Eliane, Claude and Rose had escaped the terrors of Europe; but life in Iran would soon change too.

The Allies – Russia, Britain and later the United States – soon occupied Iran and the country's economy took a dive. Suddenly there were shortages of everything, even drinking water, food and medicine. Prices soared and inflation took hold. With Iran's economy near collapse, its political system undermined and the authority of the state shattered, sanitation suffered and epidemics broke out. Without adequate food, vaccines and medicine, infectious diseases became rampant.

Rose, the youngest of Morady sisters, was increasingly unhappy. She had left Paris and her boyfriend reluctantly. Leaving behind the young man she loved had been hard on her as the two had planned to marry. He had begged Rose not to leave, but she had yielded to her parents' assurances that the war would not last long. As it dragged on and the prospects for a quick return proved increasingly remote, despair replaced all hope. George finally asked her to forget Paris and marry a friend of his in Tehran. She resisted but George and the family continued to try and persuade her. She finally relented, perhaps acquiescing to a family obligation to do so. Her wedding photograph reflects her resignation.

Eliane was soon enrolled in second grade at a French Catholic school, Ecole Jeanne d'Arc. She found good friends at school from the very first Day,[274] many of whom she is still in contact with. Despite the shortages and the difficulties of daily life in wartime, George and Tal'at were attentive to their children's needs and the youngsters enjoyed a pleasant, nurturing environment. Eliane's recollections and those of her friends are generally happy for they had been shielded from the effects of Iran's occupation. Her classmates were mostly Muslim, with a few Iranian Armenian and Russian Armenian children amongst them. Eliane and several friends and relatives attended a ballet school named after its founder Sergej Djambazian, himself a Russian Armenian immigrant.[275] 'We did not have a problem being brought up in Tehran. We practised our religion as did all my friends. We would go to our synagogues as we pleased; and best of all, we felt free and without fear,' Eliane recalls.[276] George and Tal'at had a third child, a baby boy, Fernand, born in Tehran. His birth brought great joy to the family but they had begun yearning to return to Paris. Life in Iran had become increasingly harsh with little prospect for improvement anytime soon. To take a rest from the daily grind, the family planned a vacation on the Caspian Sea. Ramsar, a recently developed resort town with an impressive European-style hotel, had become a fashionable holiday destination. While the family was in Ramsar with its forested mountains and luscious green scenery, tragedy struck. Tal'at and Eliane became badly ill but little medication and no antibiotics could be found in town. George interrupted the vacation, threw everyone in his car and drove quickly back to Tehran. Eliane recovered but Tal'at did not.

Tal'at was a victim of a typhoid epidemic that had arrived with war refugees through the Soviet Union, and which had spread rapidly throughout Iran.[277] The Soviets, after partitioning Poland in alliance with Nazi Germany in 1939, forcibly expelled an estimated 1.7 million Polish civilians labelled 'socially dangerous anti-soviet elements' from their homes. They were packed into cattle cars and dispatched to labour camps in Siberia and Kazakhstan in the course of several mass deportations.[278] After the Germans attacked their former Soviet allies in June 1941, Stalin released the Polish General Wladyslaw Anders from Lubyanka prison in Moscow to mobilise a Polish Army to fight the Nazis. About half of the Poles in Soviet labour camps had perished by then and few who had survived were fit for soldiering. Finally, between 25 March and 5 April, and again from 10–30 August 1942, some 115,000 Poles, 18,000 of them children, were allowed to leave the Soviet Union through Krasnovodsk on the Caspian Sea to reach the Iranian port of Pahlavi (now renamed Anzali). A smaller group arrived in Mashahd from Ashkabad in Turkmenistan on trucks. The Iranian Army erected over 2000 tents on the Pahlavi shoreline to accommodate the refugees. Weakened by two years of maltreatment and starvation, they suffered from malaria, dysentery, skin infections and typhus. A camp hospital and quarantine were set up immediately as 40 per cent of the patients admitted were already suffering from typhus. Accustomed to a starvation diet in Russia, many died on Iranian soil of over-eating upon receiving normal food rations. There were numerous children amongst the refugees, many orphaned or separated from parents. Several orphanages were set up, in Pahlavi, Mashhad, Tehran, Isfahan and Ahvaz. Eventually Isfahan was chosen as the main centre to care for the Polish children. In Tehran at Dowshan Tappeh Air Force Base a camp housed over 2500 Polish refugees, of whom 2156 were Jewish and 1012 children. The children were cared for in Tehran until eventually transported to Israel. Those Jewish children are affectionately known as 'the Children of Tehran' and the Polish children were commemorated by a stamp issued on 10 June 2008 in Poland. The colourful stamp depicting a Polish child in school uniform is titled 'Isfahan: The City of Polish Children'.

Most Polish men and women capable of military service enlisted and gradually went to Lebanon through Kermanshah to join the Polish forces being organised there. One convoy found an orphaned bear cub near Hamadan on their way to Lebanon. They adopted it and the cub grew up to become a six-foot, 500-pound companion to the men who served in the 22nd Transport Division (Artillery Supply) of the Polish Second Army Corps during the Battle of Monte Cassino in Italy in 1944.[279] The world may have forgotten the Polish-Iranian episode but reminders are abundant. Several Polish cemeteries in Iran are testament to the tragedy that the late Iranian author and filmmaker Khosrow Sinai has memorialised in a documentary film, *The Lost Requiem*.[280]

George Senehi and his three young children were devastated by their loss. The family had escaped Nazi-occupied France for the peace and safety of Iran but Iran was subsequently occupied as well. The Senehis finally returned to Paris in 1947 hoping to salvage what they could of their lives. In Paris, George and his children sought to mark their return with a family portrait at a photo studio. The happy family photograph belies the sadness they felt. The truth is, Eliane recalls, it took them several days of practice to finally strike a happy pose. Eliane, a teenager at the time, was visibly overtaken by emotion when looking at the photograph in 2004.[281] Several other family members also relocated. Their cousin Rahim and his wife Qodrat had already left Iran for Israel in 1943.

Another family with a harrowing experience was the Nasseris. Solayman-Khan Nasseri owned a carpet store on Haussmann Boulevard in Paris. An informant had identified Nasseri as a Jew, making him a target for possible deportation to a labour camp. Frightened, he rushed to the Iranian legation. Sardari received him warmly, calmed him down and assured him that all would be well. After making sure that Nasseri had all the papers he required and a valid passport, he began to prepare an argument on his behalf. A tribal leader in Iran is commonly called 'the khan of the tribe'. Sardari used the convention to eventually claim that the name 'Khan' as a suffix to Solayman's first name indicated that Solayman-Khan was an Iranian tribal leader. As such, he suggested, his status was worthy of princely respect traditionally reserved for Iran's nobility. As a tribal chief, Sardari argued, Solayman-Khan had to be an Aryan. Sardari's argument worked and Solayman-Khan was left alone; but the story did not end there.

His own safety assured, Solayman became ever more conscious of the threats to his French friends. He had fallen in love with a Jewish girl living alone in the city, and despite enormous difficulties and the danger of blowing his cover, he was determined to help her. He secured a hiding place for her on a farm in a nearby village out of town and visited her as often as he could, always riding a bicycle in a training outfit and carrying some food. To counter suspicion, the 'tribal leader' claimed that his 'status' required proper physical fitness, and bicycling in the countryside was essential to his regimen. Carrying food on the day-long cycling tours was therefore seen as a legitimate necessity to satisfy his athletic appetite. He visited his girlfriend at least once a week, taking different routes and whatever food and supplies he could manage to carry nonchalantly on his bicycle. The ordeal lasted several years but the couple persevered. The two married soon after France's liberation.[282]

Andre Musa was also an Iranian in Paris, operating an import-export business out of an office. Working with no retail outlet and maintaining low visibility, he had tried to avoid ethnic identification, but an informant in his building reported him anyway. He was detained by the Gestapo but Sardari intervened to free him. He, too, was never harassed again.

The atmosphere of imminent danger affected Haji-Rahim Nakhi-Musa and his brother Ezra-Neman Nakhi-Musa. Haji Rahim's Iranian friends, as already mentioned, called him Paw-Pahn (wide-feet). During France's occupation he embraced the nickname as his last name and transformed it to Papan in an attempt to avoid Jewish identification. Some friends would tease that all he needed was an added affliction to gain a 'von' prefix too (as in von Papen). His brother Neman did not let the Nazi threat destroy his sense of humour and love of cooking; everyone loved to come to his dinners. His brother, perhaps more of an introvert, was so fearful of the Nazis and protective of his son Maurice that he tried to hide the youngster at home for the entire duration of the war.

Another family, the Sassoons, originally from Isfahan, had an established antiques business. A young nephew, Seon Cyrus Sassoon, arrived from Iran in 1940 to study electronics and radio signal engineering. He could not do so in German-controlled areas, as the Nazis had banned the study of signal communication electronics for anyone without a German security clearance, so Seon travelled to southern France to continue his education in the unoccupied zone. He was caught by the French Police who were collaborating with the Nazis and was sent to a labour camp. When his family appealed to Sardari, he first stored their stock of valuable antiques in the cellar of the legation building and in his own apartment's garage for safekeeping. He then helped the family with food rations. He was particularly concerned for families with infants and small children who needed milk and basic foodstuffs. He was so conscientious in acquiring and distributing the rations that the Sassoons believed Iran's King, Reza Shah, had struck a deal with Germany and ordered the Iranian legation to assure that Iranians were adequately fed. 'It was inconceivable that Mr Sardari had done everything on his own initiative,' Hayem Sassoon, a college student and compatriot of his nephew Seon Cyrus, recalled years later. In reality, Sardari had offered the explanation that the Sassoon name implied that they were descendants of the Iranian Sassanid dynasty and thus Zoroastrian, not Jewish. To strengthen the argument he asked the Sassoons to acquire a testimony from a Zoroastrian temple in Iran. To acquire the certificate, an uncle residing in Isfahan travelled to the Zoroastrian Centre in Yazd.[283] The Centre's leaders promptly issued the certificate to be sent to Paris, as they recognised its significance. With the Zoroastrian certificate and a relentless effort, the young Seon Cyrus Sassoon was freed and returned to Paris in 1943.[284] His case was not unique; another student, Menache Ezrapour from Iran's western city of Hamadan, had been similarly trapped in 1941 in Grenoble in southern France.[285]

Seon completed his college education in 1947, returned to Iran as an electronics engineer, but chose painting as his vocation. He later travelled to the United States for further training as an artist and returned to Iran to open his own gallery. He lived and worked in Iran as an artist until his death in 1981. His nephew, Hayem Sassoon, with whom he began the study of electronics in Paris, worked as an engineer upon graduation and helped Sardari with his gadgets at his home and at the legation. In 1947, at Sardari's request, Hayem installed a new high powered radio transmitter/receiver at the Iranian Embassy, then elevated in status from a legation. In an interesting parallel, Hayem too embraced art and began a career as a sculptor in Paris after he retired as an engineer. A third nephew became a professor of architecture in Iran, but also operated his own art gallery.

The Sassoons, having closed the antiques business during the war, oganised a second-hand clothing venture out of their home. Fabrics and clothes were in very short supply but many sought to sell what they could. The Sassoons' pre-war store of antiques re-emerged from the legation building's cavernous cellar and Sardari's garage as soon as the German forces had departed. Sardari returned everything intact. 'My father then tried to present a gift to Mr Sardari but he would have none of it,' Hayem recalled. The refusals went on for a long time before Sardari finally accepted a lacquered papier-mâché box as a souvenir. Hayem remembered that it was painted in miniature style, depicting a mythical story from Shahnameh, *The Book of Kings*. 'My father begged to pay him, at least for the use of his garage space, but Mr Sardari would not even consider it.'[286]

Jean Mikaeloff, another survivor, first arrived in France as a teenager. He moved to Lyon, started a carpet and antiques business, married a French woman and prospered. A few months after Germany had occupied northern France, Iran's envoy Anoshiravan Sepahbody was accredited as ambassador to Turkey. Sepahbody and his family were to move to Marseille on the Mediterranean to board a ship for Istanbul. His son, Farhad, a teenager at the time, recalls his 'uncle Sardari' gave his father several passports when the family stopped in Paris before leaving for Marseille. Sardari asked Sepahbody to deliver the passports by hand to fellow Iranians in Lyon. Farhad remembers that Jean Mikaeloff gave a lavish reception in their honour in Lyon. Mikaeloff received one of the passports issued in his name, and escaped Nazi intrusion throughout the war.[287] Weeks later he received a warning call from a friend at the Lyon Police Department that his French wife had been identified as Jewish and was to be arrested. Jean gathered his family immediately and drove to a hideout, a cottage he had acquired in a farming village far away from the city. The family reappeared in Lyon after the war and prospered once again.[288]

Collaboration policies in France had made the occupation less costly for the Germans. Without collaborators the occupation would have required large numbers of German officers, bureaucrats, police and soldiers that the Reich could not afford. The Reich officials conducting their 'supervisory administration' numbered 200 in Paris and fewer than 1000 in the entire occupied zone. The ratio of one German to 15,000 local administrators in France, compared to one to 790 in 'the Protectorate' zone, illustrates the advantage that collaboration offered. Yet the policy had its opponents in Germany. Faced with a potential food shortage in Germany, Reich Field Marshal Hermann Goering, at a meeting attended by heads of occupation administrators in Berlin in 1942, demanded much harsher measures in occupied territories. 'I could not care less if you tell me your people [in occupied territories] are collapsing from hunger. They can do that by all means so long as no German collapses from hunger.' He opposed collaboration and dismissively quipped 'Collaboration is a thing which only Mr Abetz does.' As it turned out the 1942 harvest proved plentiful, averting a food crisis in 1942–43. Abetz continued to warn Berlin that disorder, riots and the resignation or overthrow of the Vichy government would be likely if collaborationist policies were abandoned.[289]

Sardari worked tirelessly against tremendous odds. As many as 100,000 Jews were deported from France to death camps, 20,000 through Drancy station outside Paris, of whom 2000 were children.[290] The Vichy regime enacted an anti-Jewish law on 3 October 1940 to ban Jews from employment in the judiciary, from teaching, the military, banking, real estate and the media. A decree on the following day called for the internment of foreign Jews. The regime devised and rigorously enforced over 140 anti-Jewish laws and decrees throughout its tenure.[291] In 1941 liquidating Jewish property was authorised and subjected to 'Aryanisation'.[292] A year later, 15,000 foreign Jews were turned over to the Nazis in August and the treatment of the Jews became progressively worse. Confidential reports dated 27 August and 2 September 1942 confirmed that

> … all foreign Jews in unoccupied France that have migrated since 1936 are being arrested. The numbers are about 12,000–13000 persons. As soon as the current campaign against the stateless and foreign Jews is complete, the police will confront Jewish profiteers and contrabandists.[293]

A secret directive by the SS Regimental Commander in Paris dated 14 April 1944 spelled out the policy of increased arrests in occupied France in great detail. All Jews were to be arrested irrespective of nationality or circumstance. The arrests had to include the entire family, parents, children, siblings, children-in-law, infants and anyone brought up in a Jewish household. All Jews in French work camps, prisons and detention facilities were also to be removed. The Jews so rounded up were destined for evacuation to the East and were to bring along all their cash, foreign currency, gold coins, jewelry, stocks, safe-deposit slips, laundry and luggage. They were to include:

Jews with citizenship from France, former Czechoslovakia, Poland, Norway, Holland, Belgium, Luxemburg, Yugoslavia, Greece, the Baltic states, Albania, Italy and all stateless Jews that may have immigrated from the Reich ... All keys to apartments, homes, businesses, etc., must be consigned to a legally accepted trustee ... Attempts at intervention, including those by foreign representatives will be futile and will be stopped at the onset.[294]

That was the social and political environment in which Sardari discharged his 'duty to God and his nation'.[295] It is true that he had begun his humanitarian mission as a diplomat representing a neutral government that had good relations with both the Allies and the Axis. In the early days of the German occupation he may have encountered little risk to himself. That all changed in August 1941, when the Allied armies invaded his country and forced the head of the state he represented into exile. His life and his work became more difficult when the new Iranian government, operating under Allied occupation, declared war on Germany on 10 September 1943 and ordered Sardari to return home. He faced an even more precarious situation when he refused to abandon his post. He remained in Paris to help his fellow Iranians and their friends despite having lost his diplomatic protection, his own government's support, and his salary. Abandoned and at the mercy of the German occupiers, he still found the strength to press on; and press on he did.

7

The Campaign

The List

Sardari had been composing a letter in his mind for weeks, perhaps months. He needed a firm basis to build a case to help his fellow Iranians, a case plausible enough to withstand ideological objections and strong enough to counter raw hatred. Sardari's concern might have begun the day the German troops entered Belgium, well before their triumphant march in Paris. A diplomat with a legal education, he might have developed the thought even earlier.[296] He might have considered what he could have done had he been posted to Austria, Czechoslovakia or Poland following Germany's earlier victories. Sardari was well connected and well informed. He knew what the Nazis had said and done. He could envision what they would do in an occupied territory. The key to his work was his understanding that racial policies were based on false assumptions and that those Nazi policies necessitated arbitrary enforcement.

The next day he drove alone to his country cottage. Tchin-Tchin remained in Paris to prepare for an upcoming performance and Sardari needed a quiet weekend. At the cottage he followed his regular routine: a walk around the property with Lilly, his big German Shepherd, an exchange of pleasantries with the gardener and his wife and warm greetings with neighbours in the surrounding gardens were his ritual whenever he visited. He was always happy to be there. The building was an attractive country home with French double doors that faced a well attended garden with flower beds, shrubberies and trees offering pleasant vistas. Although sparsely furnished, the cottage was comfortable. He saw the property as his sanctuary, where he could relax and refresh himself.

He spread his notes on his ornate desk and uncovered his portable typewriter. The notes had been jotted down on an odd assortment of cocktail napkins and pieces of paper torn off a variety of notepads. He sat down to write. The thoughts had spun around in his head for so long that organising them was difficult. As he recalled his own arguments, bursts of activity on the keyboard followed long pauses. After numerous false starts and repeated alterations he finally settled on a draft the following day. It began with the title *Les Iraniens de Confession Mosaique* – Iranian followers of Moses. He introduced his argument with some historical background presenting an overview of Iran's population as predominantly Muslim, yet inclusive of the Shiites, Sunnis and Mosaique. The latter were indistinguishable from the rest in culture, language and even their observance of national and cultural celebrations such as No-Rouz that marked the beginning of spring, the first day of the Iranian solar calendar, and the anniversary of the Iranian Empire's founding in 550 BC.[297] The Mosaique, he emphasised, did not speak Yiddish, nor did they celebrate separate holidays. Furthermore, they did not have any similarities with European Jewry. Their nationality was Iranian and their race, as was the case with all Iranians, Aryan. The group's distinction, he argued, had historic roots unrelated to racial inferences. The Mosaique mixed and married with fellow Iranian Muslims and were engaged in each and every profession. Their common names were typical Muslim names. They resembled the *Djougoutes* of Afghanistan or Boukhara or Turkistan – all of Iranian origin.

The name Djougoute may have been inspired by the Persian words 'Johoud' or 'Yahudi' and their similarities to the German 'Jude' and 'Juden'.[298] The text thus drafted was not the first salvo from Sardari's arsenal but it was the most extensive to that date. It was accompanied by a covering letter and a list that named the '*Iraniens de Confession Mosaique Demeurant a Paris*'. When it was finally ready to be delivered on 12 August 1942, it was addressed to 'Monsieur Krafft von Dellmensingen, Secretaire de l'Ambassade d'Allemagne, 78. rue de Lille, Paris.'[299] The documents were received at the German Embassy, and filed on 21 August 1942 under number 1821/42.[300]

5. rue Fortuny – 17th District

Paris, 12 August 1942
Mr Krafft von Dellmensingen
Secretary, German Embassy
78, rue de Lille
Paris

Monsieur le Secretaire,

I am pleased to inform you that upon my instruction to comply with the orders of the German authorities, Iranian Israelites have already registered at police stations in their districts.

Some Iranians, whose names and addresses are enclosed, have informed me
that German authorities do not consider Georgian and Afghan Israelites to be
Jews. Considering that the Iranian Israelites' situation is the same, they request
that the stamp 'Jew' be removed from their identity cards.

The Iranians have sent a statement to that effect to the German authorities, a
copy of which is attached. They have requested that I support their case before
the German authorities. Since the exception has been made for the Georgians
and the Afghans, I respectfully request that you kindly grant their request.

I thank you in advance for your consideration in resolving this issue.

Most respectfully,

A. Sardari

The List of Iranians of Mosaique Faith Residing in Paris and Suburbs

Last Name	First Name	Date of Birth	Place of Birth	Present Address
Acheroff	Ibrahim	1904	Tehran	12. Cite' Trevise, Paris
Aziz	Soleiman	1906	Tehran	108. Bld. Voltaire, Pris
Dorra	Vitalis	15.12.17	Chiraz	42. rue de la Tour D'Auvergne, Paris
Dorra	Clement	4.3.19	Damas	same
Dorra	Sami	30.3.19	Beyrouth	same
Dorra	David	5. 1.00	Damas	42. rue de Trevise, Paris
Dorra	Elie	26.7.01	Damas	32. rue de Liege, Paris
Dorra	Nazli	27.9.81	Damas	42. rue de la Tour d'Auvergne, Paris
Haghani	Nouroullah	1893	Kachan	164. rue Montmartre, Paris
Lazarian (Lazar)	Mikael	19.2.14	Tehran	6. rue Lallier, Paris
Lazarian	Morure	24.1.08	Tehran	same
Lazarian	Sivar	1866	Tehran	same
Morady	Rayhan	1872	Tehran	8. Fracois Adam, Parc Saint Maur (Seine)
Morady	Soltan	1885	Tehran	same
Morady	Habibollah	14.7.09	Tehran	same
Morady	Ibrahim	28.1.14	Tehran	same
Morady	Djahanguir	22.6.22	Tehran	same
Nehorai	Edris	2.7.92	Tehran	29. rue Meslay, Paris
Naccache	Menache	18.2.69	Damas	4. rue Noel Saint Maur-Creteil
Naccache	Jacob	14.8.94	Damas	same
Naccache	Isaac	15.12.86	Damas	same
Naccache	Yousof	8.10.12	Damas	2. Bld. Jules Ferry, Paris

Naccache	Abdo	3.1.04	Damas	118. Bld. Richard. Lenoir, Paris
Naccache	Tofic	13.3.97	Damas	57. Bld. Barbes, Paris
Naccache	Abdo	8.2.05	Damas	10. rue Pont aux Champs, Paris
Papahn	Rahim	1902	Tehran	68. Fbg. Poissonniere, Paris
Papahn	Aschraf	1919	Tehran	same
Benaron	Marco	20.04.89	Orumieh	9. rue Mazagrand

Iranians of Zoroastrian Confession

Sassoon	Mirza Ibrahim	6.95	Ispahan	90. rue Lafayette, Paris
Sassoon	Zoleyka	12.7.07	Ispahan	same
Sassoon	Emanuel	25.9.22	Ispahan	same
Sassoon	Hayem	13.9.25	Ispahan	same

Karaime Confession

| Suleyman | Ruth | 29.4.1900 | Stamboul | 10. Cite Trevise, Paris |

Muslim Confession under evaluation at Provincial Police

| Louy | Ezatollah | 1900 | Tehran | 14. Av. Maistrasse Suresnes (Seine) |

Orthodoxe Religion under consideration at Provincial Police

| Chileri | Farrok | 3.11.98 | Kieffe | 71. rue Lecourbe, Paris |

The following explanation accompanied the letter and the list:

Mosaique Iranians
'Les Iraniens de Confession Mosaique'

Iranians are mainly Muslim. The majority are Shiites with some Sunnis among them. Some of the sixteen million Iranians, all brothers and sisters of the same origin and racial stock, are converts to the Mosaique faith. There are approximately ten to twelve thousand Mosaique Iranians throughout the Iranian Empire.[301]

Mosaique Iranians are deeply and fervently attached to their native country, Iran. They never emigrate except to travel to some major cities of Europe or America on business or to study. They may take up residence there temporarily with the intention of returning to their homeland. This attachment to one's native country is very characteristic of Iranians, whether Muslim or converts to the Mosaique faith.

The habits, customs and morals of Mosaique Iranians are indistinguishable from those of Muslim Iranians. They have grown up speaking only the one national language, Persian, and they do not speak any Hebrew or Yiddish. They live the same life style as other Persians, eat and dress as Persians, and live and are educated within the Persian community. They also have the same rights and duties as Muslim Iranians. Their attachment to the Iranian culture and literature, Ferdowsi, Omar Khayyam, Sa'di, Hafiz and the magnificent history of the Persian Kings, is profound.

They are indeed, Iranian patriots and obliged to perform military service and civic duties just as other Persians. They observe and celebrate Persian national holidays such as 'Norouz' (New Year) on 21 March every year, as do all Iranians. They commonly reside in rural areas and small towns and engage in craft industries or agriculture. There are no ghettos in Iran as Iranians do not consider the Mosaique converts to be different from them. They do not impose any constraints on them and do not discriminate against them.

Iranian women of Mosaique faith dress as their Muslim counterparts, and wore the veil until very recently (when it was abolished). As is the case with Muslim Iranian households, Mosaique women reside in the inner courtyards.[302] Mosaique men may take second or third wives, but based on Koranic instructions only if the legitimate rights of the first wives and their children are not compromised; just as is the case with Muslim Iranians.

Mosaique Iranians have never intermarried with Western Jews since it had been almost impossible to enter Iran until recently, or in any case take up residence in Iran. The process of Iran's modernisation and Europeanisation goes back only 20–25 years. As a consequence, Iranians have realistically not had enough time to mix with Westerners.

From an anthropological standpoint, Mosaique Iranians have the same features and appearances as Muslim Iranians. They may have a different spiritual belief but their faces are oval with evenly distributed features, relatively low foreheads, straight noses, red or light brown lips that are often thin, and frequently blue eyes. The eyes are always very expressive.

The Iranian Mosaicque are not considered either in fact or by law to be an ethnic minority in Iran. They are seen as merely followers of a minority religion.

Mosaique Iranians are justified in believing and have every reason to believe that they have the same historic and ethnological origins as their fellow Iranians. In other words, they are descendants of the Aryan Indo-European race, with no relationship to the European Jewish race.

Mosaique Iranians frequently marry Muslim Iranians and Muslim Iranians do the same. Some even profess both faiths at the same time. The names of Mosaique Iranians, for instance, Abdallah, Nazli, Nouroullah and Ezathoulah, etc., etc., are typical Muslim names. In all respects, Iranian Mosaique resemble the Djougoutes of Afghanistan, Bukhara and Turkistan, almost all of whom are of Iranian origin.

A copy of Sardari's letter was forwarded to Berlin seeking instructions. In a note dated 21 August 1942, Dellmensingen requested that Bureau DIII of the German Foreign Office (Referat DIII, Abteilung Deutschland) consider an attached copy of a letter by 'the former Iranian consul who looks after Iranian interests under the supervision of the Swiss Consulate and the German Embassy, and express an opinion.'[303] The letter prompted inquiries by Franz Rademacher of the bureau of Juden Politik–Jewish Affairs – from August to October. Rademacher addressed the Reich Minister of the Interior, the Race Policy Office, the Institute for the Study of the History of New Germany, the World Service Institute and the Reich Institute for the Study of the Jewish Question with his inquiries. Addressing 'party comrades' and making a reference to prior correspondences he concluded by requesting that 'you oblige us with an examination of this issue and a report of the results.'[304]

The Reich Minister of the Interior, in a letter dated 2 October 1942 and signed by Dr Feldscher, replied to Rademacher declaring that 'an examination of the general question' was desirable. He then requested a report from the Foreign Office in reference to Sardari's letter of 12 August to indicate whether it had any information on the Iranian Jews and Afghan and Georgian 'Mosaiques'. He ended his letter by stating 'I would be grateful if you could recommend a known expert who could give an opinion on these issues.'[305] On 15 October Rademacher sought the assistance of the Race Policy Office, Reich Institute for the Study of the History of New Germany. He wrote:

Dear Party Comrade Gross

The question of the treatment of Iranian Jews in occupied France has led the Ministry of the Interior to examine this issue in general terms in light of the position of the Iranian Consulate in Paris which maintains that Iranians of the Mosaic faith are not Jews but rather non-Jews of Iranian extraction. In addition, the Ministry has inquired whether anything is known of the racial origins of the Mosaic Georgians and Afghans. It has also asked for referral to an expert who could give an opinion on those matters.

We would appreciate an examination of the issues and look forward to the results of the evaluation.

Heil Hitler!
Rademacher[306]

Walter Gross replied to Rademacher as 'Dear Very Honoured Legation Councillor' on 23 October 1942. 'From an anthropological perspective,' Persia's Jews displayed 'semi-Asiatic Semitic characteristics,' showing no specific Jewish features through lacking Slavic blood and mixed blood attributes. He opined that the consciousness of the members of the Jewish race was expressed in

religious terms, which remained unswervingly strong among the Mosaics, for
'they know and follow the Talmud.' He asserted that the Persian Mosaics – and
undoubtedly their descendants in Afghanistan – were racially, religiously and
politically connected to the rest of the world Jewry and closer to it than the
Jews of the Caucasus. Nevertheless, a unique racial, sociological and political
development had separated them from world Jewry.[307]

Other reports followed. One signed by Dr Otto Paul of the Institute for the
Research of the Jewish Question dated 27 October 1942 is of particular interest.
Dr Paul wrote to the German Foreign Office that the question raised was very
important but also very difficult to answer, for it required a thorough study and
additional resources. 'The entire area [of research] is a task of the Institute and
will be taken up, as soon as we have the proper personnel.' He suggested that 'it
was always irritating' to deal with 'a clever Jewish camouflage'. He then offered
the names of three experts: 'For Iran: Mr Davoud Monchi Zadeh, Ministry of
Propaganda, For Georgia: University Professor Dr Gerhard Deeters, University
of Bonn, For India, Afghanistan and Baluchistan: University Professor Dr Walter
Wust, Rector of the University of Munich.'[308]

In the meantime, Sardari composed another letter dated 29 September
1942, addressed to the German Embassy's chief of protocol. It was more
detailed and most probably typed by Madame Daruvar, one of the two
legation secretaries, as it appears neater than the first with a more even print.
Madame Daruvar would prove very valuable to the Jewish community,
and her colleague Madame Grisard was equally agreeable, dependable and
professional. The legation concierge and gatekeeper, Monsieur Belleperche,
who lived on the legation grounds with his wife, was also helpful. He had
fought in the French Army in the First World War and was gassed by the
Germans, against whom he harboured bitter feelings.

Sardari and his dwindling French staff were united in their unspoken
objective to save as many lives and livelihoods as possible, and did so with
dedication. The common objective had never been discussed, yet was clearly
perceived by each as a silent, sacred vow they shared.

5, rue Fortuny – 17th District

Paris, 29 September 1942

Dear Chief of Protocol,

Further to my letter of 12 August 1942 concerning the case of Iranian
Djougoutes, I have the pleasure of informing you that I have just learned that
pursuant to instructions from appropriate occupation authorities, a few Iranians
known to be Djougoutes have been asked to report to police headquarters and
the 'Jew' stamp has been removed from their identity cards.

Now that this decision is made, I am obligated to start a file for the people whose 'Jew' stamp has been removed. Consequently, I would like to have an official document from proper authorities to state the basis for this change that has occurred, so that I can attach it to their file.

Allow me to express my great appreciation to the Chief of Protocol in advance for your considerate cooperation.

A. Sardari[309]

Monsieur le Chef du Protocole
Ambassade d'Allemagne
78, rue de Lille
Paris

The letter precipitated continual correspondence between the German Embassy and the Swiss Consulate in Paris on the one hand, and the Swiss Embassy and the German Foreign Ministry in Berlin on the other. The Foreign Office in turn requested further explanation from Sardari as it continued to seek 'expert opinions'. Despite his bravado, Sardari's position had been dangerously weakened ever since the Allied invasion of Iran in August. Germany had had good reason to cultivate relations with Iran, as Iran had been a valuable trading partner and maintained strict neutrality. The Russo–British invasion of Iran changed all that. When Iran's government severed relations with occupied France in 1942, Sardari's position was further undermined. Iran, trying to safeguard its territorial integrity, declared its alliance with the occupiers in September 1943. The ground beneath Sardari's feet crumbled again. A directive by Mohsen Ra'iss, the Iranian Minister in Vichy, dated 11 February 1942, ordered Sardari to close the legation, terminate the staff, turn over everything to the Swiss Consulate and depart for Vichy with other Iranian diplomats as soon as possible. He was thus under orders – as of February 1942 – to leave France. A letter addressed to the French Foreign Ministry requested authorisation for Mr and Mrs Mohsen Ra'iss, their child and a nurse, Mr and Mrs Ardalaan and their child, Mr Sardari, Mr Shahryar and Mr Borhaan to withdraw their bank deposits and leave the country.[310] Sardari followed the instructions, terminated the staff with the exceptions of Monsieur Belleperche the gatekeeper and Madam Daruvar and requested permission from the German Embassy to leave Paris. The reply he received revealed his new status.

The German Embassy acknowledges the receipt of your letter of 30 April 1942 and is unable to grant your request to leave Paris at the present time. This letter is to inform you that you no longer enjoy any diplomatic and consular immunity and are recognised as a regular private person. For that reason, your request will not be granted.[311]

Sardari might have welcomed the denial of his request for he had already resolved to stay and had promised Ibrahim Morady that he would. His decision of course had serious consequences. He lost his diplomatic protection and would soon lose his own government's support, including his salary when he failed to return to Tehran. Yet, he continued to carry out his responsibilities, relying on his own resources and connections to do so. He had a sizable inheritance, and he used what was accessible in Paris and had assistance from friends when necessary.[312] A confidential 1944 letter by Iran's ambassador to Turkey addressed to Iran's Prime Minister Mohammad Sa'ed Maraghei (who also held the portfolio of foreign minister) is most revealing:[313]

Your Esteemed Excellency the Prime Minister and Foreign Minister:

You are aware that Mr Sardari, the former secretary at the Imperial Legation in Paris in charge of consular affairs, remained in Paris on my instruction when the legation was vacated [moved to Vichy], in order to assist Iranian nationals whenever necessary.

All Iranians and non-Iranians, Jews, Muslims, Armenians and the like who have contacted me and spoken to others, as well as impartial international officials, confirm that Sardari has, with the highest competence, protected the interests of Iranian nationals during the difficult times [of the German invasion] and the years that have followed.

After Iran severed relation with France, I understand he was to leave France but the Germans did not allow his departure. Nevertheless, the Ministry of Foreign Affairs stopped paying his salary. Yet, he has continued to serve Iran's citizens with due diligence and considerable sacrifice. I have observed him in that condition [from afar] for two-and-a-half years, but because he is a relative of mine have refrained from a recommendation on his behalf to avoid the misperception of nepotism. In all fairness, he has been subjected to gross injustice. Since I view all Foreign Ministry employees who have worked with me the same way, I feel compelled to express what I know about him.

One of the directors general of the Turkish Foreign Ministry who has visited Paris recently and met Sardari there, brought me a letter from him that is most distressing. Sardari has lost [sold, bartered] all his belongings, to the point of requesting clothes [from me for personal use]. He swears that he is not allowed to leave the city under any circumstances. Despite his distress, he toils in an office without heat and often on an empty stomach. He works tirelessly with the Swiss consul to help Iranians as much as possible.

I respectfully request consideration for the hardship he has suffered and the service he has rendered to all Iranians in the past two years. Please do not allow him to be abandoned to hardship, hunger and destitution, and reinstate his salary. I hope that this impartial proposal receives Your Excellency's attention. I look forward to your response by a telegram.[314]

One can only imagine the privation Sardari must have endured. The man who would not settle for anything less than the best – whether in clothes, food or drink – had been reduced to asking his brother-in-law for clothes, and to make do without heat and adequate food. Remarkably, he maintained his public persona and continued to perform his duties without interruption.

Sardari's lot took a still more dangerous turn when Adolf Eichmann, Chief of Unit IV- B4 of Reich Central Security Office (Referat IV- B4, RSHA, in charge of Jewish affairs), wrote a three-page letter directly addressed to Dr Karl Klingenfuss at the Foreign Ministry in December 1942. Referring directly to Sardari's letter, Eichmann's opening sentence was devastatingly clear. 'In the report on the Iranian Jews "Iranians of the Mosaic Confession" we have a case of the usual Jewish tricks and attempts at camouflage.' Eichmann argued that from its historical golden age to 1920–1921 (the ascendance of Reza Shah Pahlavi to power) 'a lively Jewish question' had been evident in Iran. It had been Reza Shah who 'in the course of the Iranian Revolution of 1920–21' had 'carried out the legal equality of the Jews with other Iranians.' Eichmann added that there was 'no reason to recognise the emancipation of Jews in Iran in areas under German control.' He concluded his letter by informing Klingenfuss that he had sent a copy of the letter to Section I of the Reich Ministry of the Interior.[315]

A similar letter by Dr Gross (Director, Racial Policy Office of the National Socialist German Workers Party – NSDAP) to the Foreign Ministry dated 7 January 1943, stated that he saw no reason for a special treatment of Persian or Afghan Jews. 'They are in my opinion to be handled the same way as all other Jews in all measures of practical racial policy.'[316] Professor Dr Kittel of Vienna argued that 'the claims regarding Iranians of Mosaic faith are in no way historically sustainable.'[317] Several other letters expressed similar opinions. The Swiss Embassy in Berlin, persuaded by Sardari's argument and on behalf of the Iranian government, asked the Reich Ministry of Foreign Affairs on 11 March 1943 to consider as non-Jew the Iranians identified as 'Mussai' (Mosaique/Mosaic – followers of Moses) or 'Djuguten'. The letter, containing a 'report' in French, was drafted by Sardari in Paris.

The Iranian government would be grateful if the Iranians who belong to the group in question, are no longer considered Jews in the entire German-controlled area, and especially in Germany. To justify this request, we put forward the following Iranian report:

Les Djougoutes de l'Iran … are not émigrés but have lived in that part of Asia for centuries. A large number of them have been totally assimilated and adopted the same way of life and dress as the Muslims, although they have accepted the Mosaique faith. Only for that reason they are recognised as 'Mussai' or 'Djougoute' in Iran. They have the same rights and civic duties, legal and military, as the Muslims and [although] some have adopted some of the rites of the Mosaique Confession, they respect the Islamic Holy Book, the Koran. Some have adopted Biblical and others Muslim names. From the racial viewpoint the Djougoutes have never wanted to nor ever mixed with the Western Semitic races for they never immigrated. Generally, they marry amongst themselves and their Muslim compatriots ...

The Djougoutes began to arrive in Europe with their brother Muslims about 30 years ago, but not to settle. They preserve their connection with their homeland where their parents live. They are [in Europe] to sell Iranian products and to buy European goods. Some of the Djougoutes in Europe returned to Iran at the beginning of the war. Others have tried to liquidate their assets to do the same but have not been able to obtain the necessary travel authorization, which Iranians have been denied. They have remained loyal to their country and observed strict neutrality in the current conflict, as dictated by the Iranian Legation prior to the cessation of [Iran-German] diplomatic relations ...

In sum, The Iranian Djougoutes can not be anything but Iranian. They are so for they respect all the rites, beliefs, laws and traditions of their Muslim brothers, as they also observe the Mosaique canon. Furthermore, no physical distinction between [Iranian] Muslims and Djougoutes is possible.

The letter ended with the words 'The Swiss Embassy would be very grateful to the Reich Foreign Ministry for a favourable review of the matter, and for appropriate measures to end discrimination against the Iranians to which the above mentioned groups belong.'[318]

It should be noted that Reinhard Heydrich had already called for a conference to determine a 'final solution' for 'the Jewish question' in late 1941. Heydrich was Heinrich Himmler's deputy and the director of the Jewish Section within the Reich Security Service (*Sicherheitsdienst*: SD). The conference, originally scheduled for 9 December 1941, was postponed to the following January. It was finally convened on 20 January 1942 at 56–58 Am Grossen Wannsee, a villa on the outskirts of Berlin. The SS policy of forced Jewish emigration had altered in 1941 when Himmler banned Jewish emigration in favor of 'deportation'. The German invasion of the Soviet Union in June 1941 paved the way for mass executions of Jews by *Einsatzgruppen*. In preparation for the conference and to assure that the Foreign Ministry would not appear less enthusiastic than others, Martin Franz Julius Luther,[319] Foreign Minister Joachim von Ribbentrop's undersecretary and director of Abteilung Deutschland, ordered one of his agency's departments, Referat DIII, concerned with the Jewish question, racial policy, German refugees and national policies abroad, to prepare a memorandum expressing the Ministry's *Wunschen und Ideen* – 'desires and ideas'.[320] The memorandum included eight propositions. The first three called for the deportation 'to the east' of all Jews of German citizenship as well as all Croatian, Serbian, Slovak and Romanian Jews. All Jews in German-occupied territories who had become 'stateless' through the recent amendment to the Reich Citizenship Law were also to be deported. The next two proposals called for the deportation to the east of Hungarian Jews turned over to the Germans by their own government, and the German government's willingness to do the same for other countries that would follow the Hungarian example. The sixth and seventh proposals called for influencing the Bulgarian, Hungarian and other European governments to introduce Jewish legislation of their own on the Nuremberg model. The final item called for the implementation of the measures 'in friendly cooperation with the Gestapo'.[321]

Heydrich opened the conference with references to an order by Reichsmarshall Hermann Goering to plan the final solution. He had already forwarded copies of the order to the participants prior to the conference. The authority to carry out the final solution was entrusted to Reischsfuhrer-SS Himmler and Security Police and SD Chief Heydrich; but it was made clear that all government agencies directly involved in the task were to render their full cooperation.[322] As early as August 1940, Ambassador Otto Abetz, in charge of all political matters in France by Hitler's direct orders, had requested cooperation from the Foreign Ministry to have Jews removed from the country.[323] It is perhaps a measure of Sardari's effectiveness that in a report to Berlin on the numbers of Jews living in France dated 15 September 1942, Abetz omitted any mention of Iranian Jews altogether. The Foreign Ministry had sought to mark and deport all foreign Jews in the Western occupied territories, and to confiscate their properties. Responding to the Foreign Ministry, Abetz reported that 500 Italian, 1570 Hungarian, 3046 Turkish, 3790 Romanian and 1416 Greek Jews lived in Paris. That Abetz had included Jews from Turkey – a neutral state with which Germany wished to maintain good relations – indicates that the omission of Iranian Jews may have been influenced by Sardari's efforts. The omission validates the late Ambassador Freydoun Hoveyda's claim that Abetz had assured Sardari that no harm would come to the Iranian Djougoutes in France.[324]

French governments had not required official registration of religion or ethnic origin by anyone until 1940, but in October of that year the Germans requested a census of all Jews in France from the French government. The latter complied by ordering Jews to register their 'Status des Juif' on 27 September 1940. Selective arrests followed in May 1941 when 3200 – mostly volunteers rejected by the French Army whose names had been found at recruiting stations – were called to report to Pithiaviers and Beaune-la-Rolande camps. In August, 4300 Jews were sent to Drancy, although some 1200 were released two months later. Indiscriminate arrests began in July 1942 when an estimated 30,000 were gathered in Velodrome d'Hiver (Winter Stadium) and moved to Drancy railway station for deportation to

Auschwitz. The first transport was on 27 March 1942.[325] Auschwitz would eventually expand to such a size that 9000 people could be gassed per day.[326]

Sardari was treading on very thin ice. Rebukes by Eichmann and Gross prompted another round of inquiries by the German Embassy in Paris. The Embassy reported to Berlin on 22 March that it had requested an 'explanation' from Sardari 'because it was thought that he had revealed to an operative of the Counterintelligence that 2400 Jews with illegal Iranian passports lived in France.' Sardari had already responded to the inquiry in a letter addressed to Secretary Dellmensingen on 17 March.[327]

5, rue Fortuny – 17th District
Paris, 17 March 1943

Monsieur L. Krafft von Dellmensingen
Secretaire de l'Ambassade d'Allemagne
Service du Protocole
78, rue de Lille
Paris

Dear Mr Secretary,

In response to your request for information, I am pleased to provide you with the following:

As stated previously on several occasions, religion is not listed in Iranian passports because no distinction is made among the various religions in Iran.

On the day that the German order of mandatory registration of Israelites was published, I convened a meeting of all Iranians living in the occupied zone. I stated then that all those who considered themselves Israelites should obey the order and report to their respective police station for registration.

On that note, I should point out that the old style passports did mention religious affiliation, but that passport format was changed long ago, and religion no longer appears on any of my country's official documents.

Obviously there must have been a misunderstanding in the information you received because:

1. It seems to me that since 1938, there have been no more than a total of 2400 Iranians living in all of France. However, we do not have precise statistics given that Iranians often come to France directly from Iran with passports valid for the duration of their visits, or that they reside in other European countries and thus do not need to report to this consulate. Consequently, we only have an estimate of the exact number of Iranians living in France, based on the number of citizens who contact this office.

2. According to my own documentation and subject to all reservations, the proportion of Israelites in the entire Iranian Empire is 200,000–300,000 in a population of about 15 million inhabitants. I should add that Iranian Israelites of the Mosaique confession born in Iran with Iranian parents and grandparents, or born in other countries of the Orient but whose parents and grandparents still live in Iran, have nothing in common with the European Jews and should not be confused with them.

3. Iranian Djougoutes are not immigrants. They are people who have lived in Iran and other parts of Asia for centuries. A large majority of them have been completely assimilated. Others have adopted some of the rites and dogmas of the Mosaique faith while at the same time live the same life and follow the same customs as Muslims. For that reason, they are known in Iran as 'Mussai' [associated with Mussa –Moses], or Djougoutes. They have the same rights and civil, legal and military duties as Muslims, and although they have adopted some of the rites of the Mosaique faith, they also abide by the Islamic Holy Book –The Koran. Some have taken Biblical and others Muslim names. What is important is that from a racial point of view, the Djougoutes have neither sought, nor been able to mix with the Western Semitic race for lack of emigration or immigration. In general, they inter-marry with fellow Muslims as well as fellow Mosaiques. Up until the time that the veil was abolished in Iran a few years ago, Djougoute women also wore the Islamic veil (see the book by Gabriel Bonvalot: *Du Caucase aux Indes`a travers le Palmyre –From Cacasus to the Indies through Palmyr,* ed. Flon, Noury and Cie, 1889, page 83). The Djougoutes speak Persian, the national language. They do not speak Hebrew or Yiddish and therefore are fully assimilated. They are considered totally Iranian.

4. Prior to the occupation [of France], a large number of Djougoutes and non-Djougoute Iranians left France. Certainly no Iranian in France, Djougoute or non-Djougoute, has rallied to a cause contrary to German interests. I know this because back when the consulate existed I received an order from my country through our legation in Vichy to instruct all my fellow countrymen and women to maintain strict and absolute neutrality. The order specified that those who could not maintain neutrality should leave France immediately. Although the interests of my country have now been entrusted to a neutral state [Switzerland], the same instructions have been strictly followed to this day.

In addition to having overseen the transmission of instructions from my country to my countrymen and women, I have ensured compliance with the directive with utmost vigilance. I would be interested to know if any one of my fellow countrymen and women has in any way failed in the duty to maintain neutrality. If anyone has any doubt, I welcome being contacted to provide reassurance.

5. During the war of 1914–1918, at a time when Iran did not see any disadvantages in granting Iranian nationality to certain foreigners, some Israelites from Central Europe received Iranian nationality. We do not, however, recognise them as Djougoutes. At present, Iranian nationality can be granted only by the decision of the Council of Ministers.

Most respectfully,

A. Sardari

P.S. Attached is the complete list of Iranian Djougoutes which you requested during our conversation.

[The same list as sent to the German Embassy on 12 August was appended, plus:]

Last Name	First Name	Date of Birth	Place of Birth	Present Address
Schalom	Ebrahim	1913	Tehran	40, rue de Nancy, Argenteuil
Amir	Simon	28.9.00	Tehran	23, rue Gramme, Paris
Youssof	Moise	18.1.97	Orumieh	1. Av. Louise de Bettignies Colombes (Seine)
Heraron	Renee	5.11.21	Vienna	9, rue Mazagran, Paris
Eliakin	Yoachim	15.9.94	Andrinople	85, rue Lafayette, Paris

(Islamic confession was added to the list of the letter)

Chilieri	Farrokh	3.11.98	Kieffe	71, rue Lecourbe, Paris

(Orthodox confession was added to the list of the letter)

Mordechay	Joseph	20.3.9	Tehran	30 rue Servan, Paris
Solayman	Samy	23.12.24	Stamboul	108, Bd. Voltaire, Paris[328]

Sardari tried tirelessly to construct plausible cases. A careful reading of accessible documents – many yet to be made available at French and Iranian archives – seems to suggest that Sardari was anticipating potential questions; it is possible that Sardari's German and French friends warned him of potential bureaucratic and ideological traps he faced. The statement on granting Iranian citizenship to non-Iranians, for instance, may have been to uphold the validity of the passports he had issued to non-Iranians. The letter dated 17 March 1943 expanded the list of Iranian 'Mussai, or Djougoutes' whom Sardari had already identified as racially, culturally, historically and linguistically distinct from, and unrelated to, the European Jewish population. Yet some names do not appear to be Iranian. The March 1943 list includes two new categories, '*Liste des Iraniens de Confession Zardocchti*,' and '*de Confession Karaime*.'[329] One young man identified as Zoroastrian was the student of signal electronics, Seon (Zion) Cyrus Sassoon, already mentioned.[330]

The German allegation of 22 March 1943 that 2400 Jews held illegal Iranian passports may have been a credible estimate after all; the figure generally corresponds with the estimated number of passports at Sardari's disposal. A passport could have been routinely issued for a family, particularly for a mother and her children. The number of blank passports available at the Legation is estimated at 500–1000, and if each was issued for an average of two to three persons, this could have saved over 2000 individuals. Remarkably, almost all the Iranians survived with their properties generally untouched. Some on the list had not been born in Iran, and others had no connection to the country at all. Two such persons were David Dorra and Sami Dorra, unrelated French carpet dealers and Ibrahim Morady's close business associates. One of them it was claimed was born in Shiraz, Iran, and the other to Iranian parents in Damascus, Syria. The March 1943 list includes the names of 17 persons whose places of birth were reported as Lebanon, Turkey, Switzerland or Russia. The list continually expanded and it is possible that more than one list may have existed.[331] By 4 May 1943 the list included 91 names, 55 of which were claimed to be Iranian, but included 23 that were Afghan, 13 Bukharan and several naturalised French.[332] Several handwritten lists of applicants for Iranian citizenship sent to the Iranian Foreign Ministry in Tehran illustrate Sardari's constant effort to save as many people as he could. The long list of applicants' names written in Persian script is most probably in Sardari's own handwriting.[333]

Karl Otto Klingenfuss at the German Foreign Ministry sought an experienced professional diplomat's advice on Sardari's petition of 18 November 1942.[334] The diplomat, German Ambassador to the Soviet Union who had returned to Berlin after the German-Soviet war had commenced, was Graf von der Schulenburg. Schulenburg had served in Iran as minister before his Moscow assignment and had had years of diplomatic experience in the Caucasus before his Tehran posting. He was considered a true expert, perhaps the best that the German Foreign Ministry had on matters related to Iran, the Caucasus and Iran's neighbouring states. He certainly understood Iranian culture and its political implications. He had also forged a close friendship with Iran's Ambassador to the Soviet Union, Mohammad Sa'ed Maraghei, during his tenure in Moscow. The two career diplomats had known each other from a decade earlier when both served in the Caucasus. Schulenburg deserves credit for an apparent turning of the tide in Sardari's favour in late April 1943. A directive signed by the Legation Councillor Eberhard von Thadden of Inland II, dated 29 April stated:[335]

> In the German controlled areas there are a number of Iranian citizens of the Mosaic faith who are being treated as Jews by the German government agencies. These persons belong to the Islamic Djugute sect, who have indeed adopted a number of characteristics of the Mosaic denomination, but essentially

follow the Mohammedan religious rules. Thus it appears that facts do not justify applying the German Jewish laws to them. In addition, it is not desirable for political reasons at the moment, to discriminate against the Djugutes.

It is therefore requested that orders be issued not to apply the German Jewish measures to the Djugutes of Iranian citizenship.

The persons listed on the two following attachments are known to be Djugutes.[336]

Von Thadden's directive was followed by a similar, carefully crafted letter by Schulenburg on 14 May.

As far as I can recall, the Djuguten are a Muslim sect who essentially follow Mohammedan principles. The scope of the theology of Moses that they have adopted is very limited. On the basis of blood, they are Iranian and not Semite. Therefore, applying the German Jewish laws to them seems unjustified. We are trying, despite all the difficulties facing us, to maintain good relations with Iran. Prejudice against the Djuguten would defeat our efforts and will give our enemies propaganda ammunition to use against us. The Political Bureau XIII [Ministry of Foreign Affairs], recommends not to apply the laws of German Jews to Djugoten, or at the very least to postpone their implementation.[337]

Von Thadden drafted a reply to the Swiss Embassy in Berlin in May 1943 in which he stated:

The Foreign Ministry is honoured to acknowledge the receipt of the letter of 11 March 1943 concerning the treatment of the Islamic sect of Djugutes.

The Foreign Ministry has [thus] asked the Reich Security Main Office to order that the Jewish policies in the German-controlled areas not be applied to Djugutes of Iranian citizenship.

A footnote added to the draft, apparently for internal departmental records, points to the interdepartmental difficulties.

The Reich Security Main Office has been asked to order – with the letter of 29 April of this year, I Inl. II A 3300 – that German Jewish policies not be applied to Djugutes of Iranian citizenship.

An identical request should be sent to the Reich Food Ministry concerning food ration cards, and one to the Reich Economics Ministry concerning clothes ration cards, in order to fulfil the Swiss Embassy's wishes. It is not possible to do this however, as just a few days ago the Foreign Office requested the above ministries not to apply Jewish policies to Argentine citizens of the Jewish race. The current position of the named ministries indicates that a positive response is not likely. It appears that it would not be promising at the moment to raise the issue of the Djugutes. In addition, this would endanger our slim chance of helping the Argentine Jews in whom we have great political interest. Therefore, we must await the results of our efforts in regards to the Argentine Jews.[338]

The bureaucracy, in trying to adjust to the bottlenecks it encountered during the war, often had to resort to arbitrary decisions. A note by von Thadden dated 26 May 1943 addressed to Counselor Jungling reflects his discussion with the Chief of Security Police concerning the letter of 24 April 1943, Inl. II A 3300. The Chief informed him 'correctly, that this was a typical Jewish trick in order to get the special treatment that was refused them last year through the back door.'[339]

A letter from the Belgian Foreign Office in Brussels addressed to Berlin, dated 31 May, sought verification that the German Jewish measures would not apply to the Djuguten of Iranian citizenship. It stated that the Military Administration had learned from a Belgian attorney that German officials in Paris had determined that all Iranians were to be considered Aryans. A telephone conversation with the embassy in Paris had not confirmed the existence of such a policy.[340] The Foreign Ministry in Berlin followed up by sending a letter of inquiry to the German Embassy in Paris on 3 June 1943.[341] Von Thadden wrote a memorandum dated 2 June 1943 (Inland II A 4328), expressing his reservations and the general confusion of the bureaucracy regarding the 'Djuguten' versus the 'Mosaischen'.[342] He responded to the inquiry from Brussels on 15 June 1943:

> With Djuguten one is dealing with a Jewish sect strongly influenced by Islam. The racial classification of the followers of this sect is not completely clear. One may assume that the Djuguten should not be seen racially as Jews ... The Foreign Office agreed in response to a petition by a number of Iranians that the Iranian Djuguten should not be treated as Jews. However, it became clear later that the same group of Iranians had appealed in another request to the Foreign Office six months earlier that they were not Djuguten, but it would be just if they were treated as Djuguten. Since this typical Jewish camouflage attempt was uncovered, the Foreign Office amended its position ... so each case is to be individually examined to determine if it involves the Djuguten.[343]

Ironically, the amended directive from the Foreign Ministry in Berlin provided the opportunity to circumvent Nazi Jewish policies because it allowed case-by-case evaluation, thus increasing the prerogative of local officials. Assessing each case individually – as opposed to a blanket application of anti-Jewish policies – allowed for a measure of flexibility. Sardari's cultivated friendships increased the possibility of favourable outcomes in such cases. The response of the German Embassy in Paris to Berlin's question regarding the Belgian lawyer's claim is terse, perhaps showing frustration.

The claim of the Belgian lawyer, that the Military Administration in France treats all Iranian citizens uniformly is not accurate. Concerning the special treatment of the Djuguten, please refer to the decrees of 4 January 1943 No. DIII 7488, 3 February 1943 No. DIII 532, and 7 May 1943 Inl. II A 3300.[344]

Sardari's efforts through the Swiss Foreign Ministry continued to the war's end. The Swiss Embassy in Berlin lodged a protest to the Reich Foreign Office about the mistreatment of an Iranian citizen in Belgium on 7 December 1943 and requested relief, even after Iran had declared war on Germany.

> As the Foreign Ministry of the German Reich is aware from prior messages by this embassy, German military authorities in France and Belgium have expressly confirmed that Iranian citizens of Islamic group of Djuguten cannot be subjected to German Jewish measures. The Iranian citizen Albert Soleyman Alfandry, born in Berlin on 27 April 1905, his wife born in Istanbul on 28 February 1906 and their two children, all residents in Brussels, Boulevard St. Michael, 131, have identified themselves as members of the Islamic sect of Djuguten. The commander of the Security Service in Brussels, however, has subjected them to the usual Jewish measures.
>
> The Embassy would be obliged to the Foreign Ministry for the affair to be investigated through the appropriate office in Brussels.[345]

Since Iranian proper names do not have the prefix 'Al,' it is unlikely that Al-Fandry was an Iranian, and a number of archival documents confirm that Iranian passport holders included non-Iranian Jews. An inquiry on 7 March 1943 to search for a Hermann Liebovitche, claimed as an Iranian citizen, is a case in point. Hermann Liebovitche of Antwerp had been detained and sent to Dossin-Malines labour camps in July 1942 and was reported by the SS on 3 June 1943 to have left Belgium on 15 September 1942. He was actually deported to Auschwitz on 15 September. Of the 1048 deportees on his convoy, 939 were gassed upon arrival on 17 September 1942. He may have been the only one under Sardari's watch to have perished at a death camp.[346]

There are other examples, such as that of Elya Goral, his wife Rebecca Baghdadlioglu (a Turkish name), their two daughters Hava and Esther and their son Benhas, all from Chemnitz, who requested travel papers from the German Foreign Ministry as Iranians, wishing to depart for Turkey in April 1943.[347] Albert Kamermann of Rustschuck, Bulgaria, holder of Iranian passport number 4393/83 issued in Bern, Switzerland on 3 June 1943, his wife and their two children had been taken to Westerbork Camp. The commandant requested instructions from Berlin by wire as to whether to send them to an internment camp in Germany. The reply from Berlin probably saved the family from deportation to Auschwitz. A note by von Thadden stated that 'In principle, Iranian citizens, even if Jewish, are not to be sent to Jewish camps but to internment camps.'The commander of the security services was subsequently ordered to send the family to the internment family camp Vittel in France.[348]

Another Iranian passport holder, Dario Molho of Saloniki, Greece, was ordered by the German occupying forces to wear the yellow patch and remove himself to the designated ghetto of Saloniki. The Swiss Embassy, on behalf of the Iranian government, requested from the Reich Foreign Ministry an 'immediate end' to such judgements. Von Thadden sent a note directly to Eichmann to urge compliance with the Swiss request.[349]

8

THE AFTERMATH

'HE SAVED MY FATHER'

All humans are parts of one being;
All in creation are of one origin.
When fate allots a single part pain,
No ease for other parts may remain.
If unperturbed at grief of a fellow man,
You're not worthy of the name human.[350]

Abdol-Hossein Sardari was not a man without faults. He drank too much at times and when inebriated could lose his temper. His overwhelming generosity did not always compensate for the hurt feelings he caused during those infrequent but dark moments. Yet, he was certainly a principled man despite his shortcomings. His dedication to press on even as his world crumbled around him is undeniable. He remained relentlessly focused even after his own country had been occupied by invading armies. He could have reasoned – as many had – that he was not responsible for the Nazi racial policies. He could have returned home to save his career and preserve his personal fortune. He certainly knew the hopelessness of his prospects after the Allied armies occupied Iran in August 1941. Yet, he persisted, and by doing so saved perhaps hundreds of families whose descendants today may number in the thousands. Some of them have remained in France, others relocated to other parts of Europe, the Americas, Israel, or returned home to Iran.

Sardari was reassigned from Paris to Brussels as chargé d'affaires after the Second World War, a position he held until 1952. His beloved Tchin-Tchin left Europe for China in 1948 to visit her parents and seek their approval to marry him. Sardari in a letter dated 6 July 1948 requested permission from the Iranian Ministry of Foreign Affairs to marry her. The Ministry granted the request for the marriage to 'Miss Yen Chow, a Chinese national'.[351] Caught up in the Chinese Revolution, she disappeared without a trace. Sardari had certainly expected her to return to him with her parents' blessings. The tragedy of her loss was compounded when in 1952 he was recalled to Tehran to face charges of misconduct and embezzlement. The charges referred to the period 1941–1946 and ranged from having issued unauthorised passports to having misused government funds. Dr Hossein Fatemi, a controversial journalist appointed foreign minister in Prime Minister Mohammad Mosaddeq's cabinet, publicly accused Sardari of embezzlement in an article in the national daily newspaper *Ettela'at*, published on 8 December.[352] Finally, Sardari was formally charged and detained on 18 June 1952.[353]

A few months later Sardari experienced another personal blow. His elder sister and protector suffered a stroke and passed away in Switzerland in 1953. Her husband, Anoshiravan Sepahbody, told their son Farhad, who at the time was attending college in the US, that she had been anguished over Sardari's troubles and the distress had contributed to her sudden demise. The charges against Sardari were finally dropped and his career had resumed by 1955.

The signing of the Baghdad Pact by Iran, Iraq, Turkey, Pakistan, Afghanistan, Britain and the United States on 4 February 1955 increased possibilities for regional cooperation in southwest Asia. Amidst that optimism Sardari was appointed Minister Plenipotentiary to lead a diplomatic mission to Baghdad as Lieutenant-General Nader Batmanglich was named Iran's Ambassador to Iraq. Sardari handpicked a young diplomat, Houshang Batmanglich, to accompany him on the mission. Batmanglich had completed his studies in England with a degree in political science and entered Iran's diplomatic service upon graduation in 1954. Batmanglich's English education was thought potentially useful in dealing with the British diplomatic corps, whose influence in Iraq was predominant. The Ambassador, General Batmanglich, was Houshang's uncle.

Sardari travelled to Iraq with his dog Lilly. Lilly had been with Sardari for well over a decade and the two were inseparable. Taking Lilly to Baghdad – the capital of Muslim Iraq – was a delicate matter, but Sardari loved the dog enough not to part with her. During the flight, Houshang Batmanglich recalls, Sardari was constantly concerned about Lilly's comfort and became even more attentive as the plane landed in Baghdad on a particularly hot day in May 1957.

Sardari proved to be an exceptionally capable diplomat once again. In Baghdad in 1957, as in Paris in 1940, he established himself as a great host. He personally cooked for his guests with impressive flair and his culinary presentations were just as grand. His parties, according to Houshang Batmanglich, were soon famous in Baghdad's diplomatic circles. Diplomats in Baghdad quipped tongue in cheek that one had to do *anything* to get an invitation! His most popular culinary production was the chicken dish *fesenjan*. As he had done in Paris, he always donned an apron prior to cooking, which delighted his guests, who saw in it the promise of serious culinary intent. Batmanglich and Sardari worked closely together for months prior to their arrival in Baghdad and continued to do so afterwards, until their mission was abruptly ended by a bloody coup in July 1958, staged by Brigadier-General Abd al-Karim Qasim. The Iraqi royals were killed and many others were put to flight. Foreign diplomats and their families quit Iraq hurriedly amidst the mayhem, taking their families and only the most sensitive documents.

Houshang Batmanglich, now a retired ambassador, remembers Sardari as generous to a fault. 'He spent every penny of his salary in pursuit of his diplomatic mission. He personally assumed the cost of many of the receptions he hosted, although the goal was to cultivate Iran's national interest.' His colleagues, indeed the entire diplomatic corps, genuinely respected him. He had acquired the trust and the friendship of Iraqi dignitaries to the point of having direct access to cabinet ministers, whom he could visit at will if necessary. 'As an envoy, he was extremely effective. Nearly all Iraqi dignitaries and every diplomat with whom we associated in Baghdad held him in high esteem – even affection.'

Sardari avoided discussions of his Second World War experiences and the subsequent investigations. Yet he offered Batmanglich a piece of counsel that he remembers well. 'The Iranian concept of sharing bread and salt never fails. If you serve your guests the best food and drink possible, you receive not only their appreciation but also affection.'

Some of Sardari's friends had been detained in France during the occupation. He would visit them and the authorities who could affect their status but would never officially demand their release.[354] He had made inroads with German and Vichy officials through cultivating personal relations. 'Only after winning their appreciation and affection,' he told his protégé Houshang Batmanglich, 'when they were ready to return favours, I would present my request ... They would almost always comply.' Batmanglich remembers him fondly. 'He had a way with people ... He would find a special place in anyone's heart.'[355]

The coup that ended Iraq's monarchy in July 1958 marked the end of Sardari's diplomatic career, already tarnished by the 1946–1953 charges and the investigations that followed. His old friend Abdollah Entezam – the victim of his police impersonation prank in Paris two decades earlier – was then the Chief Executive Officer of the National Iranian Oil Company (NIOC). After Iraq, Sardari left the diplomatic service, joined NIOC and moved to London in 1958.

Sardari was kind to his German friends after the war ended. Many were in dire straits back in Germany and in need of assistance. Properties had been confiscated, accounts frozen, jobs lost, cities bombed and residents of undamaged buildings evicted. Many former officials had lost everything and were at times even short of food. Sardari would help them when he could; after all, had it not been for his German friends' assistance he could not have been as effective as he had been.[356] Sardari had many friends in the French military and foreign ministry as well. General Andre Beaufre had been one such helpful officer whose friendship with Sardari continued throughout their lives. Finally, Sardari helped the French Resistance and had numerous involvements with the members.[357] He is also said to have had excellent relations with Americans, Swiss and British individuals. The American residents of Paris numbered about 5000 in June 1940, but they were not to be affected by the occupation for the US maintained neutrality for a further 18 months. Many of the Americans left Paris within the year but some 2000 remained. To help keep abreast of the latest developments, Sardari had a massive short wave radio installed in his apartment by Hayem Sassoon, the Iranian Jewish electronics engineering student.[358] As Sardari was always a gadget enthusiast, the receiver, although massive, was not out of place.

Sardari kept his Paris studio, leased from the Paris Municipality for about $300 a month. However, he made the apartment available to his nephews Farhad Sepahbody and Fereydoun Hoveyda respectively, as they were posted to the Iranian Embassy in Paris. Fereydoun Hoveyda recalled his uncle had offered him the use of the apartment for the cost of the original lease and the utilities. At the end of the first year he received a bill from the Paris city morgue, so he contacted his uncle to inquire. The bill, it turned out, had been for Tchin-Tchin's late brother's body, still kept frozen at the morgue. Sardari was adamant that he had made a promise and the promise would be kept. Hoveyda paid the hefty bill annually until 1955, when he received a letter from the morgue declaring that the fifteen-year legal limit for keeping a body in cold storage had expired and the body had thus been buried.[359] Sardari's other nephew, Farhad Sepahbody, who had left Paris as a teenager, returned there in 1970 as a diplomat. He moved into Sardari's apartment with Angela, his American wife. Sardari eventually transferred his lease to Farhad in a document dated 6 July 1974. Farhad had joined Iran's diplomatic service in 1954 upon graduation from college in the US. His assignments at the Iranian Embassy in Paris included Economic Councillor, Minister Councillor and Chargé d'Affaires from 1970 through 1974.[360]

Sardari, having joined NIOC in 1958, sold or left behind in France almost everything he had owned there. The only items he took to England with him were the Revol bust of Tchin-Tchin and the Rodin sculpture he had always treasured. When Farhad Sepahbody took over Sardari's lease and Angela redecorated the apartment, she discovered that the platform on which the grand piano had stood had a hidden space underneath. Intrigued, she found a rolled-up rug inside. Sardari had apparently hidden it there but forgotten about it.

Sardari rented his cottage in Moulineuf to a brother-in-law as he was leaving France after the war. He decided to sell the property in 1958, but his tenant, having planted some apple trees on the land, resorted to a French law concerning cultivators' rights to challenge Sardari's exclusive ownership. A bitter court case followed that finally forced Sardari to sell the cottage to the tenant at a price below its market value. The incident left behind bitter memories, and family members avoided talking about the case and urged others to do likewise. The fate of his studio apartment was similarly sad. Sepahbody sub-leased the redecorated atelier to a friend, Francois Dautresmes, a wealthy French businessman, at the end of his posting in Paris in 1974. Dautresmes failed to pay the rent to the city as stipulated in the sublease. The city thus revoked the lease and eventually tore down the building in 1982 to make way for a new construction project. The leaseholders in good standing received new apartments in the new building but Sardari's lease conveyed to Sepahbody had been lost.

The loss of property that Sardari suffered after the war is even more poignant given the fact that besides his actions on behalf of Jews already described, he may have taken additional personal risks. A prominent French professor has confided that his late father accompanied Sardari to a night club one evening in 1941. A young acquaintance appearing distressed, asked to join them as they were leaving the establishment in the early hours of the morning. A *Gheheime Staatspolizie* (Gestapo) officer, who apparently had the young man under surveillance, stopped them at the door demanding that the young man accompany him to Gestapo Headquarters. Sardari offered to drive them and persuaded the officer to accept the ride. The diplomatic licence plates gave Sardari certain privileges at security checkpoints during curfew hours. The officer and the suspect sat in the back of the four-door Citroen, and Sardari engaged the officer in small talk as he drove and offered him a cigarette. While the officer was trying to light up, the young suspect opened the door and shoved him out of the moving car. Sardari brought the car to an immediate halt. The young man jumped out, grabbed the stunned officer's service revolver, fatally shot him and disappeared in the dark. Whether Sardari knew the extent of the young man's activities or his possible connection to the Resistance is a matter of speculation.[361]

Similarly, Mouchegh Petrossian told Farhad Sepahbody whilst Iran's councillor in Paris in 1971–74 that Sardari had saved his life. The Gestapo had arrested him for involvement with the French Resistance, but Sardari appealed to a German general friend who in turn arranged Petrossian's release. Petrossian was convinced that he would have been executed otherwise. Sepahbody heard similar testimonies from others. Once he walked into a bank in Paris to deposit a cheque in Sardari's account. The young bank teller recognised the name. 'Ah! Sardari! … Had it not been for him I would not have existed … He saved my father,' he told Sepahbody.[362]

Sardari had retired from NIOC and moved to an apartment at 22 Park Crescent, London, around 1965. No longer the gregarious man of the earlier days, he lived alone and except for his daily walks with his two dogs, he seldom ventured out. The unassuming hero so kind to so many all his life, did not receive the kindness (or luck) he deserved in return. He had had an unfortunate childhood and an onerous career. The love of his life, Tchin-Tchin, had disappeared during the civil war in China. Finally, the violent 1978 revolution in Iran snatched away his pension and his favourite nephew's life. The nephew, Iran's former Prime Minister Amir Abbas Hoveyda, was executed by the revolution's infamous hanging judge, Ayatollah Sadeq Khalkhaali, on 7 April 1979.[363]

At the first news of the revolution, Sardari determined to fly to Iran to salvage what he could of his assets. He urged a friend and neighbour to purchase his apartment with its contents before he left for Iran. The friend, an attorney, did so, but begged Sardari not to leave. The last time the friend saw him, he was on his way to the airport in London.[364] Sardari received an urgent message at the airport that persuaded him not to board the plane. He had been informed that his property had been seized, his Tehran home boarded up and that the regime would arrest him, or worse, if he returned.

Sardari finally moved into a rented room in Croydon in south London. When he heard of Hoveyda's execution he was overcome by uncontrollable grief and rage. Hoveyda had been a favourite relative; it was through him, when a junior diplomat posted to Germany after the Second World War, that Sardari had helped his German friends with food and funds. Sardari paced back and forth in his room for days lamenting his nephew's ordeal as tears rolled down his face. He died soon after. His meagre belongings, the bust of Tchin-Tchin, the Rodin sculpture and the silver plate from the Jewish community of Paris, simply vanished.[365] His life, already tragic, had in the final days turned cruel. Despite moments of self orchestrated exhilaration, Sardari had not experienced much happiness.

In contrast, Rayhan Morady's descendants (Rachel, Yousef, Malek, Habibollah, Showkat, Ibrahim, Tal'at, Jahangir and Rose) flourished on three continents. Rayhan, the family patriarch and his wife Soltaneh continued to live in their Paris villa at 77 Boulevard de Montmorency after the war.[366] Rayhan passed away in Paris in 1956 at the age of 96. Soltaneh then moved to Los Angeles and a year later to Caracas, Venezuela, where two of her sons and their families had chosen to reside. She died in Caracas in 1964 at the age of 94. Rayhan and Soltaneh's eldest son, Yousef, married to the Parisian Giselle in 1929, died unexpectedly in 1931. Giselle still resides in Paris but has maintained close contact with Yousef's extended family. Rayhan's second son Habib Morady, his English wife Victoria and their son Robert migrated to Caracas in 1948 to join Victoria's family. They had two daughters in Caracas, Danielle and Evelyn. Danielle now lives in Israel with her husband

and children, and Evelyn and her family live in Spain. Robert, whose circumcision in Paris had resulted in her mother's frightening encounter with the Gestapo, tragically died of cancer in his twenties. Habib managed a successful oriental carpet business in Caracas until his death in 1996, after which Victoria continued the family business until 2007, when she retired to live with her daughter Evelyn and her family in Barcelona. She and Evelyn attended a family reunion in Israel in 2008 when Victoria was 97 years old.

Rayhan's third son Ibby (Ibrahim Morady), a businessman, fell in love with Bahie Haqqani of Iran in 1948. Bahie was in Paris for a week, on her way to the US with her parents. The attraction proved mutual. He proposed marriage within days and she accepted. Resolved to stay with Ibby in Paris, Bahie declined to accompany her parents to America and the couple married a few months later. The wedding, Ibby fondly recalled, was particularly memorable, for Sardari and Tchin-Tchin had driven from Brussels to Paris to attend. Ibby thought that Tchin-Tchin and Sardari had already married, but only a short time later Tchin-Tchin left Europe for China, never to return. Bahie and Ibby had a son Fred, born in Paris in 1949. The family moved to Forest Hill, New York, in 1952 and had a second son Claude before moving to California in 1960. They made Los Angeles their home and opened an oriental carpet showroom. Ibby, friendly, generous and remarkably gracious, passed away in June 2006. Although 94 years old and using a walker to get around, he was healthy and hospitable to the very end with a wonderful sense of humour. Fluent in Persian, French and English, he would switch from one language to another effortlessly. He is survived by his wife Bahie and two sons Fred and Claude. Fred is a recognised heart specialist, electro-physiologist and a professor at the University of Michigan Medical School. He and his wife Paulette have two daughters, Ilana and Aviva. Claude, an accomplished gemologist, is involved in appraisal, purchase and sales of antique and estate jewelry. He, his wife Jennifer and their son David live in Los Angeles. Surprisingly, Ibby's children did not know of his heroic efforts during the Second World War when first interviewed. Ibby, just as had been the case with Sardari, must have preferred not to reminisce about those unhappy days.[367]

Jahangir (Jean) Morady, the youngest of Rayhan and Soltaneh's sons, married an Iranian in Paris in 1952 and moved to Iran. They had a daughter in 1956 named Roya, but the couple separated and Jean moved to Caracas. There he married a Romanian Auschwitz survivor, Nelee. Jahangir remained an active businessman in Venezuela, importing and marketing oriental carpets.[368] Roya married David Kravetz and the couple moved to Argentina where they had a son, Nico. Years later Nico and his parents moved to San Diego, California. Rachel, the eldest of Rayhan and Soltaneh's daughters, returned to Iran after the war, married, and had five children. Rachel's sisters, Malek and Showkat, also returned to Iran and married there. They also had five children each.

Eliane, the daughter of George Senehi and Tal'at, while visiting Iran in the summer of 1953 met and married Nasser Cohanim, a dashing young businessman. They lived in Tehran and their family grew as they built Iran's first true supermarket – an impressive multi-storey place with a very popular restaurant on the top floor. The success of the market prompted the Cohanims to plan a supermarket chain and construct an architecturally notable building to house the second super store. However, the planned inauguration was foiled by the Revolution. The building was later seized and turned into a museum. The family, including three sons – Philip, Robert and Edward – moved to Paris in 1979, and later to Los Angeles. Philip and Edward married Josiane and Lora respectively. Both couples have three children each, live in Los Angeles, and together operate an import and distribution company of their own. Robert moved to St Paul, Minnesota, where he has developed a variety of homeopathic and natural remedies and a string of outlets. Nasser Cohanim, a gracious and charming man, has become a well respected banker in Los Angeles.

Eliane's brothers Claude and Fernand graduated from the University of Neuchatel in Switzerland. Claude, having studied physics and mechanics, became a flight communication specialist and a pilot. He married Martine and they settled down in Switzerland. They had two children, Christophe and Graciane, both of whom married and settled in Neuchatel. Tragedy struck the family in 1986 when Martine passed away, aged only 32. It is in her memory that Graciane named her daughter Tia Martine. Claude fell in love again when he met Laurence and they had a son, David. Fernand studied chemistry and became a quality assurance engineer. He married Marika and they have two children, Laurent and Caroline. Laurent, an economist with a doctorate, is a chartered financial analyst in Geneva. Caroline received a Master's degree in Business in 2007, and chose to remain in Neuchatel.

Rose, the youngest of Rayhan and Soltaneh's daughters, married Lotfollah Montakhab in Tehran. They had three children, two daughters and a son, but the daughters died when only six and eight years old. Although Rose and her family visited their relatives abroad, including Caracas several times, Tehran remained their home. Rose died in 1997, two years after her husband. They are survived by a son in Tehran.

Rahim Senehi, the good-natured musician and hairstylist who spent two years in detention in Germany, left Europe for Tehran in 1940. He served in the Iranian Army and married Qodrat while still a conscript. The couple migrated to Israel in 1943 and had three daughters and four sons. They made Tel Aviv their home, where Rahim died in 1970. Qodrat and six of their children still live in Tel Aviv and own and operate a construction company. One of Rahim and Qodrat's seven children, their daughter Ilana, became a teacher and moved to Texas with her husband. By the year 2007 Mrs Qodrat Senehi had been away from Iran for over 60 years and her children had never seen their ancestral home. Yet, their interest in Iran, the Persian language, cuisine, art, music and cultural traditions is avid. A visiting Iranian could not help but feel at home amongst them.[369]

Whilst I was searching for Sardari's acquaintances in France, the name Jean Mikaeloff came up more than once. Jean Mikaeloff became a prominent business leader in Lyon and once had an interesting chance meeting with the late King, Mohammad Reza Shah Pahlavi. The Shah had been sitting in a hotel lobby in Lyon during a royal visit when an elderly gentleman offered his greetings in fluent Persian. The Shah, surprised, commented on the gentleman's linguistic ability. 'I am an Iranian who has lived in France since childhood, Your Majesty,' he responded. The monarch invited him to sit down and inquired about his work and family. He had been a businessman, specialising in antiques and carpets. Married with three grown children, two sons and a daughter, he proudly mentioned that one son, a cardiac surgeon, had collaborated with Dr Christian Barnard (the famed South African surgeon who performed the first heart transplant). The Shah told an attendant on the spot, 'See to it that Dr Mikaeloff is invited to Iran,' which was done. Jean Mikaeloff is survived by two sons and a daughter – the heart surgeon, a businessman who runs the family enterprise and a talented artist.[370]

The other family of note in the story of Sardari is the Lazarians, who left Paris for New York in 1947. Their two children Claude and Janine have thrived and have families of their own. Claude and his wife Phyllis celebrated their 40th wedding anniversary in November 2004. They have two sons and two grandsons. One could find many other descendants, as every name mentioned on Sardari's list represents an extended family with members residing mostly in the United States, Iran and Israel.

Sardari was not the only Iranian diplomat to answer a calling higher than his bureaucratic duties. The expulsion of Axis diplomats from Iran under Allied occupation prompted reciprocal closures of Iranian legations abroad. The difficulties that Iran's chargé d'affaires faced in Paris were also experienced in Rome and elsewhere. The Iranian diplomat left behind in Rome was also a young bachelor, named Abdollah Khosravi. Khosravi's predicament was similar to Sardari's. He too used his access to blank passports and visa stamps to rescue as many Jews as he could, but his efforts attracted the attention of Nazi officials who sought to stop him. He was finally arrested and packed off to a minimum security detention camp in Germany for the remainder of the war. Another Iranian diplomat, Rahmat Ataabaky, Iran's envoy in Beirut, Lebanon, similarly helped Jewish refugees with Iranian birth certificates and passports. Iran's former Ambassador to Norway, Hashem Hakimi, asserted in December 2007 'I am certain that my other colleagues at the Imperial Ministry of Foreign Affairs behaved in a similar humanitarian manner, in keeping with our historic background … but never bragged about it.'[371]

Finally, a sinister misconception about the late King Reza Shah Pahlavi ought to be put to rest, as he is often accused of having been pro-Nazi or a Nazi sympathiser. The allegation that Reza Shah changed the country's name from Persia to Iran to please Hitler is ignorant nonsense.[372] Reza Shah certainly played up the Aryan heritage of Iran and maintained good relations with Germany and Italy to counterbalance continuous Russian and British interference.[373] He wished Iran to reassert its sovereignty; but evidence suggests that he had little patience with Nazi ideology. There is much anecdotal evidence, such as the time the Shah cut short an audience with the Hitler Youth leader Baldur von Shirach, who visited Tehran in December 1937, and gave a royal tongue-lashing to the cabinet minister who had scheduled it.[374] On another occasion, with the passage of the National Conscription Law, conscripts were allowed a few breaks only for recognised national holidays. Dr Loqman Nahurai, a Jewish Majles representative, had contacted the Ministry of War to seek leave authorisation for Jewish conscripts on their religious holidays, without success. When he sought and received an audience with Reza Shah, the King readily agreed to the request and wrote an order in his own handwriting to that effect on the spot. Twelve Jewish religious holidays including the first day of Rosh Hashana, Yom Kippur, two days at the start of Succot, and eight days for Passover observances were thus ordered to be recognised as official holidays for Jewish conscripts by the Conscription Bureau.

Another example was when the governor-general of Lorestan concocted false charges to expropriate desirable properties belonging to several wealthy Jewish residents in the province. The commander of the Army of the West (Lashgar-e Gharb), Lieutenant-General Ahmad Ahmadi, was ordered to Lorestan to investigate. As the result of the investigation, the governor was charged, tried, convicted and executed. Dr Habib Levy, a Jewish historian and former Iranian Army officer comments:

> If the Shahanshah did not specifically favour the Jews, he certainly did not disfavour them. No one could instigate against Jews, for it was the will of the King that governed the country, and Reza Shah would not be influenced by anyone.[375]

Mistreating minorities for financial or political gain – tolerated under the Qajar regime – came to a decisive end under the Pahlavi monarchy. A classified document signed by the chief of national police confirms Levy's assertion.[376]

Some of the slurs against Reza Shah may be traced to the propaganda that accompanied the invading British and Russian armies that in 1941 trampled on Iran's declared and strictly observed neutrality. What is particularly galling is that the accusers, so willing to defame others, are not disposed to take a critical look at their own governments and themselves.

Winston Churchill criticised the British government's White Paper that banned Jewish immigration to Palestine in Parliament in 1939 but did not change the policy when he became Prime Minister. When the US Treasury Department attempted to transfer funds to ransom Jews in Nazi-occupied Europe, Churchill's government tried to prevent the effort, for his officials were 'concerned with the difficulties of disposing of any considerable number of Jews should they be rescued from enemy occupied territory.'[377] Churchill asserted on 1 August 1946, 'I must say that I had no idea, when the war came to an end, of the horrible massacres which had occurred; the millions and millions that have been slaughtered. That dawned on us gradually after the war was over.' That the German Enigma code had been broken by British Intelligence in December 1940 and summaries of SS operations were sent to the Prime Minister regularly every week does not lend credence to the statement.[378] Such details are often too easily and conveniently dismissed as *force majeure* contingencies of war.

EPILOGUE

'PERSIA CAN NEVER GO UNDER'

Iranians resisted the ideological epidemics of the nineteenth and twentieth centuries that infected Europe, Asia, Africa and the Americas. Western ideologies did of course attract Iranian intellectuals and some even saw themselves as self-appointed leaders with a calling to move the masses. Yet the ideologues and their ideologies failed to persuade the general population. Iranians were simply more interested in shaking off the Europeans' domination of their country than the promises of liberation offered by the ideologies of those same Europeans. Fascism never made a popular impact in Iran and attempts to create a political party did not amount to much.[379] Even communism, despite Iran's proximity to the Soviet Union and active recruitment of factory workers, did not gain much of a following, and when it did organise cells in some cities in 1941–1953 they were more energised by espionage or propaganda than by personal onviction. The frustration of the Soviet Minister to Tehran, Theodor Rothstein, in failing to indoctrinate Iranians in 1921 is illustrative of the Iranians' nationalist cultural sentiment. Rothstein, a former journalist on the *Manchester Guardian* in England, told the visiting American journalist Vincent Sheean in Tehran:

> Persia is fundamentally sound. They take money from anybody; from the British today, from the Russians tomorrow, or from the French or the Germans or anyone else. But they will never do anything for the money. You may buy their country from them six times over, but you will never get it. I say that Persia can never go under. Persia is fundamentally sound.[380]

Two decades later, Nazi propagandists were also disappointed; Iranians were 'not warlike' enough and found the war's destructiveness repulsive.[381] In a secret report the German Embassy in Tehran advised Berlin to emphasise religion in its propaganda aimed at Iranians, to use the clerical communication network to influence the Iranian masses – and to claim Adolf Hitler to be the Shiites' hidden Imam – whose return the faithful expect. This was a variation on the rumours being spread in the Arab world that Hitler had converted to Islam after meeting Haj Amin Al-Hussaini of Palestine, would reveal his true Muslim identity as Haydar (the brave one) after the war, and that Mussolini was in reality an Egyptian named Mussa al-Nilli (Moses of the Nile).[382] The audacity of the propaganda and the attempt at enticing clerical collusion are indeed disturbing but in keeping with Hitler's own convictions. Hitler said of the masses in *Mein Kampf* that 'in view of the primitive simplicity of their minds, they more easily fall victim to a big lie than to a small one, since they themselves lie in little things, but would be ashamed of lies that were too big.'[383] In a secret report dated 2 February 1941 on the subject 'Propaganda Opportunities in Iranian Communities, Considering Religious Expectations of the Shiites' the German legation in Tehran advised the Foreign Ministry in Berlin that

> The realisation that certain religious expectations are alive among Iranians even today is important for our own propaganda. The greatest and highest of these expectations is the belief in the appearance of the Twelfth Imam, who is to come as the saviour of the world. The worse the condition of the masses, the stronger is the belief in the coming of the saviour.
>
> The legation has been receiving information from the most varied sources for months that clerics have appeared throughout the country reporting mysterious dreams and prophesies that could be interpreted to mean that the Twelfth Imam has descended onto the world in the form of Adolf Hitler. It should not be assumed that the stories are told on orders from superiors … but the fact remains that the religious establishment has not forbidden it. Moreover, it is the state that intervenes from time to time and arrests the mullahs who go too far in this.[384]

The report emphasised that 'The statements of the mullahs make a deep impression on the believers who hear them.' It also referred to the voluminous material that the legation's propaganda chief had collected on the reported dreams and prophesies throughout the country.

> If we could succeed in bringing the majority of the clergy of the country under the influence of German propaganda, most people would follow … Everything will be ruined however, if we offend the deep feelings of the believers by lack of elegance. A way to do this is to highlight the struggle of Mohammed against the Jews in the ancient time and that of the Fuhrer at present … Evidence should be collected and published to show that the British are the lost tribe of Israel.

The report concludes by suggesting that certain passages in the Koran should be used in Persian language radio broadcasts in parallel with Hitler's own words, such as the quotation:'I believe that today I act in the spirit of the Almighty creator in that I resist the Jews, I struggle for the work of the Lord' (*Mein Kampf,* page 69).[385]

One may ask whether Sardari's behaviour was an aberration. Those who think so mistake Iran's post-Revolution decades for its entire history. Iran was not created in 1978! Sardari's heroic conduct had a cultural context with an inspiring history. Iranian Jews have been an integral part of Iran since the state's founding in 539 BC. When Cyrus laid the foundation of the country's governance, he introduced principles that gradually melded with the national culture. The last will and testament of Darius who ruled from 522 to 486 BC confirmed that the founder's guiding principles had already taken hold. His son and heir, Khashaayaar Shah – known as Xerxes in the West and mentioned as Ahasuerus in the Bible – is associated with the festival of Purim celebrated annually to the present day.[386] Although Esther, the favourite of Ahasuerus, and the festival of Purim are commonly known, the Biblical connection to Iran is often overlooked.

The tomb of Esther and her uncle Mordecai, renovated and expanded in 1970 in conjunction with the commemoration of 2500 years of Iranian monarchy, are preserved in Hamadan, northwestern Iran. Hamadan – the ancient Ecbatana – was the summer capital of Iran, one of the three capital cities of the Achaemenid dynasty (650–330 BC). The other two were the administrative capital, Susa (Shushan) and the ceremonial capital, Persepolis – the city of the Persians.[387] It has been proposed that Alexander's victory and the Hellenism that followed it destroyed the spirit of tolerance that the Achaemenids had cultivated in the region. 'Never again do we see in that part of the world, or anywhere else for that matter, another empire based on tolerance as was that of the Achaemeinds.'[388]

Iran's governmental policies towards Israel have taken an antagonistic turn since the Revolution of 1978 and the effects on Iranians, particularly Iranian Jews, have been devastating.[389] Repeated threats, counter-threats and warnings of inevitable preemptive war, have made matters worse. Yet, the histories of Iran and Iranian Jews are so intertwined that a clerically imposed divorce is not possible. The cultural fusion has been comprehensive and Iranian Jews have been historically active partners in the nation's cultural, literary, philosophical, scientific, political, economic and technological development. Aside from the legendary Esther and Mordecai, there are the prophets Daniel, Ezra, Habakkuk, Haggai and Nehemiah, political and social leaders Bagohi, Mar Zutra and Queen Shushandokht (Susandokht) – Queen to Yazdgerd I and King Bahram's mother – significant leaders in Iran's pre-Islamic history. The famed 'Elephantine Papyri' (495–399 BC) in which a Jewish marriage contract guarantees the right of both spouses to initiate divorce if necessary, is associated with Bagohi's service.[390] It is worthy of note too that the Babylonian Talmud, perhaps Judaism's second most important document on theology and jurisprudence, was written by Iranian Jews during the Sassanian (Sassanid) period (226–642). Persian was introduced in Jerusalem at about the same time, where it soon flourished as a literary language.[391] The Arab conquest of Iran in the mid-seventh century (644–651) and the subsequent mass conversion to Islam divided the populace into Muslims and the *dhimmi*. The division granted Muslims a privileged status and political control, but the non-Muslim remainder could maintain their traditions and religious convictions. The distinction was discriminatory but the non-Muslims were protected by the state as long as they accepted the state's political hegemony and paid certain taxes not applicable to Muslims. Although that was the conquerors' command, evidence suggests that the discrimination did not take hold amongst Iranians until the late sixteenth century when reintroduced under the Safavid Dynasty (1501–1731).[392]

The hierarchical society that the Arab invaders and their followers created did not prevent interaction between Iranians of different faiths. The great Muslim philosopher, physicist, mathematician, astronomer and theologian Abu Rayhan Biruni (973–1048) – a contemporary of Avicina – is known to have consulted his Jewish counterparts on theology and scriptural analysis, and is on record as having expressed his indebtedness to them more than once.[393] Of distinguished Iranian Jews through the nineteenth century one can name numerous theologians,[394] poets,[395] scholars,[396] physicians[397] and financiers.[398] In the political realm too, Iranian Jews achieved high ranks; Rashid al-Din Fazlollah (d.1318), served as vizier to two kings, Ghazan (1292–1304) and Mohammad Khodabandeh Oljaytu (1304–1316). Sa'd al-Dowleh was vizier to Il-Khan Arghun (1284–1292).[399] The ruler of Shiraz at the time was Shams al-Dowleh, called by the Shirazis 'Malek al-Yahudi' – the Jewish king – and considered a most capable governor known for fairness and moderation. He is said to have cultivated relations with Muslim theologians and protected their followers' interests.[400] The Safavid Dynasty's theocratic origin and its policy of forcible conversion to the Shiite sect had an impact not only on the minorities but the entire nation. Iranian Jews, despite persecution and forced conversion, flourished. Their rich legacy in the arts and literature during the Safavid period is an undeniable testament to their profound attachment to their homeland.[401]

Iran's music and cuisine have also been enriched by Iranian Jews; a gastronome is more likely to find dishes of authentic ancient Iranian recipes in an Iranian Jewish home than anywhere else. Similarly, the student of Iranian music finds astonishing contributions by Iranian Jewish composers and musicians. Islam may have associated music with moral laxity but the Safavids' Shia predominance went further by attempting to ban all non-liturgical music completely. The resulting moral and religious condemnation

Brigadier-General Reza Khan Sardar-Sepah and his officers.

Yahya Moshir al-Dowleh, third husband of Naser al-Din Shah's sister, Princess Ezzat-Dowleh. One of the couple's three daughters, Afsar-Saltaneh, married Solayman Abib al-Saltaneh Sardari. They had three daughters and four sons.

Sardari (left) at Bois de
Boulogne lake, Paris, 1946.

Admiral Gholam-Ali
Bayandor (left),
Mrs Malekeh-Qods
Sepahbody and Iran's
Minister to Italy
Anoushirvan Sepahbody
at the launching of *Niroo*.

Niroo, the Iranian Navy's first gunboat.

AUSWEIS Nr. 3150

LAISSEZ-PASSER N.

Nicht uebertragbar. Nur gueltig in Verbindung mit einem mit Lichtbild versehenem amtlichen Personalausweis.

"Cette carte, strictement personnelle, est incessible. Elle n'est valable qu'accompagnée de la carte d'identité officielle avec photo."

1. a) Name / Nom	a)	Sepahbodi			
b) Vorname / Prénoms	b)	Abdolhossein			
c) Geburtstag- und Ort / Date et lieu de naissance	c)	1890 (Tag/Jour)		Teheran (Ort/Lieu)	
d) Beruf / Profession	d)	Iranischer Minister in Frankreich			
e) Wohnung / Adresse	e)	Paris (Ort/Lieu)		5 rue Fortuny (Strasse/Rue)	
f) Staatsangehörigkeit / Nationalité	f)	Franzose	Iran		
g) Personalausweis / Pièce d'identité	g)	Dipl.Pass (Art/Espèce)	(Nr./No.)	(Behoerde/Autorité)	(Ausstellungsart-Tag) Lieu et date de délivrance
h) Kraftwagen / Voiture	h)	Buick (Art/Espèce)	C.D. (Fabrikat/Marque)		(Kennummer/Immatriculation)

2. Ziel der Reise / Lieu de destination		Vichy
3. Grund der Reise / Motif du voyage		endgültige Ausreise
4. Berechtigung: / Autorisation		Fuer einmaliges Ueberschreiten der Demarkationslinie hin und zurueck. Pour un seule traversée aller et retour de la ligne de démarcation.
Grenzuebergang: / Traversée de frontière		Grenzkontrollstelle: Moulins Contrôle à la frontière
5. Gueltigkeit / Validité		26.10. - 31.10.40
6. Bemerkung / Observations		Wird begleitet von seiner Gattin, seinem Sohn und dem spanischen Chauffeur Gilles

Paris, den 23.10. 1940.

Dienststempel: / Cachet

Passierscheinstelle: / Le Service des laissez-passer   VI

Unterschrift / Signature

The Nazis give permission to the Iranian envoy to leave Paris with his immediate family, October 1940.

Left to right: Amir Abbas Hoveyda (Sardari's nephew, at the time in charge of Iranian Affairs in occupied Germany), Fatemeh Sepahbody, Tchin-Tchin, Fereydon Hoveyda and Farhad Sepahbody, Paris, 1946.

Tchin-Tchin in Paris, 1946.

Left to right: Fereydoun Hoveyda (then attaché at the Iranian Embassy), Tchin-Tchin and a Sardari cousin, Amir Sardari MD.

Sardari's dog, Lilly, Paris, 1946/1947.

The letter in which Sardari transferred his Paris apartment to Farhad Sepahbody in 1974.

TEL: 01-730 8255
TELEX: 261544

CABLES: NAFTMELLI, LONDON

NATIONAL IRANIAN OIL COMPANY

132/5 SLOANE STREET,
LONDON, SW1X 9BG

REF ....

DATE ___6.6.74.___

JE SOUSSIGNE ABDOL-HOSSEIN SARDARI DONNE TOUT
POUVOIR A MON NEVEU SON EXCELLENCE FARHAD
SEPAHBODY, MINSTRE-CONSEILLER DE L'AMBASSADE
IMPÉRIALE DE L'IRAN A PARIS, EN CE QUI CONCERNE
MON APPARTEMENT SIS 112, BOULEVARD MALESHERBES,
PARIS XVII, TANT POUR L'OCCUPATION, LE TRANSFERT
A UN AUTRE LOCATAIRE, QUE LA RESILIATION DU
CONTRAT S'IL LE JUGE NECESSAIRE.

A. H. SARDARI

Farhad Sepahbody posing with Sardari's elaborate radio in his Paris apartment, 1946/1947.

Farhad Sepahbody astride Sardari's 1938 Peugeot motorcycle, aiming his uncle's German .22 calibre carbine, in a picture taken at Sardari's country cottage in 1946.

Tal'at and George Senehi, Normandy, France, 1932.

Eliane, Claude and Tal'at Senehi in Paris, 1937.

Habib and Victoria Morady's wedding in Paris, 22 November 1936.

Rose Morady's wedding to Lotfollah Montakheb, Tehran, 1941. Left to right: Alice Senehi, Khanom Senehi, Yvonne Michailof-Senehi, Morteza Senehi, Rose, George Senehi, Lotfollah, Tal'at Morady-Senehi, Eliane and Claude Senehi.

The Djambazian School in Tehran, 1943. The teacher and master was Mr Djambazian, a Russian immigrant. Seated at the front, third and fourth from left, are Alice Senehi and Parvaneh Cohanim. Eliane Senehi is seventh from left; years later she married Parvaneh's brother.

Left to right, front row: unidentified mother and child, Eliane and her aunt Rose Morady. Second row: Habib Morady and his wife Victoria, Margarete Golchi, Calude, Tal'at Morady, Soltaneh Morady and Ibby Morady. Third row: Ne'man Papahn, Margarete's husband Mr Golchi, Lotfollah Victory, John Elghanian, Khanbaba Fatoullah, an unidentified friend and Ebrahim Rokhsar. Jean Morady stands at the back.

Morteza Senehi and his bride Khanom, Eshagh Cohanim (a family friend), Sara Senehi and Benjamin Senahi. The children, Mishel and Rachel, are Sara's grandchildren from a daughter in Iran, and were brought to France to go to school. Khanom passed away in January 2008. She was 96 years old and lived in Washington DC.

77 Boulevard de Montmorency, Montemorency, Seine and Oise.

Claude, George, Eliane and Tal'at Senehi at their Paris home, 1937.

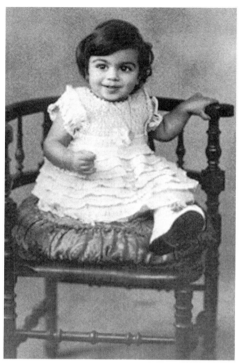

Eliane Senehi, Paris, 1934.

Eliane Senehi at her grandparents' riverfront home in Paris, 1938.

Rayhan stands between Rose, Tal'at and Sotaneh in the centre. Solayman Michailof stands fourth from right at the back. Yvonne Michailof-Senehi kneels on the right and Rahim Senehi sits on the left. Paris, 1933.

Left to right, seated: Simon and Khanom Senehi, Khanom's moth-in-law, Sara, holding Alice Senehi, Sotaneh, Jean and Rayhan Morady. Second row: Ne'man Papahn (holding a tray), Ibrahim Acherof (holding a chalice drum or tonbak), Rahim Senehi with a 'tar'. His brother Benjamin stands directly behind him. Rose Morady is on the far left of the third row. Solayman Michaelof is holding up a glass at the back.

Yusef, Jean(?), Rayhan and Soltaneh Morady, Paris, 1926.

Celebrating 'Seezdabedar', the thirteenth day of the Iranian New Year, Paris, 1938. Seated: Ibrahim Acherof, Rahim Senehi and George Senehi with musical instruments. Sara Senehi sits on the far right. Standing: Solayman Michailof, Yvonne Senehi, Tal'at Senehi and Jean Morady.

Rahim Senehi in Germany before his detention by the Nazis, Berlin, 1934.

Rahim Senehi in military uniform with his future wife, Kodrat, while serving in the Imperial Iranian Army, Tehran, 1940.

Ibby Morady standing in front of his Paris shop, 1934.

Ibby at his office in Los Angeles, 1998.

Ibby and his wife, Los Angeles, 1996.

Eliane Senehi Cohanim at her uncle Ibby Morady's Los Angeles home, 2004.

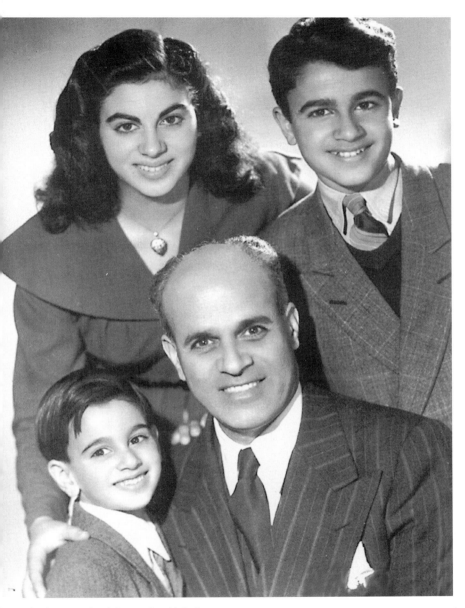

iane, Claude, Farnand and George Senehi, Paris, 1947.

Eliane and Uncle Ibby, Los Angeles, 2004.

Ibrahim Morady checking an old address book for names from the Paris days, Los Angeles, 2004.

Lady Afsar-Saltaneh, Abdol-Hossein Sardari's mother.

Front row, left to right: Pari Farbod (standing), her mother Malekeh Saba (Sardari's eldest sister), Mohammad Hassan in police uniform (Sardari's brother), Habibollah Hoveyda, Lady Afsar-Saltaneh (Hoveyda's mother-in-law) and Maryam Farbod. Taken in the 1930s.

Anoushirvan Sepahbody, Iran's Minister to Switzerland and dressed in diplomatic uniform, is followed by Abdol-Hossein Sardari, Ali Motamed and Abdollah Entezam, in a picture taken at the Bern Federal Palace, Switzerland, 1930.

Minister Anoushirvan Sepahbody with an unknown colleague and Abdol-Hossein Sardari, Bern, 1931.

The Morady family in Paris, 1924. Standing: Habib, Yuself, Tal'at. Seated: Rose, Soltaneh, Rayhan, Jean and Ibby.

Rayhan Morady, Paris, December 1952.

Mouchegh and Irene Petrossian in Paris.

Claude and Eliane Senehi, Paris, 1938.

George Senehi in his garden, Paris, 1939.

George Senehi with his daughter Eliane, just before leaving for Iran, Bretagne, France, 1940.

Ibby Morady at his Los Angeles home, 2004. Ibby passed away on 6 June 2006.

Ibby Morady at his father's store, Paris, 1932.

Ibby Morady showing off the costume he wore at his father's shop in Paris in 1932; Los Angeles, 2004.

Hayem Sasson in Paris, 2008, who was an electronic engineering student during the Second World War. His father's valuable antiques were stored by Sardari during the German occupation of France and returned without charge.

could have ended Iran's musical tradition, had it not been for the non-Muslim Iranians. Thus the nation's Zoroastrians, Armenian Christians and Jews preserved, performed, taught and composed Iran's music for several centuries. Some notable Jewish maestros include Ostad Zohreh, a woman from Shiraz who directed an orchestra of about 25 female artists at the Qajar courts of Fath-Ali Shah (1772–1834) and Mohammad Shah (1808–1848). She travelled with the two royal households on their excursions.[402] Morteza Khan Neydavud was another master musician and teacher whose musical education had begun with his father Baalaa Khan, a musician in the court of Nasser al-Din Shah Qajar. Neydavud recorded 'the first and only existing complete repertoire of classical Persian Music's extensive *radif* (order or chain) system. This unprecedented monumental undertaking yielded nearly 300 hours of recorded music, one full copy of which is stored at Iran's Ministry of Education in Tehran and another at Jerusalem University's music library.'[403]

It is of interest that Nasser al-Din Shah, when visiting Paris in 1873, proposed a Jewish homeland to Baron Rothschild on 12 July, in the presence of the French diplomat Adolph Cremieux. Rothschild and Cremieux had sought an audience to seek the King's assent to establish 'Alliance' schools in Iran. Cremieux, who presided over 'Alliance Israelite Universalle', received Nasser al-Din Shah's approval at the audience; 35 years later 2200 students were attending eleven Alliance schools in several Iranian cities.[404] Their graduates became active participants in the socio-political awakening that ushered in the Constitutional movement, and the blossoming of the country's twentieth-century economic development. Ambassador George V. Allen of the United States in a confidential dispatch to the US secretary of state dated 6 October 1947, explained:

> Although Jews in Rezaieh speak a dialect of Aramaic and Jews in Yazd use a sort of Pre-Persian Pahlavi vernacular, the only common language Jews in separated portions of Iran have with each other is Persian, which is the mother tongue of most Jews in Iran. This is in sharp contrast with the other minorities of Iran –the Armenians, the Assyrians, the Kurds and the Arabs – which have their own languages and speak Persian usually with an accent. This linguistic identification of the Iranian Jews with other Persians is an important factor in the high degree of assimilation of the Jews in Iran. Until a few months ago, when several newspaper articles on the question of Zionism raised the issue, there was no indication that the Jews in Iran were ever considered a minority in any other than a strictly religious sense, as is and has been the case with the Armenians and the Assyrians.[405]

A decade after the Second World War, Iranians began to enjoy increasing standards of living. There were improvements in employment, income, educational opportunities and nearly everything else, including daily per capita meat consumption. The Iranian Jewish community was not left behind. An Iranian-born Israeli scholar's research conducted before the 1978 revolution concluded that Iranian Jews were 'free, proud and rich'. There were at least 80,000 Jews in Iran (0.25 per cent of the population) 60,000 of whom resided in Tehran. 'On per capita terms they may well have been the richest Jewish community in the world.' Of the country's 4000 university professors, 80 were Jewish and of the 10,000 physicians, some 600.[406]

Statistics, names and numbers are mere facts. Truth on the other hand, as the late Professor Richard Weaver observed, may be perceived by the intellect at a level higher than sensory perception. Facts therefore, are about here and now, but truth remains eternal.[407] The gains from the enduring embrace of Iranians going back over 2500 years, the mutual joy of cultural enrichment (artistic and scientific achievements, shared cuisine, unsuppressible love of music, poetry, literature) and undivided affection for the country, although not quantifiable, are deeply felt by every Iranian – irrespective of religion. It is that unquantifiable reality that explains Sardari's actions best.

There is every reason to believe that this remarkable historic partnership will endure.[408] A revolution turned Iran upside down over three decades ago. That is of course an undeniable fact. Thirty years in the life of a nation endowed with several thousand years of history on the other hand, is a blink of an eye; that is a more profound truth.

Those oblivious to Iran's history may find Iranians enigmatic. The Iranian national psychology may defy logic, but not to those who take the time to contemplate the long-term multi-dimensional factors. Iranians, defining their identity through their history, find any exhortation to forget the past suspect. Having experienced devastating misfortunes, they have preserved their common identity through their language, culture and mythology. The Iranian capacity to mix reality and myth seems baffling to the children of the industrial age but the Iranians intuitively distinguish mere facts from fundamental truths. Their secret of survival throughout their long and often sad history is their refusal to become prisoners of the moment. It is for this reason that Iranians resort to poetry more readily than facts when making a crucial point. A keen observer may notice the phenomenon, whether at casual gatherings of friends or at technical scientific conventions. The Iranian capacity to remain conscious of eternal truths is an ingrained intellectual means to turn misfortunes into transitory impediments.

Those who congratulated themselves for having undermined Iran's government at the Doha OPEC Conference of 1976 to lower oil prices, or hailed the Iranian Revolution of 1978 to halt Mohammad Reza Shah's alleged megalomania, should not have found the results surprising.[409] Latching on to short-term advantages has often resulted in misplaced bets and long-term disasters. Proponents of military confrontation with Iran ought to recall that recent past and consider not only their prescription's immediate impact, but its long-term consequences. The unexpected outcomes will surely upset national, regional and possibly global interests for years.

Iran's mythology may suggest answers to the country's current political questions. The essence of responsibility and good governance is indeed embedded in the myths of Jamshid, Zahak, Fereydoun and Kaykhosrow, all recorded in Ferdowsi's monumental *Shahnameh* – the Book of Kings.[410] Iranians have always been proud of their historical heroes. Cyrus is idolised by many, reflecting their deepest cultural feelings. The policies and pronouncements of extremists are but a thin crust of ice destined to melt away at the rising of the sun. The sun will shine again, as it has after every previous national disaster Iran has faced. Dr Roy Mottahedeh, a scholar of Islamic History, observed in 2002 that Khomeini and his revolution had shocked the Iranian intellectuals,

> ... who at first had loved the revolution as their own, believing that the masses under the leadership of Khomeini had finally spoken up to what they, the intellectuals, had always wanted. About three years ago a poem was passed hand to hand throughout the intellectual community of Tehran in which the poet exalted Zoroaster as the prophet who 'never killed nor ordered anyone to be killed'. The poem is addressed to 'our ancient land and soil':
>
> You, O ancient elder, eternally young,
> It is you I love if anything I love;
> Of Ferdowsi, that castle of legend that he raised
> To the heavens of might and glory I love;
> Of Khayyam, that anger and complaint that eternally
> affects the heart and soul I love.
>
> These words echo one of the most self-consciously dramatic episodes in the intellectual history of the nineteenth century ... The Iranian poet who praised Zoroaster had also come to feel that what he loved in his land, that 'ancient elder, eternally young,' was its partly rediscovered ancient past, which to him no longer seemed emotionally unconnected. For some Iranians, particularly among the intellectuals, this past had at last taken root; they had been forced by the dialectic of events finally to say whether the Iranian image of the hero was Cyrus or Hosain [the Shiite's martyred third Imam], and they had answered: Cyrus.[411]

And here lies the ironic accomplishment of the Iranian Revolution. It has awakened the cultural consciousness of Iranians to see beyond the historic horizon of the Arab conquest in 642. Cyrus was Persian but his message remains universal. The new generation of Iranians may have completed an intellectual circle. From the fashionable criticism of 'Westoxication' and rejection of Western culture championed by many, if not most, intellectuals before 1978, they have arrived at a new appreciation of Aristotle, Dante, Goethe. Much to their surprise and delight, they have rediscovered with fresh eyes the teachings to be remarkably in concert with their very own pre-Islamic heritage. Shahrokh Meskoob, a leading Iranian intellectual, refused to join the popular crusade against the West for his understanding of history was not selective. He stated that 'after suffering defeat at the hands of the Arabs and after converting to Islam, the Iranian people also returned to the past. They turned back from one great historic event to history.'[412]

Most political aspirations for good governance, tolerance, liberty, rule of law and justice, can be found in the ideals that Cyrus promoted long before Magna Carta. To promote that understanding is an intellectual tectonic shift that deserves international attention. Furthermore, since the ideas did not originate in Washington, London, Paris, Berlin, or Moscow, they cannot be easily dismissed as ideological impositions of the West on the rest. The Iranian soul yearns for respect for its cultural greatness. It seeks recognition for its contributions to humanity in the arts, literature, philosophy, religion, mathematics and science.[413] The British Historian Edward Browne has observed that 'what is generally called Arabian science,' is mostly 'the work contributed by Persians.'[414] How many outside Iran today are aware that what they utilise daily and call 'Arab numerals' arrived in the West in the ninth century through algebra texts of the Iranian mathematician Mohammad Kharazmi?[415] How many recognise that the famed Muslim philosopher Abu Nasr Mohammad Al-Farabi is actually an Iranian who was also an authority on music and theology? How many appreciate Avicina as the remarkable Iranian physician, chemist, mathematician, philosopher and musical theorist that he was? How many understand that what is considered Middle Eastern music is historically Persian, the result of an intense development of musical theory between the ninth and fifteenth centuries? *The Great Book of Music* by Farabi, the writings of Avicina on *Harmonic Consonance and Dissonance* and the subsequent works by others guided musical development not only in the Middle East, Turkey, North Africa and India but also China and Spain.[416]

Iranians – despite accusations to the contrary – do not harbour territorial ambitions but strongly desire respect and distinction.[417] These are cultural aspirations that are both attainable and legitimate. The crucial point is differentiating between Iran's rulers and Iran's population. Proponents of military action are proposing war not only against Iran's rulers but against all Iranians. Such rhetoric validates what the current rulers have claimed all along, that the West is exploitative, arrogant and a predatory enemy of Iran and Iranians. The Iranian Revolution may be traced at least in part to the humiliating perception that the Shah's policy of alliance with the West had failed, for despite his accommodations with the United States, neither he as Iran's Head of State nor his nation's aspirations received the respect they deserved. The Shah, instead of being accorded respect as a valuable ally, appeared 'as a petitioner at the court of the great republic of the West'.[418] The insult directed at the person was felt by the nation.

A condition for the sale of US military hardware to Iran in March 1962 – Status of Forces Agreement (SOFA) – was politically odious for it recalled the Western imposed Capitulation Agreements, terminated amidst national celebration and fanfare by Reza Shah on 11 May 1928. Iranian political leaders were understandably reluctant to accept the conditions but the United States was insistent. Prime Minister Assadollah Alam, under pressure from the United States and bowing to the Shah's desire to acquire American weapons and training for the Iranian Armed Forces, asked Foreign Minister Abbas Aram to draft a bill to address the American requirement in early 1964. At a following cabinet meeting objections to the measure were intense enough to abandon its discussion. Finally, a few days before leaving office, Alam presented the bill to parliament. Although signed by himself, Foreign Minister Aram and Minister of War Assadollah Sani'i, the bill had not been discussed or approved by the cabinet. The Majles and the Senate passed the bill under questionable circumstances in October 1964, when Hassan-Ali Mansur had already replaced Alam as prime minister. Prime Minister Mansur was assassinated on 21 January 1965 as he was entering the Majles. The murderer, Mohammad Bokharaii, a 17-year-old high school student, had awaited his victim's arrival carrying a copy of the Qoran, a picture of Khomaini and a handgun.[419] Thirteen years after the US achieved its desired agreement (SOFA) in Iran, its most vociferous opponent – Ayatollah Khomaini – established the Islamic Republic there with himself as the infallible Supreme Leader.

The Iranian national sentiment is neither militarist nor expansionist. Doubters would be hard pressed to find an Iranian monument glorifying war or victory in the entire country; nearly all statues and monuments in Iran honour poets and philosophers. Iran has always been a major regional power, yet managed to coexist with much smaller, less powerful neighbours. Encouraging distrust and hanging on to bilateral treaties perceived as insurance policies tethered to the United States provides limited security only for the short term. A security system in which all countries in the region – including Iran and Israel – participate would be more likely to foster a lasting balance. As shifts of power within the region are likely, flexibility within a collaborative, genuinely regional security arrangement would facilitate the necessary adjustments to maintain the overall long-term equilibrium, without military confrontation.[420]

Considering the current turmoil in much of the world is fuelled by religious interpretations, it is fitting to conclude with an observation made over a decade ago that remains applicable to international relations today:

In the period of the Old Testament, the world ... consisted of a few hundred miles around the Near Eastern Centers. No one had ever heard of the Aztecs, or even the Chinese. When the world changes, then the religion must be transformed. But my notion of the real horror today is what you see in Beirut. There you have the three great Western religions, Judaism, Christianity and Islam – and because the three of them have three different names for the same biblical god, they can't get on together. They are stuck with their metaphor and don't realise its reference. They haven't allowed the circle that surrounds them to open. It is a closed circle. Each group says, we are the chosen group, and we have God.[421]

Sabre rattling will neither make friends nor ensure the submission of 'the other'. Even apparently decisive victory will not guarantee resignation as the vanquished may submit only long enough to sharpen their knives for the next round. The concept of liberty is not limited to voting rights or even good governance. We must condition ourselves to tolerate the liberty to dream, the liberty to aspire and the liberty to become great not only for ourselves, but for others as well. National aspirations long blocked are analogous to mighty rivers permanently dammed. Just as accumulated pressure can burst through a dam causing devastation, national humiliation long festered can precipitate explosive extremism.[422]

Foreign interference, whether in support of dissidents or in pursuit of regime change, will have horrendous long-term consequences. The calls for 'US involvement' by well meaning intellectuals, exiles and political activists, are unfortunately based on three misguided assumptions: that Iranians trust foreign intentions; that the nation will refuse to see factions favoured by foreigners as traitors; and that Iranians are a nation of marionettes given to dancing at the whims of conductors abroad.[423] Seeking national security through military advantage over neighbouring countries ought to give way to a new understanding of security in which the entire neighbourhood feels secure. Just as free trade proved a better approach than mercantilism to global commerce over a century ago, inclusive collective security arrangements could prove better and more stable than exclusive arrangements based on zero-sum calculations.

Level-headed observers capable of shedding emotional attachments and prejudices may see through the Islamic Republic's self-generated confusion. The inflexible theologians, once in power, had to resort to expediency – *maslahat* – to prolong the Islamic Republic's survival.

> In fact, the attempt to tie Islamic law to daily governance through maneuvers such as the adoption of maslahat may actually freeze religious thought and diminish the tendency of Islamic jurisprudence in Iran to support pluralistic interpretations. Moreover, by empowering an Islamic critique of the state and exposing the fragility of the state's genuine religious legitimacy, the ruling

leaves the state vulnerable to exactly the sort of challenge that created it. The invocation of maslahat was meant as a doctrinal vindication for *raison d'etat*, but was nonetheless quite incongruous coming from a man who had made his career criticising secular rulers for disregarding divine law. Khomeini thus undermined the very foundation of the theocracy he had hoped to establish in Iran.[424]

Iranians, already burdened by experiences of their past, are unlikely to be moved by catchy statements and attractive political promises. What is needed is patient, continuous, even grinding effort, to convince Iranians through positive action rather than fancy locution. When the West assures Iran's population that its legitimate national interests are respected and the only barrier in the way to their realisation is the policies of the country's disagreeable rulers, liberty and good governance will loom in sight, and if outside interference is avoided, within reach. Neither bombs nor sanctions will be necessary.

The Arab Spring

In 2011 the world witnessed a political tsunami that swept through Tunisia to Egypt, Libya, Yemen, Bahrain and Syria. The phenomenon that has come to be known as 'the Arab Spring' does not show signs of abating any time soon. Does the Arab Spring have any relevance to Iran and the Iranian experience? Does it have relevance to any other non-Arab country? The answer to both questions is that it does, because the underlying cause of the upheaval is universal, even if overlooked, ignored, misrepresented or misdiagnosed. The undercurrent of resentment that propelled the seemingly sudden uprisings had been accumulating strength, while pushing against static political barriers for many years.

Poverty, inadequate political representation and foreign intrigue have been commonly blamed for the sudden surge. Economics, politics and foreign relations are important, but dignity trumps all! The Arab Spring reflects a crisis, and it is all about dignity. Humans have a tremendous capacity for enduring economic and political deprivation, but humiliation is another matter. Even the poor, the powerless and the illiterate demand a degree of respect, which in essence is seeking recognition of their humanity. That is not much to ask. Yet obliviousness to human dignity persists.

The protests in Tunisia, Egypt and elsewhere surprised most governments and their analysts, but they should have known better. To put it simply, the societal arrangements that existed, and many more that still do, were not and are not sustainable. The surging torrent after a broken dam will surprise and devastate, but it always comes with a history of force accumulation. The causes of stability, security, peace and prosperity will be better served through respect for our common humanity. To seek stability through support for an oppressive government, or peace through security for some at the expense of insecurity for others is to mortgage tomorrow's stability and peace for today's limited advantages. Those who passionately and often sincerely inquire why certain nations behave the way they do, are likely to find the answer in those nations' pasts. People are now more educated, more informed and better connected than previous generations. They are therefore more sensitive to, and less tolerant of, unjustified indignity directed at individuals, minorities, majorities or entire nations, whether by their governments or by foreign interests.

Viewed from that perspective, the relevance of the Arab Spring to Iran is obvious. The crisis of dignity is applicable to Iran and is accentuated by the country's educated youthful population. In dealing with Iran – as is the case with other countries – the distinction between the government and the nation is crucial and sensitivity to Iranian national dignity is imperative. Whether dealing with the Persian Iran or the Arab Egypt for instance, the international community's cognizance of what Iranians or Egyptians may perceive as policies of national denigration is of utmost consequence. To put it bluntly, what political leaders in Washington, London, Paris, Berlin or Beijing say is not nearly as important as that which is heard in Iran or Egypt. Knowing the difference is important, but gaining that knowledge requires familiarity with the nations' recent histories and their interpretation of past major events. The same applies to declarations emanating from Tehran, Riyadh, Jerusalem or Manama directed at others.

What is certain everywhere is the gradual assertion of national interest to replace the interests of the ruling elite. People have never been as educated, as informed and as confident as today. Relative improvements in living standards, health care and education have created new socio-political realities worldwide, and with them new aspirations. People want to have a say in their own governance, in determining their national interests and in the policymaking processes of their countries. The leaders endowed with the vision to see that reality will be today's national statesmen and tomorrow's national heroes. They could also act as teachers and mentors as their nations take charge of their representative, lawful governance. The leaders who try to stem the tide will not succeed or their successes will be short-lived. Being on the winning side in such a case is morally right with long-term political, economic and security advantages to boot. A statesman would appreciate both, but even a lesser politician ought to recognise the latter.

NOTES

1   Moslehoddin Sa'di put it in verse as: 'Adam's children are parts of one being, for in creation are of one origin/If fate causes one organ pain, other organs could not at rest remain/If thou aren't touched by others' pain, you aren't worthy of the human name.' For a different translation see Chapter 8.

2   Much of the failure in dealing with Iran may be the direct result of such obliviousness to its historical culture, resulting in repeated stereotypes, misunderstandings and disappointments.

3   Robert Satloff, *Among The Righteous: Lost Stories From The Holocaust's Long Reach Into Arab Lands* (New York: Public Affairs, 2006).

4   Abbas Milani, *The Persian Sphinx*, in Persian (Washington, DC: Mage, 2001), pp. 89–91. The English edition was published in 2000.

5   The high school friends – fellow graduates of Tehran's Alborz High School – are Nasser Shariati and Majid Azizi. I am grateful to them and to their wives Shohreh Shariati and Yassi Azizi who put me in touch with Mrs Eliane Senehi Cohanim. I cannot thank Mrs Cohanim enough for introducing me to her late uncle Mr Ibrahim Morady in Los Angeles, two other uncles' widows in Caracas and Tel Aviv, and her third and youngest uncle, also in Venezuela.

6   Parviz Esmailzadeh and the author met in Tehran, conscripted in 1973. Both received Basic Training in the same company. Parviz introduced the author to the Sassoon family in Paris.

7   Elaine Sciolino, *Persian Mirrors: The Elusive Face of Iran* (New York: Free Press, 2000), p. 157.

8   Katayun Amirpur, 'The Future of Iran's Reform Movement,' in Walter Posch ed. *Iranian Challenges*, p. 34.

9   Suzanne Maloney, *Iran's Long Reach: Iran As A Pivotal State In The Muslim World* (Washington DC: United State Institute of Peace Press, 2008), p. 84. The survey suggested that 75 per cent did not pray, and it was even worse among young students, 86 per cent. 'Drugs and Prostitution Rampant among Youth: Government Report' Agence France Presse, 5 July 2000.

10 Amirpur, p. 39.

11 Ray Takeyh, *Guardians of the Revolution: Iran and the World in the Age of the Ayatollahs*, (New York: Oxford University Press, 2009), p. 182–183. Velayat-e Faqih – Guardianship

of the Islamic Jurist – was a new interpretation asserted by Khomaini, although rejected by numerous Grand Ayatollahs and lesser theologians.

12 Elaine Sciolino, *Persian Mirrors*, p. 74, 62.

13 The reference is to the official seal of the Iranian government, a protective lion holding up a sword in the right hand with a shining sun appearing on its back. The golden 'Lion & Sun' appeared at the centre of Iran's tri-coloured flag until the Islamic Republic replaced it with a graphic depiction of God's Arabic name, Allah. Research for this book was in part conducted at the Library of Congress and facilitated by the gracious and helpful staff of the Near East Reading Room and the the Second World War German Documents Collection at the US National Archives.

14 Iran at the time exchanged ambassadors only with its neighbouring countries. The highest ranking envoys to other countries including Britain, France, Germany and the United States were ministers plenipotentiary.

15 Petain was born in April 1856. He died in July 1951.

16 Mark Mazower, *Hitler's Empire: How the Nazis Ruled Europe* (New York: Penguin, 2008), p. 107.

17 Farhad Sepahbody, the ambassador's son's recollections. See http://users.sedona. net/~sepa/vichy.html.

18 Recollection of Ambassador Anoshiravan Sepahbody's son, Farhad Sepahbody, who became an ambassador himself; personal interviews.

19 Mark Mazower, *Hitler's Empire*, pp. 419–423.

20 Abdol Hossein Sardari de Tehran (Iran), Licencie en droit de Tehran, *L'Apprentissage en Droit Suisse:Thèse presentée a la Faculté de droit de l'Université de Génève pour obtenir le grade de docteur en droit*, Thèse No 401 (Liège: Imprimerie Georges Thone: 1937).

21 His friends, such as the Petrossian brothers, assisted with provisions and catering. The famed Parisian hairdresser Alexandre might have helped with the entertainment and the guest lists; Alexadre's 'Salon de Coiffure,' was very fashionable. Correspondence with Ambassador Hoveyda, 1 September 2003.

22 I am indebted to Mr Houman Sarshar for pointing out that in some legal documents the adjectives 'kalimi' or 'yahudi' were attached to people's names, usually as middle names, to indicate their Jewish faith. The custom became less prevalent and was abandoned in later years with the passage of the Law of Identity and Personal Status on 5 May 1925. The fact remains that specific identifying information with regard to race and religion was not included in Iranian passports and other government documents.

23 Ahmad Mahrad, 'Sarnevesht-e Iranian-e Yahudi Tey-e Jang-e Jahani Dovvom dar Orupa –The fate of Iranian Jews During the Second World War in Europe,' *Yahudian-e Irani dar Tarikh-e Moaser – The History of Contemporary Iranian Jews* v.3, (Beverly Hills, CA: Markaz-e Tarikh-e Shafahi-e Yahudian-e Irani –Center for Iranian Jewish Oral History, 1999), pp. 86–87.

24 Ahmad Mahrad, 'Sarnevesht,' p. 87.

25 Ahmad Mahrad, 'Sarnevesht,' p. 88–91. Also, primary German Second World War documents: Eichmann to Foreign Ministry, Political XIII to DIII 2345, Berlin 14 April 1943, German Foreign Ministry Archives, US National Archives, T-120 K1509 Microfilm Publication T-120, serial K1509, roll 4668, frame K346220.

26 Mark Mazower, *Hitler's Empire*, p. 183.

27 Abbas Milani, *Mo`amaye Hoveyda* (Washington, DC: Mage: 2001), p. 91. For an English edition see Abbas Milani, *The Persian Sphinx: Amir Abbas Hoveyda and the Riddle of the Iranian Revolution* (Washington, DC: Mage, 2000). Ambassador Fereydoun Hoveyda confirmed during interviews with the author that Sardari had received such a letter. Abetz was the German Ambassador to Vichy from 1940 to 1944, after he had been expelled as persona non grata in 1939. He had joined the NSDAP in 1931 and had been assigned to France as a member of the German Foreign Service from about 1935. He was convicted of crimes against humanity in France in 1949 but served only

five of his 25-year sentence. He did not enjoy his freedom for long. He burned to death in 1958 in a traffic accident on an autobahn in the Ruhr. He was 55 years old.

28 Abetz was not an aristocrat, nor was Ribbentrop who had acquired his aristocratic 'von' before his last name, through his wife. Abetz, a Francophile art teacher, joined the National Socialist Party in 1937, when he applied to the German Ministry of Foreign Affairs. Ribbentrop, a wine merchant, joined the party in 1932.

29 Christopher R. Browning, *The Final Solution And The German Foreign Office: A Study of Referat D III of Abteilung Deutschland 1940–43* (New York: Holmes & Meier, 1978), p.29. See Chapter Seven for more on Abteilung Deutschland, Referat D-III.

30 File 2345 ZU III. Schulenberg had served as ambassador to the Soviet Union 1934–1941, and had been a close friend of Iran's Ambassador to Moscow, Mohammad Sa'ed Maraqei, who would become prime minister.

31 Political XIII to DIII, No. 2345, Berlin, 14 April 1943, Serial K1509, frame K346220; US National Archives Microfilm Publication T-120, roll 4668. Ahmad Mahrad, p. 96. Iranians use the words 'Yahudi, Johud, or Kalimi,' to mean Jewish. The coinage of the German term 'Djuguten' may have been based on a transformation of the Persian 'Yahudi, or Johud.' Both 'Yahudi' and 'Kalimi' are respectful terms although 'Johud' has acquired derogatory connotations. Yahudi is a Persian term for Jewish and Kalimi an Islamic one that refers respectfully to God's spoken words and the concord with Prophet Moses.

32 For a brief biography see http://www.gdw-berlin.de/b13/bio/b13-bio13-wsl-e. htm. While the Nazified bureaucrats justified their actions as patriotism in wartime, many nationalists opposed Nazi ideology. The Kreisau Circle was a gathering of such nationalists, organised by Count Helmuth James von Moltke and his wife Freya Deichmann. Count Helmuth von Moltke was hanged on 23 January 1945 in Berlin; Mrs Von Moltke passed away at the age of 98 in Norwich, Vermont. Iran's Ambassador to Moscow Mohammad Sa'ed Maraghei, who knew Schulenberg well, considered him a genuine friend of Iran. The friendship of the two diplomats had a long history going back to the days they had both served in Georgia around 1910. Sa'ed served in the Caucasus from 1904 to 1924 and is reported to have given protection under the Iranian flag to numerous potential victims of the Russian Revolution. Schulenberg was convinced that Germany's interest required maintaining good relations with Russia. He confided to Sa'ed that if Germany attacked the Soviet Union, 'its defeat would be certain and costly in the extreme.' Rumours of an imminent German attack began circulating in the diplomatic corps in Moscow several weeks before it happened. Sa'ed sent a secret coded dispatch to Tehran three weeks prior to the attack, correctly predicting it and the most likely date of its commencement – the anniversary of Napoleon's invasion, 21 July. Mohammad Sa'ed Maraghei, Baqer Aqeli ed. *Khaterat-e Siasi* [Political Memoirs] (Tehran: Namak Publishing, 1994), pp. 7–8, 45–61, 77, 81, 84, 85, 86. Sa'ed served as foreign minister and prime minister after his ambassadorial tenure in Moscow.

33 Personal interview with Ibrahim Morady, 23–25 February 2004, Los Angeles.

34 The author has seen a reference to 1500 passports and rumours of up to 3000. The late Fereydoun Hoveyda, Sardari's nephew and a seasoned diplomat himself, thought the number would have been closer to 500–1,000. Telephone interview, 10 June and communication dated 5 September 2003. Ambassador Ahmad Tavakoli stated storing 500 blank passports at an embassy would have been possible, 1000 unusual, and any number above 1000 unlikely. Telephone interviews, 28 August, 7 September 2003.

35 S. Djalal Madani, *Iranische Politik und Drittes Reich* (Frankfurt am Main: Verlag Peter Lang, 1986), p. 41. Also, Pol. Arch. Juden Iran 1941–44, Deutsche Botschaft Paris an AA, 22 Marz 1942; Iranischer Konsul Paris an Deutsche Botschaft in Paris, 29 September 1942 – 22 Marz 1942.

36   German archival documents suggest that Sardari had managed to exempt 2400 Iranian
     Jews from German racial laws. Since the number of Iranian Jews in France was by far
     less than a thousand, there is no doubt that Sardari provided Iranian identity papers to
     non-Iranian Jews. See Pol. Arch. Juden Iran 1941–44, Deutsche Botschaft Paris an AA, 22
     Marz 1942, quoted in S. Djalal Madani, *Iranische Politik und Drittes Reich* (Frankfurt am
     Main:Verlag Peter Lang, 1986), p. 41. Fereydoun Hoveyda entered Foreign Service upon
     completion of his doctorate and was assigned to the League of Nations. He was Iran's
     Ambassador to the United Nations when the 1978 Revolution ended his diplomatic
     career. He was the younger brother of Prime Minister Amir Abbas Hoveyda, executed
     by Iran's Islamic Republic.
37   Mrs Ra'iss, Paris. Telephone interview, 31 January 2004. Mohsen Rai'ss, a career
     diplomat, had served as Minister to Rumania before his assignment to Vichy.
38   Ministry of Foreign Affairs, Third Political Department, Number 3052, dated 21/8/1321
     (11 November 1942), in Marzieh Yazdani ed. *Asnad-e Mohajerat-e Yahudian-e Iran beh
     Felestin: 1300–1330* Records on Iranian Jews Immigration to Palestine: 1921–1951,
     (Tehran: Records Research Center Publication, 1996), number 97, p.75.
39   German Foreign Ministry Archives, Stamping 'Jude' on Identification and Ration
     Cards of All Jews in France, Berlin, 7 January 1943, Serial 1509, frame K345212,
     National Archives Microfilm Publication T120, roll 4661.
40   See http://www.wiesenthal.com/social/press/pr item.cfm?ItemID=9276. The
     recognition was facilitated by this author's research.
41   Abbas Amanat suggests she was only thirteen. Abbas Amanat, *Pivot of the Universe: Nasir
     al-Din Qajar and the Iranian Monarchy, 1831–1896* (Washington, DC: Mage Publishers,
     1997), p.107. Fereydoun Adamiat, *Amir Kabir va Iran* (Tehran: Kharazmi, 1348), p.24.
42   The King might have been tricked into giving assent to the execution order while drunk.
43   It is speculated that he was offered 'qahveh Qajar,' poisoned coffee, a royal offering of
     the Qajar kings and princes to the nobility they disfavoured. A royal offering of a cup
     of coffee could not be refused. Abbas Milani, *Moamaye Hoveyda* (Washington, DC:
     Mage: 2001), p.50.
44   Yahya, as the eldest son, inherited his father's title of nobility Adib-al-Saltaneh.
45   Anoshiravan Sepahbody had an illustrious public life. He joined the Iranian Ministry
     of Foreign Affairs in 1907, served as vice consul in Vladikavkaz, Imperial Russia in
     1910, permanent representative to the League of Nations and minister plenipotentiary
     to Switzerland 1929–33, minister to Italy, Austria, Czechoslovakia and Hungary
     1933–36, ambassador to the USSR 1936–38, minister to France & Spain 1938–40,
     ambassador to Turkey 1940–43, ambassador to Egypt 1943–45, minister of foreign
     affairs 1945–46, minister of justice 1946, ambassador to France 1946–47, minister of
     foreign affairs 1947. He then served as a senator 1951–53 and passed away in 1982 at
     the age of 94.
46   Firouzeh Ensha, personal inquiry, 15 July 2004.
47   Habibollah Hoveyda had the title 'Ain al-Molk,' meaning 'eye of the state'.
48   Angela Sepahbody, interview, 8–10 June, Sedona, Arizona.
49   Some speculated that Tchin-Tchin may have been married or engaged in China
     before coming to Paris and her brother had been sent to warn Sardari to stay away.
     Ms. Firouzeh Ensha, conversation on 23 April 2004. If this is true, Tchin-Tchin and
     Sardari knew that the relationship was doomed from the start.
50   Khan should not be mistaken for a last name. The term may have entered Persian usage
     as the title of the kings of Khata and Tartary, then referring to a prince or lord. Later it
     was commonly used as 'mister'. It was also a respectful manner of addressing officers
     prior to 1925.
51   Ali Ansari, *Modern Iran*, second edition, (London: Pearson Longman, 2007), p.344; FO
     371-11481-E397, Lorraine's Assessment of Reza Shah, 18 January 1926.

52 Laleh means tulip and lalehzar, a field of tulips.

53 Ibrahim Morady, Rayhan's son, personal interview, Los Angeles, California, 25 February 2004.

54 Literally, 'from under soil'.

55 Pronounced Ess-haagh (Issac).

56 F. Steingass, *A Comprehensive Persian-English Dictionary* (London: Routledge, 1988), p.601, c. 1.

57 Jahangir's name appeared as Djahangir in a list prepared in 1942 that suggested he had been born in Tehran. See Chapter Seven.

58 The Russo-British accommodation was in part due to the 1905 Russian defeat by Japan and a desire to avoid confrontation between Russia and Britain on the one hand and concern over a German plan to construct a railway to the Persian Gulf on the other. The German railroad would have challenged the Russo-British dominance of the region.

59 He had succeeded his father when Nasser al-Din Shah was assassinated on 1 May 1896.

60 Some sources have reported the date of his death as 9 January 1907.

61 Edward G. Brown, *The Persian Revolution of 1905–1909* New Edition (Washington, DC: Mage Publishers, 1995), p.207. Baharestan – spring garden – is the name of the property donated to Parliament in 1906.

62 Saifollah Vahidnia, *Khaterat-e Siasi va Tarikhi – Political & Historical Recollections* (Tehran: Ferdowsi, 1362 = 1983–84), pp.175–184.

63 Edward G. Brown, p. 292.

64 Ibid, p.293.

65 Habib Levy, *Tarikh-e Yahoud-e Iran (History of Iranian Jews)* v. 3, (Beverly Hills, CA: Iranian Jewish Cultural Organization of California, 1984), pp.841–843. The noted Tehran cleric Sayyed Jamaladdin Va'ez visited the Hadash Synagogue on a Saturday and in a historic address to his fellow Iranians spoke of the Constitution's promise of liberty, encouraging them to support the movement. See Levy, p.820.

66 Morgan Shuster, *The Strangling of Persia* (Washington, DC: Mage Publishers, 1912, 1987), pp.xlv, xlvii; Edward G. Brown, pp.269, 440, 441.

67 A particularly gruesome incident was a riot engineered by a notable tribal chief titled Sowlatodowleh in Shiraz in November 1910 aimed at discrediting the Provincial Governor Qavamolmolk. His instigators followed by a crowd carried a corpse to the Government House, accused the Jewish community of the slaying and demanded immediate justice from the governor. Qavam asked that the corpse be left there for forensic evaluation and invited others to await the outcome of the investigation at the Justice Department. The crowd did neither, ran amok and proceeded towards the city's Jewish residential area. Looting broke out, government troops intervened but the rioters returned to the Government House to threaten the governor. The governor came out of the building rifle in hand. Shots were fired and the crowd dispersed only to regroup and return to looting. Qashqaii tribesmen were involved in the riot and plunder. The British consul reported that Qavam and his cabinet may have panicked at that point, closed the gate of the Government House and gone into seclusion. Although initially effective, government troops failed to safeguard the victims and their properties, and some of them may have joined the rioters. Eleven people lost their lives and some 50 homes were looted. The corpse, it turned out, had been the body of a Jewish girl who had died and been buried hours earlier. Ironically, the German Legation and the German Jewish community expressed interest in helping and protecting the victims in Shiraz, while the British diplomatic corps urged their German colleagues not to reveal that Sowlatodowleh had been responsible. Diplomatic Notes, 1911, German Foreign Ministry Archives, Serial K698, frames K182719-20; National Archives Microfilm Publication T120, roll 4337.

68 Cyrus Ghani, *Iran and the Rise of Reza Shah: From Qajar Collapse to Pahlavi Power* (London: I.B.Tauris, 2000), p.14.

69 Ivo J. Lederer ed. *Russian Foreign Policy* (New Haven: Yale University Press, 1962),

p.519. Also, Firuz Kazemzadeh, *Russia and Britain in Persia, 1846–1914: A Study in Imperialism* (New Haven: Yale University Press, 1968), p.634. The incident was a serious betrayal that would unfortunately be repeated.

70   Cyrus Ghani asserts that Iran declared its neutrality after Turkish occupation, p.16.

71   Cyrus Ghani, p.16.

72   Cyrus Ghani, p.17; Donald Wilber, *Riza Shah Pahlavi* (Hicksville, New York: Exposition Press, 1975), p.17

73   Harold Nicholson quoted in Cyrus Ghani, p.17.

74   William J. Olson, *Anglo-Iranian Relations During World War I* (London: Routledge, 1984), p.223.

75   Cyrus Ghani, *Iran and the Rise of Reza Shah: From Qajar Collapse to Pahlavi Power* (London: I.B. Taurus, 2000), p.23; DoS, Caldwell to Secretary of State, 12 September and 1 October 1919.

76   Hassan Vosouq's title of nobility 'Vosouq al Dowleh' may be translated as 'Confidence of the Empire'. He was born in 1868 and died in 1951. His younger brother Ahmad Qavam –Qavam al Saltaneh (the Pillar of the Crown) would become prime minister five times. The titles of Vosouq's two cabinet ministers were: 'Saarem al-Dowleh'(Sword of the Empire) and 'Nosrat al-Dowleh' (the Victor of the Empire).

77   Cyrus Ghani, pp.26, 33, 54, 55, 89, 114; FO 371/2862, George P. Churchill to Curzon, 29 July 1919.

78   Cyrus Ghani, pp.162, 163, 158; FO 371/6427, Pierson Dixon to Curzon, 14 May 1921.

79   Cyrus Ghani, p.146.

80   Ibrahim Safaii, *Zamineha-ye Ejtemaii-e Kudeta-ye 1299 [Social Backgrounds of the Coup of 1920]* (Tehran: n.a., 1353/1971), p.240.

81   Safaii, p.243.

82   Safaii, pp.245–249.

83   Cyrus Ghani, p.192. A member of the British financial advisory body in Tehran at the time wrote 'One thing, I believe, may be affirmed with absolute certainty – namely, that the movement was not engineered either by or with the knowledge of the British Legation.' Peter Avery reflects that 'It is to be regretted that, when it suited their purpose in the Second World War, British Information Services themselves issued statements to the effect that it was the British who had made possible Reza Shah's rise to power.' See Peter Avery, *Modern Iran* (New York: Frederick A. Praeger, 1965), pp.227–228.

84   Curzon informed the British minister in Tehran, Herman Norman that creating a new bank in Iran would challenge the Imperial Bank and hiring US nationals would be prejudicial to British interests. [The] 'intention [to create a national bank and hire American advisors] of the Prime Minister [Seyyed Zia] … gives ground for utmost distrust of his protestation of [being] an Anglophile.' In another dispatch to Norman he stated 'The cosmopolitan policy pursued by the Prime Minister is doomed to failure. An army under officers of a single nationality, preferably British, has always impressed me to be in Persia's interest.' See Cyrus Ghani, pp.208, 209, 211; FO 371/6403, Curzon to Norman, 18 April 1921.

85   Peter Avery, *Modern Iran* (New York: Frederick A. Praeger, 1965), p.266.

86   The young army officer was Habib Levy, the Jewish author of *Tarikh-e Yahoud-e Iran; The History of Iranian Jews*, v. III (Beverly Hills, CA: Iranian Jewish Cultural Organization of California, 1984) p.942.

87   Habib Levy, *Tarikh-e Yahoud*, v. 3, p.943.

88   Habib Levy, *Tarikh-e Yahoud*, pp.941–944. I am indebted to Mr Massood Haroonian for the gracious gift of the four-volume history in 2005. Sadly, he passed away in 2006.

89   Literally, a combination of Arab and ostan. Ostan is the Persian word for province.

90   Called 'the most eminent order of the Indian Empire for chivalry', it was founded by Queen Victoria in 1877. The order included three classes: 1. Knight Grand Commander

(GCIE), 2. Knight Commander (KCIE) and 3. Companion (CIE). Cyrus Ghani, pp.334–337.

91 Ibn Saud defeated the Hashemite family and declared himself the first king of the Kingdom of Saudi Arabia in 1924–25. Britain offered the Hashemite family the thrones of the newly created states of Iraq, Jordan and Syria. The French, however, did not support the British design for Syria.

92 Cyrus Ghani, pp.267, 269; FO 416/72, Curzon to Loraine, 10 May 1923 & FO 371/9024, Loraine to Curzon, 17 May 1923.

93 Zahedi had served in the Persian Cossack Brigade with Reza Khan. His rise in the ranks from Captain to Brigadier-General had been meteoric, gaining three promotions in the campaign against the Bolshevik separatists in Gilan in 1921. See Cyrus Ghani, p 241; FO 371/6435, Intelligence Summary no 13, 30 July 1921; Ahmad Ahrar ed. *Khaterat-e Ardeshir Zahedi (Memoirs of Ardeshir Zahedi)* v. I, (Bethesda, MD: Ibex Publishers, 2006) p 22. He became Prime Minister in 1953.

94 Cyrus Ghani, pp.334, 335, 340, 341, 344, 345.

95 Cyrus Ghani, p.353.

96 Cyrus Ghani, p.360.

97 Taqizadeh, son of a cleric, was a nationalist elected to the first Majles. He went to Europe in 1910, became a proponent of modernity, was excommunicated by some theologians, returned to Iran in 1924 and was reelected to the Majles. He served as provincial governor, cabinet minister, ambassador, senator and senate president. Ala, son of a diplomat, was educated in London and joined the Ministry of Foreign Affairs in 1906. He served as cabinet minister in several governments, delegate to the Paris Peace Conference 1918–1919, Minister to Madrid and Washington, Member of Parliament, Head of the National Bank, Ambassador to Washington 1945–1950, Prime Minister twice, Minister of Court and Senator. Mosaddeq, a descendant of the Qajar royalty, was educated in Iran, France and Switzerland. He began his public life in 1906, was elected to the Majles in 1923 and 1925, but clashed with Reza Shah and was exiled in 1927. Reelected to the Majles in 1943, he became prime minister following Prime Minister Haji-Ali Razmara's assassination in 1951. Allied with Ayatollah Abol-Qasem Kashani (who supported the Fadaiyan-e Islam group that had assassinated Razmara) and the Tudeh Party (pro-Soviet communist), he governed until 1953. Dismissed on 15 August 1953, Mosaddeq refused to step down. The Shah left Iran but Mosaddeq was overthrown and arrested on 19 August. He was tried and served three years followed by house arrest. Dowlatabadi studied theology but was accused of apostasy. He established several secular schools in 1897–1905 to promote modern education in Iran. He was elected to the Majles twice, left Iran in 1927 and returned in 1939.

98 Patrick Clawson & Michael Rubin, *Eternal Iran: Continuity and Chaos* (New York: Palgrave-Macmillan, 2005), p.53.

99 Richard F. Nyrop, ed. *Iran: A Country Study* Foreign Area Studies, The American University (Washington, DC: US Government Printing Office, 1978), p.53.

100 Capitulation was particularly odious and humiliating to Iranians for it exempted all foreigners, their employees and anyone claiming to be under the protection of a foreign legation from prosecution under Iranian law. Ayatollah Khomeini referred to the Status of Armed Forces Agreement that the United States had persistently requested, ratified by Iran's two Houses of Parliament after considerable pressure in 1964, as a renewal of capitulation. In a well distributed sermon he accused the government of having 'degraded Iranians to less than an American dog'. Khomeini was exiled in 1964 but his charge remained potent. Mansur was assassinated by a Khomeini supporter on 27 January 1965.

101 Peter Avery, *Modern Iran* (New York: Frederick A. Praeger, 1965, pp.283–284.

102 Markaz-e Amar-e Iran (Iran Centre for Statistics), *Bayan-e Amari-e Tahavolat-e Eqtesadi*

... (Statistical Indicators of Economic & Social Changes in the Pahlavi Reign), (Tehran: n.p., 1976), p 287.

103 Peter Avery, *Modern Iran* (New York: Frederick A. Praeger: 1965), p.276.

104 Julian Bharier, *Economic Development in Iran 1900–1970* (London: Oxford University Press, 1971), pp.37, 38. Cyrus Ghani, p.399. David Menashri, *Education and the Making of Modern Iran* (Ithaca: Cornell University Press, 1992), pp.91–162, states the education budget increase from $100,000 to $12 million.

105 Morteza Kaveh, *Charting Educational development 1922–1977* (Doctoral Dissertation: University of Kansas, 1982), p.110. Cyrus Ghani, p.399.

106 Cyrus Ghani, p.276.

107 Arthur C. Millspaugh, *Americans in Persia* (Washington, DC: Brookings Institution, 1946), p.26fn. Donald N. Wilber, *Riza Shah Pahlavi: The Resurrection And Reconstruction of Iran* (Hicksville, New York: Exposition Press, 1975), p.123. Peter Avery, *Modern Iran* (New York: Frederick A. Praeger, 1965), p.263.

108 Peter Avery, *Modern Iran* (New York: Frederick A. Praeger, 1965), pp.302–303. From L.P. Elwell-Sutton, *Modern Iran* (London: 1941), p.94, quoted in Peter Avery, pp.303. Richard A. Stewart, *Sunrise at Abadan: The British and Soviet Invasion of Iran, 1941* (New York: Praeger, 1988), p.10.

109 Safaii, p.91.

110 Bharier, pp.172, 173.

111 Richard A. Stewart, *Sunrise at Abadan* (New York: Praeger, 1988), p.10; Raj Narain Gupta, *Iran: An Economic Study* (New Delhi: The Indian Institute of International Affairs, 1947), p.73.

112 Oddvar Aresvik, *The Agricultural Development of Iran* (New York: Praeger Publishers, 1976), p.42.

113 Bharier, pp. 3, 5, 14, 27, 197; Jane W. Jacqz ed. *Iran: Past, Present, and Future* (New York: Aspen Institute for Humanistic Studies, 1967), p.33; Gupta, pp.140, 141.

114 E'zaz Nikpay, *Taghdir ya Tadbir: Khaterat-e E'zaz Nikpay* (*Destiny or Determination*) First Edition (Tehran: Ibn-Sina, 1347/1968), p.62.

115 'His aim was to shatter the obsession with foreign influence under the spell of which so many of his compatriots laboured and to make the country stand on its own feet. When he had performed these tasks, then Iran would be able to deal with foreign powers on its own, not on their terms. The idea was repugnant to him that Iran must somehow survive simply because it was of so much importance to people like the British that they would never allow it to be obliterated. His Iran would survive because it had a right to do so and was capable of surviving by its own effort.' See Peter Avery, *Modern Iran* (New York: Frederick A. Praeger: 1965), p. 235.

116 William H. Forbis, *Fall of the Peacock Throne: The Story of Iran* (New York: McGraw-Hill, 1981), p.26.

117 Pronounced Kaashaan.

118 The Fin Royal Garden had become Amir Kabir's home after his dismissal as prime minister on 11 November 1851. He was killed two months later on 10 January 1852 while taking a bath in the garden's bathhouse. See Abbas Amanat, *Pivot of the Universe: Nasir al-Din Shah Qajar and the Iranian Monarchy, 1831–1896* (Washington, DC: Mage Publishers, 1997), p.118.

119 His name was Mulla Binyamin Ben-ha-Mulla Mishael, commonly called Benyamin Ben Mishael Kashi. He is also referred to more respectfully as the Honourable Rabbi Mulla Benyamin, son of the Honourable Rabbi Mulla Mishael. See Amnon Netzer, 'The Jewish Poet Amina of Kashan and His Sacred Poems,' in Shaul Shaked & Amnon Netzer, *Irano Judaica: Studies Relating to Jewish Contacts with Persian Culture Throughout the Ages* vol.V, (Jerusalem: Ben-Zvi Institute, 2003), p.71.

120 Shaked & Netzer, p.72.

121 Richard Weaver too has argued, 'To labour is to pray, for conscientious effort to realise an ideal is a kind of fidelity.' Richard M. Weaver, *Ideas Have Consequences* (Chicago: The University of Chicago Press, 1984), p.73.

122 Kamal means perfection, molk means territory, land, country, thus 'perfection of the country'.

123 Baqer Aqeli, *Zoka al-Molk-e Furuqi va Shahrivar-e 1320* (Tehran: Elmi & Sokhan, 1367/1988), pp.267–285.

124 A person from Kashan is called a Kashi.

125 Lalehzar means a field of tulips, Golestan means a field of flowers, and Baharestan means a place of ever-present spring.

126 A framed net mesh that could be snapped up to stay horizontally if a lady wearing one wished to examine something closely or converse with a female friend. It could snap down by a light touch to cover the face, with a mechanism similar to that of welders' protective masks.

127 E'zaz Nikpay, *Taghdir ya Tadbir: Khaterat-e E'zaz Nikpay* (Destiny or Determination: Recollections of E'zaz Nikpay) First Edition (Tehran: Ibn Sina, 1968), p.42.

128 Bahie Haqqani's family had stopped in Paris on the way to the US when Ibby and Bahie met. The two fell madly in love. Bahi declined to accompany her family to America and the couple soon married.

129 Interview with Ibrahim Morady, 23–25 February 2004, Los Angeles, California.

130 He was still impressed by his friends' response to his suggestion when we met in 2004. 'Not a single one of them objected,' he told the author repeatedly with intense emotion, amazement and visible pride.

131 The French officer in charge of 'Jewish Affairs' in the Bordeaux region was Maurice Papon. Papon, who died on 17 February 2007 at the age of 96, rose to become a cabinet minister in 1978–1981. He was finally brought to court and convicted of collaboration with the Nazis on 2 April 1998 and sentenced to ten years imprisonment. After serving three years he was freed on the grounds of failing health on 18 September 2002. *The Economist*, 24 February 2007, p.99; *Washington Post*, Sunday 18 February 2007, p.C7, c.1.

132 Ibby Morady's recollection. He could not recall Solayman's full name. Morady was over 90 years old at the time of the interview in 2004.

133 Guy-Charles Revol (1912–1991) was one of the signatories to the 'Appeal of France', *L'Appel de la France* addressed to '*Son Eminence L'Ayatollah Khomaini*' to save Iran's former Prime Minister Amir Abbas Hoveyda.

134 Ambassador Farhad Sepahbody recalls his uncle Abdol-Hossein Sardari as a Leica aficionado. Sardari gave his nephew Farhad a Leica camera as a gift, when the latter was a teenager (Farhad Sepahbody interview, 23 March 2007). Leica's parent company, E. Leitz Inc., a family owned firm that popularised the 35 millimetre film, used Leica's international status to save numerous Jews. The company, headed by the Protestant patriarch Ernst Leitz II, instituted a 'Leica Freedom Train' employing Jews and sending them abroad as Leica representatives and sales staff. See James Auer, 'Leica Freedom Train,' *Milwaukee Journal Sentinel*, 9 October 2002; Frank Dabba Smith, *The Greatest Invention of the Leitz Family: The Leica Freedom Train* (New York: American Photographic Historical Society: 2002).

135 When Farhad Sepahbody was chargé d'affaires in Paris in the early 1970s, Mrs Sepahbody —Angela — once entertained 300 guests in that apartment. I am indebted to Mrs Angela Sepahbody for describing the apartment and its layout in detail. Interview, 8–10 June 2004, Arizona.

136 The late Terrence O'Donnel described in a journal an aristocrat he met in Iran, 'I knew that the Prince mended his own shoes but I had assumed that this was simply an eccentricity on his part. It did not occur to me that it might be a normal accomplishment for an Iranian prince, yet it is perfectly understandable when one

reflects on the turmoil of Iran's three thousand years of history, at so many points of which a prince one day might be a pauper the next.' See Terrence O'Donnell, *Garden of the Brave in War: Recollections of Iran* (Washington: Mage Publishers, 2003), p.203.

137 Interview with Ambassador Fereydoun Hoveyda, 23 April 2004. Hoveyda had witnessed the incident.

138 Fereydoun Hoveyda, 21, 23 April 2004.

139 The late Ibrahim Morady remembered her as tall and stunning when she accompanied Sardari to his wedding.

140 Communication with Mrs Petrossian through her son Armen, September–October 2003.

141 Sardari's personnel file at the Iranian Ministry of Foreign Affairs contains the original copy of a letter by him requesting 'permission to marry Yen Chow, a Chinese national.' His request was approved on 15 Tir 1327 (6 July 1948).

142 Their eldest brother Dr Armenak Petrossian, a physician, lived in Iran until the Second World War, moved to Paris and then left for the United States in 1945. I am indebted to Mr Armen Petrossian for the information. Armen had no recollection of Sardari's relations with his father, but agreed to interview his mother. Mrs Petrossian confirmed that her husband catered at Sardari's receptions at cost or possibly at no charge. Mouchegh and his younger brother Melkom studied in Moscow and spent some time in Armenia before moving to Paris. Mouchegh was arrested by the Gestapo and charged as a member of the Resistance. Sardari rose in his defence and called upon his friends in the German military. Mouchegh told Farhad Sepahbody in Paris in the early 1970s that Sardari had saved his life. Melkom passed away in 1972 and Mouchegh in 1981. Communication with Armen Petrossian, 6 September and 11 October 2003.

143 Mark Mazower, *Hitler's Empire: How the Nazis Ruled Europe* (New York: Penguin Press, 2008), pp.425–432.

144 Irene Nemirovsky's novel *Suite Francaise*, reflects the Germans' conduct in the early phases of occupation. Tragically, Nemirovsky, born in Kiev to a Jewish family of bankers who left for France during the Russian Revolution, fell victim to Nazi atrocities and perished in 1942.

145 Mark Mazower, *Hitler's Empire*, p.229.

146 Ibrahim Morady could not remember his first name but recalled the last name as Atchildi. Several others have confirmed his role, but they too had difficulty recalling his first name and did not know that he had been from Central Asia and Jewish. Some believed he had been from Kiev. The author heard repeated references to his popular 'hydrotherapy' and his German customers, not at all mentioned by Atchildi in his own writings.

147 Asaf Atchildi, 'Rescue of Jews of Bukharan, Iranian and Afghan Origin, in Occupied France (1940–1944),' in Nathan Eck and Aryeh Leon Kubovy eds., *Yad Vashem Studies on the European Jewish Catastrophe and Resistance* (Jerusalem: Jerusalem Post Press, 1967), pp 257–281.

148 Several states in the Caucasus declared their independence in 1918 after the fall of Imperial Russia and received international recognition but were later invaded by the Red Army and incorporated into the Union of Soviet Socialist Republics by 1921. In his article, Atchildi does not name his Afghan source of inspiration, and claims credit for the saving of Central Asian, Afghan and Iranian Jews almost exclusively.

149 The name appears to be the Persian family name Asqarzadeh – descendant of Asqar.

150 Asaf Atchildi, 'Rescue of Jews,' pp.246, 268, 247–248.

151 Ibrahim Moradi, who had been an Iranian Jewish leader and close friend of Sardari, recalled Dr Atchildi as a close associate of Sardari. So did Fereydoun Hoveyda, Sardari's nephew. Both recalled that his clinic was frequented by German officers who found his 'hydrotherapy' much to their liking.

152 German Embassy in Paris to the German Foreign Ministry (Berlin, DIII, Nr. 726/42),

23 January 1942, frame K345063; Letter from the 'Association Culturelle Sephardie de Paris,' 13 January 1941, frames K345067-82; Letter from 'Die Hohe Schule' in Frankfurt/M, 12 February 1942, frames K345083-5; Letter from Rademacher in the German Foreign Ministry regarding the treatment of the Sephardi, 13 February 1942, frames K345086-7; Report of the German representative in Saloniki, 26 February 1942, frames K345088-95; Rademacher's determination of policy, 6 March 1942, frames K345096-8; German Foreign Ministry Archives, Serial K1509; National Archives Microfilm Publication T120, roll 4661

153 Conversations with Ambassador Fereydoun Hoveyda.

154 The cylinder, discovered in an excavation in Babylon in 1878, is kept at the British Museum in London.

155 For a version of the recipe see Najmieh Batmanglij, *Food of Life* (Washington, DC: Mage Publishers, 1986), p.142.

156 Sir Winston Churchill, 'Small nations must not tie our hands when we are fighting for their rights and freedom,' *The Second World War: Gathering Storm* (Boston: Houghton Mifflin, 1948), p.547.

157 Zavod Imjeni Stalina (ZIS) was later renamed Zavod Imjenie Likhacheva (ZIL) after Stalin's demise.

158 Nearly all traditional Iranian homes have a 'mehmaan-khaaneh,' guest-room, set aside for receiving and entertaining visitors.

159 Mohammad Khanmalek Yazdi, *Arzesh-e Massaii-e Iran Dar Jang: 1939–1945 (The Value of Iran's Efforts in the War: 1939–1945)* v.1, (Tehran: Ministry of Agriculture Press, 1324/1945), p.51. Richard A. Stewart, *Sunrise at Abadan: The British and Soviet invasion of Iran, 1941* (New York: Praeger, 1988), p 107.

160 The document was signed by accredited representatives Afghan Foreign Minister Faiz Mohammad Khan, Iraqi Foreign Minister Dr Naji Al-Aseel, Turkish Foreign Minister Dr Toufiq Roshdi Aras and Iran's Foreign Minister Enayatollah Samii. See Hossein Makki, v.6, pp.346–350.

161 Ali Dashti, a member of parliament at the time, has suggested that had a strong character such as the seasoned politician and scholar Mohammad-Ali Furuqi rather than Mansur been prime minister, the tragedy of Iran's occupation by the Allies would have been avoided. See Ali Dashti, *Panjah-o-Panj*, Fourth Edition, (Los Angeles: Entesharat-e Dehkhoda, 1381), p.150; Cyrus Ghani, p.406.

162 Richard A. Stewart, *Sunrise at Abadan: The British and Soviet Invasion of Iran, 1941* (New York: Praeger, 1988), p.139; translated from Davood Mo'ayed Amini, *Az Sevvom ta Bistopanjom-e Shahrivar 1320* From 25 August to 16 September 1941 (Tehran: n.a., 1942), p.3; Nasrollah S. Fatemi, *Oil Diplomacy: Powder-keg in Iran* (New York: Whittier Books, 1954), pp.192–193. At the time Iran exchanged ambassadors with neighbouring countries but ministers plenipotentiary with all others.

163 Five merchant ships belonging to the Hanza Line were thus trapped in the Iranian port of Bandar Shahpour in the Persian Gulf. Iran depended on commerce with Germany. See, Richard A. Stewart, pp.13–16. Hossain Makki, *Tarikh-e Bist Saleh Iran* vol. 6, pp.443, 449.

164 The German Minister in Tehran warned Berlin that Soviet pressure on Iran would force the country to embrace the Allies. See US Department of State, *Documents on German Foreign Policy*, Series D, Vol. 8 (Washington, DC: Government Printing Office, 1956–64), p.355.

165 US Department of State, *Documents on German Foreign Policy* vol. 8, p.419.

166 Her Majesty's Public Records Office, Chiefs of Staff Report, 23 February 1940, War Cabinet Minutes, CAB 66, vol. 5, W.P. (40) 18; Richard A. Stewart, *Sunrise*, p.17.

167 Her Majesty's Public Records Office, Appreciation by Chiefs of Staff Committee, 6 October 1939, War Cabinet Minutes, CAB 66, vol. 2, W.P. (39) 73; Richard A. Stewart, p.17.

168 Her Majesty's PRO, Review of Military Policy in the Middle East, December 1939, War Cabinet Minutes, CAB 66, W.P. (40) 18; Richard A. Stewart, p.18.

169 Her Majesty's PRO, Chiefs of Staff Report, 23 February 1940, War Cabinet Minutes, CAB 66, W.P. (40) 66; Richard A. Stewart, p.18.

170 Richard A. Stewart, *Sunrise*, p.20.

171 General Maxim Weygand, *Recalled to Service* (Garden City, NY: Doubleday, 1952), pp.40–41; Richard A. Stewart, Sunrise, p.22.

172 US Department of State, *Documents on German Foreign Policy* vol. 9, p.95; Richard A. Stewart, p.24.

173 US Department of State, vol. 12, p.686.

174 US Department of State, vol. 12, p 835.

175 US Department of State, vol. 12, p.835; Richard A. Stewart, p.60.

176 Telegram Nr. 438, 2 June 1941, German Foreign Ministry Archives, Serial K1509, frame K346168; National Archives Microfilm Publication T-120, roll 4668.

177 Mohammad Khanmalek Yazdi, *Arzesh-e Massaii-e Iran dar Jang-e 1939–1945* (*The Value of Iran's Efforts in the War, 1939–1945*) vol. 1, (Tehran: Ministry of Agriculture Press, 1326/1945), p.51. Richard A. Stewart, *Sunrise*, p.63.

178 Hossain Makki, *Tarihk-e Bist Saleh Iran* (*A Twenty Year History of Iran*) vol. 7, (Tehran: Elmi, 1363), p.29; Cyrus Ghani, *Iran and the Rise of Reza Shah*, p.405.

179 US Department of State, *Foreign Relations of the United States: 1940–1946* (Washington, DC: Government Printing Office, 1958–69), 1941, vol. 3, pp.388–90; Richard A. Stewart, p.75.

180 Stewart, p. 76; Her Majesty's Public Record Office, FO371-27201-E4541.

181 Stewart, p.85; US Department of State, *Foreign Relations of the United States, 1941.* vol. 3, pp.397–98.

182 Anoshiravan Sepahbody's son, Farhad Sepahbody, and Fereydoun Hoveyda, both seasoned diplomats, report finding Anoshiravan Sepahbody's warning (itself based on a confidential meeting with Turkey's President Ismat Inonu) in the Iranian Foreign Ministry's Archives in Tehran, initialled in the margin by Prime Minister Mansur, indicating that he had seen it but not necessarily informed Reza Shah. Mohammad Sa'ed, Iran's Ambassador to Moscow, warned Tehran as well. Iranians have speculated about Mansur's intentions and loyalty (although his inattention may have been due to an overwhelming workload). On the other hand, he might have held a grudge as he had been charged with corruption when Minister of Roads and Transportation in 1936, detained, tried and acquitted. Mohammad Ali Furuqi suggests that Mansur was not above lying. Furuqi was named Prime Minister on the day Anglo-Russian forces invaded Iran. Mansur was assigned Governor of Khorasan, but also wanted the trusteeship of the holdings of Imam-Reza's Shrine Foundation in Mash-had (Meshed), a position already promised to Furuqi's son-in-law Ali-Akbar Assady whose father had been wrongly accused of rebellion and executed while holding the same office. Finally, Furuqi told him to seek Assady's acquiescence. Mansur did so by promising Assady the combined posts of deputy governor and [deputy] trustee of the foundation. Both met Furuqi in his office to announce the agreement. Mansur thus received the trusteeship and departed for Khorasan but Assady's promised appointment never came. A month later Assady contacted Mansur in Mash-had. 'I made the promise in Tehran, but I am in Mash-had now ...' he told Assady. See, Baqir Aqili, *Zoka al-Molk Furuqi va Shahrivar-e 1320* (Tehran: Elmi, 1989), pp.252–253. Hossain Makki, *Tarikh-e Bist Saleh Iran* vol. 6, p.286.

183 Their genuine friendship did not prevent von Papen from employing Sir Hugh's butler, Elyeza Bazna (code named Cicero) as a spy. The top-secret information he delivered to von Papen and in turn passed on to Berlin was so astonishing that the Nazi high command did not believe it.

184 Mohammad Khanmalek Yazdi, pp.41–43. Yazdi estimates that Iran's National Railways employed 32,000–35,000 people, moved 3619,728 tons of armaments and ammunitions to the USSR and in doing so sustained a loss of 1,078,948,000 rials ($1=17 rials). In addition to the tonnage carried by rail, 1,380,272 tons of material was shipped to Russia by truck, bringing the total shipped from 1941 to September 1944 to about 5,000,000 tons. See p 159.

185 Cyrus Ghani, p.406; DoS, 740.0011, Louis G. Dreyfus Jr. to Secretary of State, 24 Aug. 1941.

186 Many Iranians found parallels to such reporting during the months leading to the Iranian Revolution of 1978. See Houshang Nahavandi, *The Last Days: The end of a reign and a life* (Los Angeles: Ketab Corporation, 2004), p.224–225. Nahavandi's background includes Tehran University professor, university president and cabinet minister.

187 Richard A. Stewart, *Sunrise*, pp.92–93. US Department of State, *Foreign Relations of the United States, 1941* vol. 3, p. 403. Hossain Makki, *Tarikh-e Bist Saleh Iran* vol. 7, First Edition (Tehran: Elmi, 1363), pp.73–75.

188 Richard A. Stewart, pp.94–95; *The Complete Presidential Press Conferences of Franklin D. Roosevelt* vol. 18:1941 (New York: De Capo Press, 1972), pp.101–102.

189 Richard A. Stewart, p.95.

190 Richard A. Stewart, p.103, 104; Henry C. Cassidy, *Moscow Dateline* (Boston: Houghton Mifflin, 1943), pp.200–201.

191 Richard A. Stewart, p.107.

192 Richard W. Stewart, p.119–122.

193 Richard W. Stewart, p. 154; Bisheshwar Prasad, ed. *Official History of the Indian Armed Forces in the Second World War, 1939–1945: The Campaign in Western Asia* (Culcutta: Sree Sarawata Press, 1957), p.327.

194 Richard A. Stewart, p.141.

195 Elder brother of Abdollah Entezam. Abdollah, a diplomat and later head of NIOC was Sardari's friend.

196 Reader Bullard, *The Camels Must Go* (London: Faber and Faber, 1961), p.227.

197 Cyrus Ghani, *Iran and the Rise of Reza Shah*, pp.292–293.

198 Iran's King, Reza Shah, to Prime Minister Mohammad-Ali Furuqi upon hearing the Russo-British ultimatum demanding the monarch's exile. Baqir Aqili, *Zoka al-Molk Furuqi va Sharivar-e 1320* (Tehran: Elmi, 1989), p.134.

199 Baqir Aqili, p.132.

200 Nasrollah Entezam became ambassador to the UN and the United States. Abdollah Entezam, a diplomat and later INOC Chairman, was his brother. Israel's first envoy to Iran, Moir Ezry in his memoirs states that Nasrollah Entezam had warmly supported a proposal at the UN in 1947 to create two states, a Jewish and an Arab state, in Palestine. See Moir Ezry, Translated into Persian by Abraham Hakhami, *Yadnameh; Kist Az Shoma Az Tamamiye Ghowme Oo*, v. 1, (Israel: self published, 2000), p.98.

201 Baqir Aqili, p.133. Furuqi told his son Mohsen the details. The story is Mohsen's recollection.

202 Baqir Aqili, p.134.

203 It is believed that Reza khan, before ascending the throne, visited Imam Reza's Shrine in Mash-had (Meshed) and prayed that if given seven sons, he would name all seven Reza. He did. Mohammad-Reza 1919–1980) was the first, followed by Ali-Reza (1922–1955), Gholam-Reza (1923), Abdol-Reza (1924), Ahmad-Reza (1925–1981), Mahmoud-Reza (1926) and Hamid-Reza (1932–1992). He had three daughters, Shams (1917–1996), Ashraf (1919) and Fatemeh (1930–1989).

204 Baqir Aqili, p.138.

205 Baqir Aqili, p.136–138.

206 Baqir Aqili, p.138, 139.

207 Mohammad Sa'ed asserted in his memoirs that Bullard exhibited an inexplicable hostility towards Iran, Iranians and particularly Reza Shah. When Sa'ed was foreign

minister in Sohaily's Cabinet that followed Furuqi's Government in 1941, Bullard
presented the prime minister with a list naming 50 prominent Iranians he wanted
arrested. Prime Minister Sohaily responded that protocol required the envoy to
contact Foreign Minister Sa'ed. Bullard presented the list to Sa'ed, who upon looking
at it recognised nearly all as prominent dignitaries and refused. Bullard angrily
threatened Sa'ed while banging his fist on the foreign minister's desk. Sa'ed retorted,
'You ought to refrain from your request, not increase people's unhappiness.' Bullard
replied, 'We don't care about public opinion ... The opinion of the [Iranian] public
has been against us since 1907.' Not able to intimidate Sa'ed, Bullard pressured the
young Prime Minister Sohaily. He finally succeeded in 1943; but his list by then
had grown to 180. Baqir Aqili, pp.23, 57, 84. Mohammad Sa'ed Maraghei, Bagher
Aghely ed., *Khaterat-e Siasi* – Political Memoirs – (Tehran: Namak Publishing, 1994),
pp.137–139.

208 Richard W. Stewart, p.197.

209 Ibid, pp.193, 200.

210 Baqir Aqili, pp.95, 96, 110, 119.

211 Richard W. Stewart, p.194.

212 Ibid, pp.195–196. Stewart cites daily journals of the Reverend M. Miller, *The Diary of
Reverend William Miller* (Philadelphia: Presbyterian Historical Society Collection, 1941).

213 Winston S. Churchill, *The Second World War: The Grand Alliance* (Boston: Houghton
Mifflin, 1950), pp. 92–493; Richard W. Stewart, p.196.

214 Richard W. Stewart, p.196; US Department of State, *Foreign Relations of the United
States, 1940–1946* 1941, v. 3, (Washington, D.C.: Government Printing Office, 1958–69),
pp.446–447.

215 Baqir Aqili, p.102. The details are recollections of Furuqi's son & confidant, Mohsen.

216 Radio Delhi reported that Reza Shah had taken the crown jewels out of the country.
See Richard W. Stewart, p.208. Some parallels in reporting during the months prior to
the Iranian Revolution of 1978 have been suggested. See Houshang Nahavandi, *The
Last Days: The end of a reign and a life* (Los Angeles: Ketab Corp., 2004) pp.224–225.

217 Baqir Aqili, p.119.

218 For the Iranian notion of chivalry see Jane W. Jacqz, ed. *Iran: Past, Present and Future;
Aspen Institute Persepolis Symposium* (New York: Aspen Institute for Humanistic Studies,
1976), p. 426.

219 Baqir Aqili, p. 131.

220 R. Azari Shahrezai, ed. *Iran and German Expert Immigrants (1931–1940)* (Tehran: Iran
National Archives Organisation, 1995). The collection includes 112 documents
on recruitment of European Jewish experts for employment in Iran. Most reflect
ministerial or cabinet level deliberations, some reported to the King, who occasionally
made recommendations. Also see Ahmad Mahrad in Homa and Houman Sarshar eds.
The history of Contemporary Iranian Jews, v. 3, (Beverly Hills, CA: Center for Iranian
Jewish Oral History), pp.98, 99. A telegram from Stockholm dated 6 November 1943
reports from the Swedish Embassy in Tehran, for instance, that Dr Hans Jurgen Israel
Katzenstein of Germany was arrested by the Soviets (Stockholm Nr. 3142 to Berlin
Pol VII 9577, Secret, 6 November 1943, German Foreign Ministry Archives, Serial
K1509, frame k346271; National Archives Microfilm Publication T120, Roll 4668).
Reza Shah's personal physician was Dr Curt Erich Neumann, a German Jew who
had practised in Berlin before migrating to Tehran. Dr Neumann decided to travel to
Germany in January 1935 to purchase some medical supplies and equipment for his
practice in Tehran. He sought assurance from the German Embassy that he would not
be subjected to harassment. The embassy cabled Berlin that Dr Neumann, the Shah's
physician, had been well respected in Iran and conveyed his request for a purchasing
trip to Germany. The German Foreign Ministry, having contacted security and police

departments, replied within ten days that 'there are no charges pending against the Jewish immigrant Dr Erich Neumann in Germany and he will not be endangered. The police, up to this point, have no political files against him.' See Ahmad Mahrad in *The History of Contemporary Iranian Jews*, v. 3, (Beverly Hills, CA: Center for Iranian Jewish Oral History, 1999), pp.71–73; Staatspoliziact, II 1 B2 60421/135/35, Berlin, 14 January 1935.

221 Baqir Aqili, pp.132, 191. It is of interest that Golshaiyan's reputation was much maligned as having sold out to the British following the infamous Gass-Golshaiyan oil agreement that Iran's Parliament rejected and the government finally withdrew. The agreement had been negotiated between Finance Minister Golshaiyan and Anglo-Iranian Oil Company's Neville A. Gass and presented to the Majles on 19 July 1949. The incident suggests the charges against Golshayan are unjustified. Golshaiyan's refusal to subsidise his country's occupation deserves recognition. Naficy has defended his actions by arguing that no devaluation had in fact occurred. The Allies' demand for Iranian currency on the one hand and Iranian government's budgetary deficits financed by borrowing from the National Bank increased the notes in circulation from 1.2 billion rials on 20 March 1941 to 3.7 billion on 21 March 1943 and 6.6 billion on 20 March 1945. The notes in circulation had increased by 53 per cent per year and the consumer price index had followed by 50 per cent per year. Naficy's argument would have been more convincing had the exchange rate been adjusted months after the occupation as a consequence of economic disarray, rather than in anticipation of the chaos that was to come. Iran's currency exchange law, passed in 1931, had made imports contingent upon exports. An exporter of 10,000 rials value would receive at Iran's border a certificate for 10,000 rials worth of exports, which he would sell to the National Bank and receive a 10 per cent premium on its face value. An importer of 10,000 rials worth of goods would have to apply to the Bank for 10,000 rials of foreign currency and pay back the 10 per cent premium plus a service charge. Thus the government subsidised exports at the expense of imports. Naficy's other argument is more compelling: 'A defeated country cannot impose its terms on the victors. Indeed the Allies had plans to issue their own money or put into circulation Indian rupees.' See Kamran M. Dadkhah, 'The Iranian Economy During the Second World War: The Devaluation Controversy,' *Middle Eastern Studies*, Vol. 37, No. 2, April 2001, p.187. Also, A. Cecil Edwards, 'Iran (Persia) To-Day,' *International Affairs (Royal Institute of International Affairs 1931–1939)*, Vol. 15, No. 2 (March–April 1936), p.255.

222 Patrick Clawson and Michael Rubin, *Eternal Iran: Continuity and Chaos* (New York: Palgrave Macmillan, 2005), p.58.

223 Richard W. Stewart, *Sunrise*, p.213. A revolutionary leader who accompanied Khomaini to Tehran, one of the founders of the Revolutionary Guard Corps and director of the Islamic Republic National Radio, stated in 2006 'Iran's Islamic Revolution is the latest mistake. The regime that resulted from this revolution, the Islamic Republic of Iran, has been defeated in many respects. It has failed not only in the economic domain, but also in its cultural, social and political accomplishments. The defeat of this regime has been not simply the defeat of an ideological, revolutionary, maximalist version of Islam but also the defeat of all the revolutionary products of Iranian intellectualism of the 1960s, whether Muslim or Marxist, secular or religious.' See Mohsen Sazegara, 'The Point of No Return: Iran's Path to Democracy,' The Washington Institute for Near East Policy, Policy Focus #54, April 2006.

224 Richard W. Stewart, *Sunrise*, p.216. Field Marshal Sir William Slim, *Unofficial History* (London: Cassell & Company, 1959), p.237.

225 Richard W. Stewart, p.217. Also, see US National Archives, Microfilm Records of German Foreign Ministry, Serial 913-294969. Internment of the Axis nationals in

Iran was not an isolated case. The US sought and achieved the expulsion of Latin Americans of Japanese descent for internment in the United States and possible prisoner-of-war exchange with Japan. See H.R. 662, the Commission on Wartime Relocation and Internment of Latin Americans of Japanese Descent Act; Xavier Becerra and Dan Lungren (US Representatives from California), 'Justice for the Forgotten Internees,' *The Washington Post*, 19 February 2007, p.A19, c.2.

226 Ibrahim Qavam Shirazi was still known by his officially discarded noble title, Qavam al-Molk, conferred by the Qajar monarchs. Britain's Legation was upgraded to embassy two years later, and so were Iran's legations abroad.

227 The Kazerooni family answered the call of industrialisation in Iran by introducing modern textile mills in Isfahan, making the family financially successful, socially prominent and politically influential.

228 Baqir Aqili, pp.190, 204, 205.

229 From Dr Mohammad Sajjady's own written recollections. See Baqer Aqeli, *Chronology of Iran 1906–1979*, First Edition, (Tehran: Goftar Publishing Corp., 1990), Appendix 32, pp.412–417.

230 Farhad Rostami, ed., *Pahlaviha: Khanedan-e Pahlavi Be-ravayat-e Asnad* (The Pahlavis: Pahlavi Dynasty According to Documents), Volume 1, (Tehran: Iran's Contemporary History Studies Institute, 1975), printed by the Foreign Ministry's Press, p.197, Document #98, [A-112-327-1]. The valet's name is not on the list, but Mahmoud and several members of the Royal Family accompanied Reza Shah into exile.

231 Farhad Rostami, p.198, document #100, [J-112-328-19]

232 'Interview with Dr Kazem Vadi'i, Statesman, Former Cabinet Minister and University Professor,' *Iranians* (Washington, DC), Vol 13, No. 407, Friday 26 December 2008, p.12.

233 Farhad Rostami ed. *Pahlaviha: Khanedan-e Pahlavi beh Ravayat-e Asnad* (The Pahlavis: Pahlavi Dynasty According to Documents) Vol. 1 (Tehran: Contemporary Iranian History Institute, 1378/1999), pp.198–199. The letter is numbered as document number 101, archived as [j-112-328-16].

234 Farhad Rostami, p.201, document number 103, [D-996-49].

235 Farhad Rostami, p.202, document number 106, [A-112-328-2].

236 Farhad Rostami, pp.205, 206, 208, document number 112, [A-112-327-6].

237 Farhad Rostami, p.207, document number 116, [A-112-327-7].

238 Foreign Minister Sa'ed advised the cabinet to send a bill to Majles to declare war on Germany. It is of interest that Bullard did all he could to obstruct the move. The bill received parliamentary approval on 9 September 1943. Mohammad Sa'ed Maraghei, Agheli ed. *Khaterat-e Siasi*, pp.141, 142.

239 Farhad Rostami, p.209, 210–211, document 120, [A-112-327-10].

240 Farhad Rostami, p.211–212, document number 121, [A-112-327-11].

241 Michael J. Cohen, *Churchill And The Jews* (London: Frank Cass, 1985), pp.262, 281, 282. Three ships loaded with Jewish refugees – SS *Pacifica*, *Milos* and *Atlantic* – arrived in Haifa in November 1940. As the *Atlantic*, the last of the three, arrived on 24 November, the passengers beginning with the earlier arrivals were transferred to the liner *Patria* for repatriation. On the 25th Hagana exploded a bomb on board the *Patria*. The liner capsized; 252 refugees and 12 British policemen died. The late arrivals onboard *Atlantic*, 1,783 refugees, were sent off to Mauritius, but the rest, in consideration of the tragedy, were allowed to remain in Palestine.

242 Kazem Vadi'i 'Interview,' *Iranians*, 26 December 2008, p.12.

243 Richard Stewart, p 215; Donald N. Wilber, *Riza Shah Pahlavi* (Hicksville, N.Y.: Exposition Press, 1975), p.217–220. S.H. Steinberg, *The Statesman's Handbook 1949* (New York: Macmillan Co., 1949), pp.1235–1236. Also see Mohammad Reza Shah Pahlavi, *Answer to History* (New York: Stein & Day, 1980), p.69. The information about the Jewish community on Mauritius was also provided to the author by a commercial pilot who had, much to

his surprise, seen a Jewish cemetery there and managed to contact a survivor who had confirmed the story of the king and the pianist. According to the pilot, the British had 'dumped' some 2500 Jewish refugees on the island during the war.

244 The remains finally arrived home for burial at a mausoleum in Ray, near Tehran in 1950. After the 1978 Revolution, the clerics, reportedly led by Ayatollah Khalkhaali, tore down the building but found the remains had already been removed.

245 Cyrus Chani, *Iran and the Rise of Reza Shah*, p.406; DoS doc. 158, Dreyfus to Secretary of State, 19 September 1941.

246 Cyrus Ghani, *Iran and the Rise of Reza Shah*, pp.401, 402, 404, 407. Ghani cites Gordon Waterfield, *Professional Diplomat – Sir Percy Loraine* (London: 1973), p.210; Lord Kinross, *Ataturk: The Rebirth of a Nation* (London: 1964), pp.461–462; Hassan Arfa, *Under Five Shahs*, p.246.

247 A. Cecil Edwards, 'Iran (Persia) Today,' *International Affairs (Royal Institute of International Affairs 1931–1939)*, Vol. 15, No. 2, March–April 1936, pp.245, 264.

248 Furuqi was bitter at his resignation but was looking forward to an ambassadorial appointment to Washington DC in 1942 when he died of a heart attack.

249 Ahmad Qavam (1875–1955), a member of the Qajar nobility, was named Minister of the Interior in 1911, Minister of Finance & Minister of Interior in 1914–1918 and Governor of Khorasan 1922–1923. He was accused of having plotted to assassinate Minister of War Reza Khan and sent to exile in 1923. The British Minister to Tehran, Sir Percy Loraine, was convinced of Qavam's conspiracy, but his American counterpart, Rabbi Joseph Saul Kornfeld, was not sure. He was granted permission to return to Iran in 1930 to attend to his extensive properties. He renewed his political activities and intrigue after Reza Shah's abdication. See Cyrus Ghani, pp.40, 279.

250 The departure was in part to soothe the feelings of Iranians who had been insulted at the Tehran Conference in 1943. The chargé d'affaires of the Soviet Embassy informed Foreign Minister Sa'ed on November 26 that Stalin and Molotov had arrived in Tehran earlier that day, and requested a meeting at the Foreign Ministry at 6:00pm. Sa'ed invited Prime Minister Sohaily to join him for the meeting with the Soviet diplomat. At 6:00pm, Molotov entered Sa'ed's office unexpectedly. Sa'ed who had last met Molotov in Moscow as Iran's ambassador the previous year, was pleasantly surprised. Molotov revealed that Roosevelt and Churchill would arrive the following day, but asked that Sohaily and Sa'ed share the information only with the Shah and the Court Minister Hossein Ala. Sa'ed awaited a similar visit by his American and British counterparts, but the diplomatic courtesy would not be forthcoming. The Shah, Iran's Head of State, decided to pay a visit to Stalin, Roosevelt and Churchill the following day since they had pointedly chosen not to visit him. The discourtesy turned to insult as the Shah was made to sit and wait behind a closed door at the Soviet Embassy where Roosevelt had stayed and where the conference was being held. He finally had a meeting with Roosevelt but on the way to meet Churchill, the British prime minister entered the corridor and exchanged pleasantries with the Shah for two to three minutes and walked away. Stalin had already informed the Shah that he would 'pay a courtesy call on His Majesty' and did so the following morning. Stalin and Molotov then met with Sohaily and Sa'ed around noon the same day as well. The British had hosted a reception the previous evening at which the gift of the British monarch to the People of the Soviet Union – The Stalingrad Sword – was presented to Stalin, but they had not invited a single Iranian government official. Sohaily and Sa'ed, incensed that Iran's Head of State – the Shah – the Iranian government and the nation had been snubbed, contacted the American and British envoys and complained. The US Minister Louis G. Dreyfus conveyed the message to Roosevelt and informed Sa'ed that the 'three leaders' had resolved to issue a declaration to assuage hard feelings before their departure. Roosevelt ordered that the declaration be shown to

Sohaily and Sa'ed prior to signing. The draft was revised by Sa'ed and Sohaily twice, insisting on guarantees of Iran's independence and territorial integrity. The three signed the document before their departure on 2 December. Stalin and Molotov also wired friendly notes of thanks to Prime Minister Sohaily and Foreign Minister Sa'ed and requested that their sentiments be conveyed to His Majesty. Mohammad Sa'ed Maraghei, Aqeli ed. *Khaterat-e Siasi*, pp.142–152. Churchill's attitude towards Iran and Iranians, as was the case with the British Ambassador Bullard, was typical.

251 Gary R. Hess, 'The Iranian Crisis of 1945–46 and the Cold War,' *Political Science Quarterly*, Vol. 89, No. 1 (March 1974), p.124.

252 Qavam, after replacing Prime Minister Sohaily on 9 August 1942, asked Sa'ed to retain his post as foreign minister. Qavam also had an explosive encounter with Bullard who pressured him for Iranian currency to be used for the expenses of the occupying troops. Printing money required parliamentary approval and Majles had already allowed 300 million rials to be issued a few months earlier. Bullard's new demands required another bill to issue an additional 500 million rials in new currency. Bullard was impatient. At a meeting with Qavam, Sa'ed and Abol-hassan Ebtehaj who would become the director of the National Bank, Bullard angrily slammed his fist on a table and shouted in French 'You are hiding behind your Majles deputies as women. Who the hell are they to be granted importance? They are a bunch of vagabonds.' Qavam was shocked and speechless. Sa'ed could not contain himself. Without seeking Qavam's permission to speak, he told Bullard, 'Who do you think you are? Who has given you permission to insult us? You have no right to utter those words. Do you think you are our master? We are not a defeated nation. Sit and speak politely!' Bullard paled. Qavam thanked Sa'ed after Bullard had left. Mohammad Sa'ed Maraghei, Aqeli ed. *Khaterat-e Siasi*, pp.140–141. The incident is confirmed by Abol-Hassan Ebtehaj in his memoirs, pp.149–152, as reported by Aqeli in the editor's Foreword, p.33.

253 Gary R. Hess, 'The Iranian Crisis of 1944–46 and the Cold War,' *Political Science Quarterly*, 89, No 1, March 1947, p.143. Hossein Ala was later to become prime minister. He survived an assassination attempt by a member of the 'Fedaiyan-e Islam' terrorist group whose mentor was Ayatollah Kashani. Ala served as the minister of the imperial court later. Fedaiyan-e Islam assassinated several important personalities, among them Prime Minister Haji-Ali Razmara, killed on 7 March 1951. Hossein Makki, v 6, pp.485–491. Richard Stewart, *Sunrise*, p.226. See Harry S. Truman, *Memoirs: Tear of Trial and Hope*, v. 2 (Garden City, NY: Doubleday & Compant, 1955), p.95.

254 William H. Forbis, *Fall of the Peacock Throne: The Story of Iran* (New York: McGraw-Hill, 1981), p.52. US Consul in Tabriz Lester Sutton sent a similar report to Tehran by telegraph: 'The pall has lifted. Just a year and a day after it was founded, the Democratic regime of Azerbaijan crumbled in a few hours yesterday … I have never seen so many smiling faces since I came to Azerbaijan.' See US Department of State, *Foreign Relations of the United States, 1940–1946* v.7 (Washington, DC: Government Printing Office, 1958–69), p.561.

255 Habib Ladjevardi, 'The Origins of US Support for an Autocratic Iran,' *International Journal of Middle East Studies*, Vol. 15, No 2., May 1983, p.229; FDR, 12 January 1944, RG-59, Numerical File 891.00/3037, NA.

256 Nathan Godfried, 'Economic Development and Regionalism: United States Foreign Relations in the Middle East, 1942–5,' *Journal of Contemporary History*, Vol. 22, No. 3 (July 1987), p 483; US, Department of State, *Foreign Relations of the United States, 1943*, 4: 330–6.

257 Ambassador Farhad Sepahbody, son of the late Anoshiravan Sepahbody confirms the episode. The surplus was finally sold to the Iranian Army.

258 Baqer Aqeli, *Chronology of Iran: 1906–1970*, p.289; Gholamreza Karbaschi, *Ruzshomar-e Ravabet-e Iran va Amrika* (Tehran, 2001), p.69; also the daily *Ettela'at*, 4th of Khordad (26 May 1947). For an estimate of the cost of transporting war material borne by

Iran see Mohammad Khanmalek Yazdi, *Arzesh-e Masaii-e Iran Dar Jang: 1939–1945* v. 1, (Tehran: Ministry of Agriculture Press, 1329/1945), p. 159. He estimated the 'loss' to Iranian railways at about 1,078,948,000 rials for having transported 3,619,728 tons of armaments to the USSR. An additional 1,380,272 tons of supplies were also moved by truck, for a total of about five million tons in 1941–44. Peter Avery reports a 'British agreement to indemnify Iran with over £5 million for use of the railways during the war and the gift in July 1949 of two frigates to the Persian Navy did not have the effect of reducing anti-British feelings … The indemnity for the use of Trans-Iranian railway was scarcely commented on in a press that was almost without exception hostile.' See Peter Avery, *Modern Iran* (New York: Frederick A. Praeger: 1965), p. 413. US Ambassador in Iran George Allen in a confidential Memorandum of Conversation with Mr Iliff, UK Treasury Rep., Cairo, dated 8 May 1947 (RG84, FSP…, Tehran Embassy, 1947: 850.6–892.3, Box 14, Entry Number 2738A, NND 765028, Subject: Allied Debt to Iranian State Railway) reported to the secretary of state that the 'Tripartite Treaty provided that a financial Agreement should be negotiated between the UK, USSR and Iran in regards to employing Iran's communication facilities during the war … The Iranians drafted a proposal, but it was unacceptable to the British Government and nothing has ever been done since towards concluding an agreement. During the war the British contributed enough to keep the railway running. When the US took over in April 1943, the US expressed reservations as to its financial responsibility. The Persian Gulf Command took the position that it was operating the railroad as an agent of the Combined Chiefs of Staff and accepted no financial responsibility. Up to now the Russians have paid nothing to fortify the railroad. The British paid everything to keep it running to 1 July 1945. The sum paid did not amount to much more than the outgoings and there is a clear liability to pay something for depreciation and return on capital … The Persians claim 380,000,000 rials in special claims. In addition they claim 100,000,000 rials in compensation for the personnel – inflated during the war and could not be discharged immediately. Illif [Britain] is inclined to offer £3,000,000 on the basis of 1.5 per cent return. The Persians are asking for £20,000,000. If the US is drawn into this, I am thinking along the lines that we refuse any request to consider this question with the Persians unless and until they regard the Soviets as equally liable in the whole matter …'

259 Only eleven tons of the gold bullion was finally returned on 1 June 1955. The Soviet Union then added a promise on 1 August 1955 to deliver gradually an additional $8.75 million worth of goods to settle the debt. See Baqer Aqeli, *Roozshomar-e Tarikh-e Iran az Mashrooteh ta Enqelaab-e Eslaami 1906–1979* [Chronology of Iranian History from the Constitutional to the Islamic Revolution, 1906–1979], Vol. 1 and 2, first edition (Tehran: Goftar Publishing Co., 1990), pp. 347–348.

260 They were Representatives Mozaffar Baqaii, Hossein Makki, Abdolqader Azad, Allahyar Saleh, Mohammad Nariman and Ali Shaygan.

261 Razmara was attending Ayatollah Qomi's funeral at the Soltani Mosque when struck. Recent revelations allege that Razmara may have been involved in the attempt to assassinate the Shah. Lieutenant-General Tahmures Agahiyan, Imperial Iranian Army, Ret., has suggested in his published recollections that documents discovered after Razmara's death linked him to the Soviet Union and a planned conspiracy. Investigating Major Adl Moqaddam's uncommon finances pointed to his frequent visits with retired Lieutenant Colonel Hamid Nezami who had served under Razmara. The Colonel was repeatedly observed meeting with a sergeant who would go to a far-away laundry to talk to the owner, followed by a rendezvous on the Karaj Road with a Soviet Embassy official who was identified as a KGB officer who had served in Afghanistan. All involved were arrested one evening as Colonel Nezami and the KGB agent were meeting at 11:00pm. The KGB officer, fearing a Siberian

punishment or worse, agreed to serve as a double agent if his arrest would remain a secret. Razmara had allegedly met with Soviet officials at least twice a week since 1943–44, had spoken Russian and occasionally asked Colonel Nezami to deliver sealed envelopes to the Embassy contacts in later years. Of particular interest are Nezami's recollections of Razmara's meetings and behaviour during the 24 hours prior to, and after, the attempt on the Shah's life. A sealed briefcase Razmara had entrusted to Nezami to bury in a safe place reportedly contained a document signed by Razmara and the Soviet Ambassador to Iran in which Razmara's ascent to power had been foreseen under certain conditions. They were: 1. Oil concessions to the USSR in northern Iran. 2. Independence of Azerbaijan 3. Independence of Kurdestan. 4. Institution of a Socialist Republic in Iran. 5. Formation of a government inclusive of the Tudeh Party leaders. 6. The cabinet must be confirmed by the leadership of the Soviet Union. 7. Trial and punishment of the Pahlavi family in a revolutionary socialist court. 8. The Government of the Soviet Union accepts Razmara's long-term command and leadership. 9. One-third of the Razmara-led coup d'etat government to be selected by Razmara. 10. Generals and senior officers of the armed forces to be tried and punished. 11. General nationwide purge by the government security. 12. Cancellation of oil concessions in the south after Razmara's government is firmly established. 13. New oil agreement with the USSR after the Anglo-Iranian deal is cancelled. 14. The Soviet government would cooperate with the reconstruction of the new regime's civil and military institutions. The KGB officer continued to serve in the consular office in Tehran for two more years. After his tour of duty and reassignment to Moscow he was turned over to the CIA. The three Soviet agents, LTC Nezami, Major Moqaddam and Sergeant Tashviqi were tried, convicted of treason and received the death penalty. The laundry owner and two others received six months to a year incarceration. See Sepahbod Tahmures Agahiyan, 'Mo'arefi-e Avamel-e Sue-e qasd-e Bahman-e 27, Daneshgah' [Identification of the Villanous Attempt of 4 February 1949 at Tehran University], *Payam Weekly Magazine* Vol. 16, issue 694, 12 December 2008, pp. 14–19.

262 See Fariborz Mokhtari, 'Iran's 1953 Coup Revisited: Internal Dynamics versus External Intrigue,' *Middle East Journal*, volume 62, No. 3, Summer 2008, pp. 457–488, for the events of 1941–1953.

263 Small teaglasses called estekaan, hold half as much as a teacup and are popular among Iranians.

264 Although mass deportation of Jews had not yet started, she must have felt a premonition; telephone interview, 19 January 2004.

265 The fact that she was a British subject, had the Gestapo known, might have been enough reason to have her detained.

266 Telephone interview with Mrs Victoria Morady, 19 January 2004.

267 Jean During et al., *The Art of Persian Music* (Washington, DC: Mage Publishers, 1991), p. 127.

268 Visiting Mrs Kodrat (Qodrat) Senehi, the late Rahim's widow in Tel Aviv in January 2007, I inquired about the musical instrument while looking at family photographs. A sunburst of a smile flashed on her son's face. 'I have it at my home,' he said. Itzhak then drove me to his home, where his father's tar was lovingly kept in its original case. He carefully opened it and brought the instrument out to show me. A few minutes later he put it back just as carefully. 'It reminds me so much of my father.'

269 It is most likely that Sardari helped in Rahim's rescue and the author has heard one such reference but has not found supporting documentation. Unfortunately, both George and Rahim had also passed away by the time of writing.

270 Joseph Ariel, 'Jewish Self-Defence and Resistance in France During World War II,' Nathan Eck and Aryeh L. Kubovy eds. *Yad Vashem Studies on the European Jewish Catastrophe and Resistance* Jerusalem: Jerusalem Post Press, 1967), pp. 227–228.

271 Eliane Cohanim, seven years old in 1941. Interview, 30 September 2004.

272 Eliane Cohanim, interview, 30 September 2004.

273 The author met her in Tel Aviv in January 2007 and owes her a debt of gratitude for wonderful hospitality, a wealth of information and her family photographs. Her name is now spelled Kodrat.

274 Empress Farah Pahlavi is a graduate of the same school.

275 Mr Djambazian's daughter runs a school by the same name in Glendale, California.

276 Eliane Cohanim, 30 September 2004.

277 Some remained in Iran but many left for a variety of destinations including Israel. The story of the Jewish youngsters among them known as 'The Tehran Children, or The Children of Tehran,' is compelling. See Deborah Umer, *Tehran Secret Operation: Rescue of Jewish Children from the Claws of the Nazis*,, Hushang Zareh trans. *Amaliat-e Makhfianeh-e Tehran: Nejaat-e Bache-haay-e Yahoudi az Changaal-e Nazi-haa* (New York: Hushang Zareh, 2005), pp.109, 129–150; http://www.zchor.org/tehran/children. htm, www.jewishgen.org/databases/Holocaust/0102_Tehran-children.html, www. jewishgen.org/yizkor/Tehran/teh000.html. On February 1943 a group of 1230 (861 children and 369 adults) finally reached Palestine. See Israel Gutman ed., *The Encyclopedia of the Holocaust* (New York: Macmillan, 1990).

278 Between 1939 and 1941 half a million Poles, mostly government officials, judges, teachers, lawyers and intellectuals had been arrested. On 10 February 1940, some 250,000 from rural areas were deported to Siberia by rail on 110 cattle cars. On 13 April 1940, some 300,000 were sent to Kazakhstan on 160 cattle cars. In June and July 1940, around 400,000 were deported to Archangelsk, Sverdlovsk and Novosibirsk. In June 1941 an additional 280,000 were deported to the Soviet Union.

279 The honey coloured cub was named Voytek. In the heat of the battle he is reported to have walked on two hind legs, paws stretched forward, loading and unloading 100-pound boxes of artillery shells tirelessly all day and every day until the battle was won. His image became the symbol of the 22nd Transport Division and he was given an official rank. He would even march upright and in step with the troops. He ended up with comrades in Scotland but when the Polish Army in exile was demobilised in 1947, Voytek was left at the Zoological Garden in Edinburgh. The Iranian bear-soldier died in captivity in 1963.

280 Habib Levy, *Taarikh-e Jaame' Yahudian-e Iran: Gozideh Taarikh-e Yahud-e Iran* (Los Angeles: Ketab Books, 1997), p.534. Iran continued to accept and assist refugees. Iraqi Jews, twice as numerous as Iranian Jewry, looked to Iran for safety and slipped through Iran's borders frequently, some for repatriation to Israel. See Sohrab Sobhani, *The Pragmatic Entente: Israeli-Iranian Relations, 1948–1988* (New York: Praeger, 1989), pp 4, 86; Uri Bialer, 'The Iranian Connection in Israel's Foreign Policy,' *The Middle East Journal* 39 (Spring 1985) pp.292–315. On the Polish exiles in Iran see Andrzej Krzysztof Kunert, *Polacy w Iranie 1942–1945* (Warszawa: Rada Ochrony Pamiec Walk I Meczenstawa, 2002), and numerous articles by Ryszaed Antolak. In an article titled 'Iran and the Polish Exodus from Russia 1942,' Antolak wrote in 2004:

Beggarly, unwell and dishevelled, the Polish refugees were nourished more by the smiles and generosity of the Iranian people than by the food dished out by British and Indian soldiers. Iran at that time was going through one of the unhappier episodes of her history. Occupied by the Russian and the British, her relations with the soldiers of these two countries were understandably strained and difficult. With the Poles, however, there was an immediate affinity which was evident from the moment they arrived and which extended from the lowest to the highest levels of society.

281 I am indebted to Mrs Eliane Senehi Cohanim for repeated interviews she so kindly granted, but am particularly thankful for sharing her family photographs and

introducing me to friends and relatives who became sources of information for this book. Her husband, Mr Nasser Cohanim, was just as kind and cooperative.

282 Mrs Mary Lou Eshaghoff, who had heard the story for the first time in Paris in 1958 from Solayman-Khan Nasseri, her father's first cousin, provided the information. She had accompanied her father Habibollah Michael Eshaghoff to visit cousin Solayman-Khan at the age of fourteen. She later met the Nasseri couple on several occasions. Telephone call, 17 March 2004.

283 A city to Isfahan's southeast.

284 Telephone interview with the 81-year-old Mr Hayem Sassoon on 29 August and 19 September 2004. The author met Mr Sassoon in Paris in April 2008.

285 Menache and his brother Edward arrived in Paris in September 1938 in pursuit of higher education. They moved south to Grenoble anticipating a European war but one that would not spread far and would not last long. When the war came, Edward returned to Iran but Menache remained in France. The Vichy regime required 'Jewish registration' in 1941 and began wholesale internment of Jews in the area in 1942. Ezrapour was sent to work camps Uriage and Shapoli before being shipped to the concentration camp Gurs, 50 miles from the border with Spain. Unlike thousands of Jews who were deported from Gurs to Auschwitz-Birkenau and Sobibor camps, Ezrapour and 40 others were sent to Meyreuil work camp near Marseilles after having survived a month at Gurs in cramped quarters on daily rations of a bowl of watered-down turnip soup and 75 grams (2.4 ounces) of bread. At Meyreuil he worked in coal mines. Two Gestapo officers sought him out one day but the camp commandant identified him as an Iranian and he was left alone. The camp was liberated by US forces in August 1944. Ezrapour returned to Grenoble to complete his studies and returned to Iran with his degree in 1946. I am indebted to Mr Karmel Melamed in Los Angeles for Ezrapour's story. He interviewed Ezrapour and published his findings in *The Jewish Journal of Greater Los Angeles* on 6 August 2004 and *The Jerusalem Post* on 14 December 2006.

286 Mr Hayem Sassoon recalled the event again during conversation with the author at a Paris hotel, on 12 April 2008.

287 The name is seen to have been spelled differently, but it is spelled Mikaeloff by Jean himself.

288 Mr Majid Azizi in New Jersey in August 2006, Mr Raymond Senehi in California in September 2006, and Ambassador Farhad Sepahbody in Arizona in 2004, contributed to piecing Mikaeloff's story together.

289 Mark Mazower, *Hitler's Empire*, pp.238, 285, 286, 287.

290 Recalled at the fourteenth Jewish Film Festival in Vienna, hosted in part by the French Embassy, where Thomas Draschen's film *Children's Memories* was premiered in December 2006. France'es highest administrative tribunal, The Council of State, ruled on 16 February 2009 that the French government had been responsible for the deportation of thousands of Jews to Nazi death camps during the Second World War. French authorities, it ruled, had helped deport Jews even without being forced to by the occupying German Army. See Edward Cody, 'France Responsible in WWII Deportations,' *The Washington Post*, 17 February 2009, p.A8, c. 1.

291 Richard H. Weisberg, *Vichy Law & the Holocaust in France* (Amsterdam: Harwood Academic Publishers GmbH, 1995).

292 The date of the authorisation was 2 June 1941.

293 Report of Mass Arrest of Foreign Jews in France to Berlin, 27 August 1942, frame K345139, Confidential Report, 2 September 1942, frame K345142; German Foreign Ministry Archives, Serial K1509, National Archives Microfilm Publication T120, roll 4661.

294 Memorandum by SS Police Colonel Dr Knochen on Increased Arrests of Jews in Occupied France, 14 April 1944, Records of the Reich Commander of the SS and Chief of the German Police [RF-SS], Serial 225, frames 2763640-2763645, National Archives Microfilm Publication T175, roll 225.

295 See Fereydoun Hoveyda's recollection on 19 April 2004 in the Introduction.

296 He received his doctorate in law from the University of Geneva in 1936. The dissertation titled *L'Apprentissage en Droit Suisse* examined the late nineteenth-century labour market in Switzerland when trades were learned through apprenticeship and apprentices had limited or no rights.

297 Iranians preserved their calendar after the Arab invasion despite their conversion to Islam. They did so by changing the base year to the one commemorating Prophet Mohammed's *hejira* – retreat from Mecca to Medina in June 622 – thus making it an Islamic calendar.

298 Johoud, meaning Jewish, is considered a derogatory term. The proper word would be Yahudi, or the respectful Moslem term Kalimi in reference to 'Kalam-Allah,' the word of God and the concord with Prophet Moses.

299 Dellmensingen, as was the case with most German career diplomats, disliked both Foreign Minister Joachim Ribbentrop and his deputy Martin Franz Julius Luther. Many diplomats referred to the two as 'the wine salesman' and 'the furniture mover', after their previous professions and implying their lack of diplomatic competence. Dellmensingen became Sardari's friend and returned to live in Paris after the war.

300 Letter from Sardari to the German Embassy in Paris, 12 August 1942, German Foreign Ministry Archives, Serial K1509, frame K346183; National Archives Microfilm Publication TI20, roll 4668. Dr Asaf Atchildi's assertion that he had not met Sardari until 11 August (see Chapter three), may have been influenced by the date of Sardari's letter to Dellmensingen.

301 10–12,000 might have been a typographic error since in another letter dated 17 March 1943, he gives the estimate at 200,000–300,000 in a population of 15 million.

302 Traditional Iranian home architecture incorporated two parts, each with a courtyard. The inner part, the 'andaroun' was the private residence where the family members lived freely, women did not cover themselves and close relatives were welcomed. The second section, the outer courtyard 'birouni' was the quarter for receiving visitors, conducting business and holding formal meetings and receptions.

303 DIII-5133, Abteilung Prot. Nr. 1821/42; 21 August 1942, German Foreign Ministry Archives, Serial K1509, frameK346181; National Archives Microfilm Publication T120, roll 4668.

304 D III-5875, Berlin, 15 October 1942, German Foreign Ministry Archives, Serial K1509, frame K346192; National Archive Microfilm Publication T120, roll 4668. Fraz Rademacher, born on 20 February 1906, joined the Party in March 1933, although a member of SA since the summer of 1932. He studied law at Munich and Rostock Universities and became an assistant judge in 1932. He entered the Foreign Office in December 1937 and was assigned to the German Embassy in Montevideo, Uruguay, in 1938 as chargé d'affaires until April 1940. He was assigned to head D III, 'Judenreferat' upon his return and through Albert Speer's office with which Luther had good relations, received a 'Jewish apartment evacuated for him through special measures' in Berlin. Rademacher hired as his deputy Dr Karl Otto Klingenfuss who had replaced him in Montevideo, and returned home in 1942 when most German embassies in South America closed down. Klingenfuss worked at D III from July to December 1942. A previous assistant, Gerhard Todenhofer, had served at D III from August 1940 to July 1941 before moving on to another position in Abteilung Detschland. His replacement, Dr Herbert Muller, was Rademacher's acquaintance from pre-Foreign Service days with a similar education and background. Muller worked at D III from 11 November 1941 to 1 April 1942, when drafted into the army. Muller had entered Foreign Service in 1939, and been posted to the German Embassy in Tehran until the Allied invasion of Iran ended that country's diplomatic relations with Germany. Klingenfuss's replacement and Rademacher's last deputy in D III, Frtiz-Gebhardt von Hahn, joined the Nazi Party

with a law degree in April 1933 and entered Foreign Service in March 1937. Hahn was assigned to the German consulate in Geneva. Consul-General Dr Wolfgang Krauel was not a Nazi and uncomfortable with Hahn at first but Hahn quickly gained a reputation for moderation. Called up for active duty in the navy in February 1940 and sent to Holland, he was wounded when a bullet shattered his arm in June 1940. While still recuperating, he returned to D III on 12 December 1941 but had to report to hospital on 5 January 1942. He was finally released in December and while on sick leave from the navy, returned to D III until he had to report for active duty again in May 1943. The 'Jewish experts' of D III – Rademacher, Muller, Klingenfuss and Hahn – were careerists with similar backgrounds who had joined the Nazi Party after it had come to power, yet ended up working at D III fortuitously. See Christopher Browning, *The Final Solution And The German Foreign Office: A Study of Referat D III of Abteilung Duitschland 1940–43* (New York: Holmes & Meier, 1978) pp.23–34.

305 Ie 193/42, 5012 – Berlin, 2 October 1942, German Foreign Ministry Archives, Serial K1509, frame K346189; National Archives Microfilm Publication T120, roll 4668.

306 Rademacher to Gross, 15 October 1942, Berlin – DIII 5875, German Foreign Ministry Archives, Serial K1509, frame K34192, National Archives Microfilm Publication T120, roll 4668.

307 Reich Institute for the Study of the History of New Germany – Munich, 23 October 1942, German Foreign Ministry Archives, Serial K1509, frame K346194-6; National Archives Microfilm Publication T120, roll 4668.

308 Institute for Research on the Jewish Question, Frankfurt-Main Branch Office, 27 October 1942, German Foreign Ministry Archives, Serial K1509, frame K346200-1; National Archives Microfilm Publication T120, roll 4668. Monshi-Zadeh was an Iranian who returned to Tehran to form the National Socialist Workers Party known by its Persian acronym SOMKA –Socialist-e Melli-e Kaargaraan-e Iran.

309 Letter from Sardari to German Embassy in Paris, 29 September 1942, German Foreign Ministry Archives, Serial K1509, frame K346244; National Archives Microfilm Publication T120, roll 4668.

310 The originals of both letters are in Sardari's personnel file at the Ministry of Foreign Affairs, Tehran; copies are in the author's possession. Carrying currency across borders was subject to severe restrictions during the war.

311 The original letter is in Sardari's personnel file, Ministry of Foreign Affairs, Tehran.

312 It is suggested for instance that some friends discreetly paid the rent of his apartment in Paris. Telephone interview with Mr Yehuda Auqel in Paris, 21 March 2004.

313 Sa'ed had served as Foreign Minister in Ali Sohaily's cabinet in 1942 and 1943, before becoming prime minister in 1944. A career diplomat, he served as prime minister and foreign minister simultaneously. Sa'ed, educated in Europe, had served in the Caucasus, Turkey and Russia for decades. He was ambassador to the Soviet Union when Iran was invaded in 1941.

314 Anoushiravan Sepahbody was named Foreign Minister in 1945. The original letter is in Sardari's personnel file at the Ministry of Foreign Affairs in Tehran.

315 Chief of Security Police & SD, IV- B4b-2032/42 – Berlin, 8 December 1942, Serial K1509, frames K346203-5; National Archives Microfilm Publication T120, roll 4668. Eichmann's letter also illustrates the common accusation that Reza Shah harboured pro-Nazi and anti-Jewish sympathies to be shamefully wrong.

316 Party Chancellery Document regarding letter of 7 November 1942 (File D III 6282), Berlin – 7 January 1943, German Foreign Ministry Archives Serial K1509, frame K346212; National Archives Microfilm Publication T120, roll 4668.

317 Dr Kittel to Reich Ministry of the Interior –Vienna, 16 February 1943, German Foreign Ministry Archives, Serial K1509, frame K346239-42; National Archives Microfilm Publication T120, roll 4668.

318 Swiss Embassy in Berlin (Schweizerische Gesandtschaft in Deutschland, Berlin), 11 March 1943, German Foreign Ministry Archives, Serial K1509, frame K346216-7; National Archive Microfilm Publication T120, roll 4668.

319 Luther's rise to prominence was due to his loyalty to the Ribbentrops and the couple's support. He had impressed them when decorating their villa in Berlin's Dahlem district before Ribbentrop was named Ambassador to London in 1936. The couple took Luther to London and his meteoric rise in the Foreign Service began. Ribbentrop became Foreign Minister in February 1938 and by the end of the year Referat Deutschland's function as liaison to NSADP was given to the newly created Referat Partei under Martin Luther. Ribbentrtrop established the new division 'Abteilung Deutschland' on 7 May 1940 with Luther as its director, who assumed Referat Deutschland's jurisdiction over Jewish affairs. The new Foreign Office Division was organised, as Luther had proposed to Ribbentrop on 16 April 1940, with the following bureaus: Referat Partei, liaison to NSADP organisations; DII, security and international police cooperation; DIII, Jewish, racial and refugee policies; DIV, production and distribution of literature; DV, international travel by German dignitaries; DVI, special construction. Two months later DVII, geographical services, was added. When Ribbentrop added to Luther's duties the study of reorganisation – heading a Sonderreferat Organisation – the latter's influence grew in leaps and bounds. Luther however tried to remove his benefactor in 1943 by denouncing Ribbentrop in a memorandum for Walter Schellenberg, head of foreign intelligence in Reich Security Main Office (RSHA), who was supposed to prepare Himmler before delivering to him the memorandum. But the letter was inadvertently delivered directly to Himmler who in turn gave it to the Foreign Minister, who showed it to Hitler. Luther was arrested on 10 February 1943 and sent to a concentration camp in Sachsenhausen north of Berlin. His agency was then dismantled and his subordinate 'Jewish Experts' –Franz Rademacher, Karl Otto Klingenfuss, Fritz Gebhardt von Hahn, Herbert Muller – were scattered or sent to the Eastern Front. Luther died shortly after the war, aged 49. Eberhard von Thadden succeeded Rademacher after the reorganisation.

320 Christopher R. Browning, *The Final Solution And The German Foreign Office: A Study of Referat D III of Abeilung Deutschland 1940–43* (New York: Holmes & Meier Publishers, Inc., 1978), pp.76, 79.

321 Christopher Browning, *The Final Solution*, p.77. Unsigned Memorandum, 'Wunschen und Ideen' Inland II g 117), 23 December 1941, German Foreign Ministry Archives, Serial 1512, frames 372043-4; National Archives Microfilm Publication T120, roll 780.

322 Christopher Browning, *The Final Solution*, p. 77, 78.

323 Christopher Browning, *The Final Solution*, p.49. Abetz to Ribbentrop (Inland II g 189) 20 August 1940, German Foreign Ministry Archives, Serial K773, frame K204577; National Archives Microfilm Publication T120, roll 4199.

324 Ambassador Fereydoun Hoveyda asserted that Sardari had received a note from Abetz to that effect. The author has not found the letter in the archives.

325 Aryeh Leon Kubovy ed., *Yad Vashem Studies on the European Jewish Catastrophe and Resistance* (Jerusalem: Jerrusalem Post Press, 1967), pp.222, 223, 231, 233. The Council of State, France's Highest Administrative Court, ruled on 16 February 2009 that the French government of Marshal Philippe Petain had been responsible for the arrests, internment and transports to transit camps for deportation to death camps. See *The Washington Post*, 17 February 2009, p.A8, c. 1.

326 Thomas Keneally, *Schindler's List* (New York: Scribner, 2000), p.307; quoting Commandant Rudolf Hoss.

327 German Embassy in Paris in reference to letter from Sardari, 22 March 1943, German Foreign Ministry Archives, Serial K1509, frame K346223; National Archives Microfilm

Publication T120, roll 4668.

328 German Embassy in Paris, 17 March 1943, German Foreign Ministry Archives, Serial K1509, frames K346243-8; National Archives Microfilm Publication T120, roll 4668.

329 The persons identified in the list as Zoroastrian were a well known Iranian Jewish family from Isfahan (also spelled Esfahan or Ispahan). The consonants F and P may be interchangeable in Persian, e.g., Pars or Fars. This is probably the result of the Arab invasion of Iran. The Arabic language lacks the consonant P.

330 Mr Hayem Sassoon, Mrs Leila Sassoon and her younger brother Parviz Esmailzadeh confirmed the story. Sardari, according to Mrs Leila Sassoon and conveyed by Parviz Esmailzadeh, had achieved such saintly status among some Jewish communities in Isfahan that the Saturday prayers at some synagogues would always end with a prayer for him. The practice may have continued in Isfahan to recent times.

331 Some German documents suggest Sardari may have exempted 2400 Jews from German persecution. Iranian Jews residing in France at the time numbered about 500 and almost certainly less than a thousand. Some may have received travel papers to leave German occupied territories, thus not appearing on any list. See Juden Iran 1941–44, Pol. Arch., 22 Marz 1942, Deutsche Botschaft Paris an AA, also, Iranischer Konsul Paris an Deutsche Botschaft in Paris, 29 September 1942–22 March 1942. See S. Djalal Madani, *Iranische Politik und Drittes Reich* (Frankfurt am Main:Verlag Peter Lang, 1986), p.41.

332 Asaf Atchildi, 'Rescue of Jews of Bukhara, Iranian and Afghan Origin in Occupied France,' facsimiles of documents between pp.264–265.

333 A copy of the handwritten list of applicants sent to the Iranian Ministry of Foreign Affairs in Tehran is in the author's possession.

334 Referat DIII 6362, Berlin, 18 November 1942, German Foreign Ministry Archives, Serial 1509, frameK346202; National Archives Microfilm Publication T120, roll 4668.

335 Eberhard von Thadden, one of the 'Jewish Experts' in the German Foreign Office, was in charge of 'Jewish Affairs' in a new bureau *Juden Politik* under Horst Wagner. Luther's Abteilung Deutschland was dissolved by the following April. Von Thadden died in a car accident in 1964.

336 Lists from Sardari to German Embassy in Paris (Inland II A 3300, Berlin), 29 April 1943, German Foreign Ministry Archives, Serial K1509, frame K346251; National Archives T120, roll 4668.

337 Schulenburg was implicated in the plot to assassinate Hitler and was executed on 10 November 1944; Political XIII to DIII 2345, Berlin, 14 April 1943, German Foreign Ministry Archives, Serial K1509, frame K346220; National Archives Microfilm Publication T120, roll 4668.

338 Inland II A draft, Berlin, 10 May 1943, German Foreign Ministry Archives, Serial 1509, frames K346254-5; National Archives Microfilm Publication T120, roll 4668.

339 Berlin, 26 May 1943, German Foreign Ministry Archives, Serial K1509, frame K346256; National archives Microfilm Publication T120, roll 4668.

340 Foreign Office, Brussels, Nr. 1249/43, 31 May 1943, German Foreign Ministry Archives, Serial K1509, frame K346232; National Archives Microfilm Publication T120, roll 4668.

341 Foreign Office, Berlin, Inland II A 4557, Berlin, 3 June 1943, German Foreign Ministry Archives, Serial K1509, frame K346233; National Archives Microfilm Publication T120, roll 4668.

342 Von Thadden regarding the Djuguten, Berlin, 2 June 1943, German Foreign Ministry Archives, Serial 1509, frame K346257-8; National Archives Microfilm Publication T120, roll 4668.

343 Inland II A 5661, Berlin, 15 July 1943, German Foreign Ministry Archives, Serial K1509, frame K346263; National Archives Microfilm Publication T120, roll 4668.

344 German Embassy in Paris, 13 August 1943, German Foreign Ministry Archives, Serial K1509, frame K346264; National Archives Microfilm Publication T120, roll 4668. The references are to a letter by Dr Gross dated 7 January 1943 forwarded to Paris in February 1943 (D III 532), letters by Professor Euler & Adolf Eichmann (D III 7488) of January 1943 and Berlin's reactions to Sardari's letters (Inland II A 3300).

345 Swiss Embassy in Berlin, 7 December 1943, German Foreign Ministry Archives, Serial K1509, frame K346267; National Archives Microfilm Publication T120, roll 4668.

346 R VIII 00638/Inland II A 3719, Berlin, 3 March 1943 – 11 June 1943, German Foreign Ministry Archives, Serial 1509, Frames K346171-78; National Archives T120, roll 4668. The inquiry might have arrived too late. See, Serge Klarsfeld & Mazime Steinberg, *Memorial de la Deportation des Juifs de Belgique*. I am indebted to the Holocaust Museum archivists for tracing Liebovitche's deportation.

347 Swiss Embassy in Berlin, Inland II B, 22 April 1943 – 1 February 1944, German Foreign Ministry Archives, Serial 1509, frames K346273-78; National Archives Microfilm Publication T-120, roll 4668.

348 Inland II A 8772, Berlin, 17 November 1943 – 10 February 1944, German Foreign Ministry Archives, Serial K1509, frames, K346280-9; National Archives Microfilm Publication T120, roll 4668.

349 Inland II A 7313, Berlin, 6 September 1943 – 10 February 1944, German Foreign Ministry Archives, Serial K1509, frames K346291-7; National Archives Microfilm Publication T120, roll 4668.

350 Iranian poet and scholar from Shiraz, Mosleh-oddin Sa'di (1194–1292). Sa'di traveled widely and visited Ethiopia, Egypt, Syria, Palestine, Armenia, Turkey, Arabia, India and parts of Europe. He was captured by Frankish soldiers in Jerusalem and sent to forced labour at the fortress in Tripoli for a time before ransomed by a friend in Syria. He eventually returned home to Shiraz where he wrote the two masterpieces, *Golestan* (Flower Garden) a collection of stories in prose and poetry and *Boustan* (Fragrant Garden) a book of poems.

351 15 Tir 1327.

352 17 Azar 1331 of the Iranian calendar.

353 28 Khordad 1331. The first round of investigation started in 1947 and ended after the dossier reached Prime Minister Ahmad Qavam's desk with Foreign Minister Anoshiravan Sepahbody's recommendation. Qavam took the case to the Shah, who issued a royal pardon. The investigation re-opened when Dr Hosein Fatemi became Foreign Minister (Mossadeq's Cabinet) in 1951. Fatemi charged Sardari with two items of fraud amounting to 78,000 and 24,000 rials, funds allegedly earmarked for arms procurement from France. Fatemi reportedly held a grudge against Sardari since a few years earlier he had allegedly been implicated in a currency smuggling case between Switzerland and France and sought diplomatic cover from Sardari. Sardari had refused. Fatemi, after becoming foreign minister, persisted on prosecuting Sardari and ordered his detention. Royal favour was sought once again, this time by Amir-Houshang Davallou, reportedly close to the Imperial Court. Sardari was freed from detention and the charges against him finally dropped. Ambassador Hashem Hakimi, an Iranian career diplomat, recalls Fatemi's first meeting with the Foreign Ministry employees a week after assuming the office of foreign minister. Without greetings or introduction Fatemi blasted the 200 employees called to meet the new minister with a tirade of insults. The insults included 'you good for nothing layabouts who spend your time in cabarets and gambling halls and do nothing worth mentioning.' The Political Joint Secretary Amir-Khosrow Afshar-Qasemlou, a career diplomat, walked out of the meeting hall in disgust. A week later the employees were called to another meeting with Fatemi at which he apologised. He had been for years influenced by adverse propaganda against the Iranian Civil Administration in general and Foreign Ministry

in particular, he explained. After having seen the Foreign Ministry at work, he had realised that his outburst and prejudice had been unjustified. That prejudice may have affected Sardari's prosecution.

354 An official demand could have triggered an official bureaucratic reaction, bringing inflexible policy or ideological strictures into play.

355 Interview with Ambassador Houshang Batmanglich, 27 April 2004.

356 Fereydoun Hoveyda and Farhad Sepahbody asserted the connection, for instance with Krafft von Dellmensingen, in several interviews.

357 Fereydoun Hoveyda recalled meeting French leftists in Beirut, Lebanon, who confirmed to him Sardari's assistance to the Resistance. Interview, 21 April 2004. Farhad Sepahbody confirmed Beaufre's continued friendship with Sardari after the Second World War. M. Petrossian confided to Sepahbody at a meeting in Paris in the 1970s that Sardari had saved his life after the Germans had arrested him for involvement with the Resistance.

358 Hayem Sassoon, interview, 19 September 2004. Sassoon contends that despite its appearance, the radio was a short wave receiver, not a two-way radio.

359 Interview with Fereydoun Hoveyda, Los Angeles, 21 April 2004.

360 Farhad Sepahbody was Iran's last Ambassador to Morocco under the Pahlavi Monarchy until 1978. He is the son of Ambassador Anoshiravan Sepahbody who left Paris with his family for Vichy on 26 October 1940, four months after the Nazis had occupied Paris in June 1940.

361 The incident was confided under the condition of anonymity and non-attribution. The story was reportedly told the son by his late father. The author has not confirmed the incident independently.

362 Communication with Ambassador Farhad Sepahbody, 16 June 2003. Mouchegh Petrossian died in 1981.

363 Khalkhaali boasted to V.S. Naipaul during an interview that he had personally executed Hoveyda minutes after having sentenced him to death. He gleefully showed off the instrument of the murder to the visiting author, a handgun he had kept on the mantel. See Abbas Milani, *Moamaye Hoveyda* (Washington, DC: Mage Persian Editions, 2001), p.454.

364 The friend is Jonathan Steinberg. He has kept the contents of Sardari's flat and has offered to exhibit them.

365 Dr Firouzeh Ensha was one of the last relatives to visit Sardari before his passing and saw the bust in his room. The author has tried to locate the plate and the bust without success.

366 Rayhan and Soltaneh had nine children, Rachel, Malek, Showkat, Ibrahim, Tal'at and Rose, were daughters. Tal'at married George Senehi.

367 The author speaking with Claude in April 2004 inquired about certain documents issued by French and German police officials in 1940–1945 related to one of his father's interventions. 'He never spoke about this! I had no idea! My father is some kind of a hero and I did not even know about it,' he said with visible excitement.

368 Telephone conversations with the author in 2004. He was then 86 years old.

369 The author had the privilege to meet the family in Tel Aviv in January 2007. I am grateful to Mrs Qodrat Senehi and her children, particularly Ilana and Itzhak.

370 Conversation with Mr Raymond Senehi, Son of the late Benjamin Senehi, September 2006, and repeated discussions with Mr Majid Azizi, 2004–2009.

371 Communication with Ambassador Hashem Hakimi, 4 December 2007. Ambassador Ataabaky's deputy, First Secretary Kaaviani, is reported to have been very helpful to Jewish refugees as well. Abdollah Khosravi returned to Italy after the Second World War, married an Italian and lived in Rome. He disregarded his ambassador's instructions to ignore the Shah and Queen Soraya who had flown to Rome in 1953 after Prime Minister Mohammad Mosaddeq had refused to give up the premiership.

Khosravi and a number of Iranian residents of Rome welcomed the royal couple at the airport and put the embassy's Rolls-Royce at their disposal. Since the Shah did not have access to funds, an Iranian –Hossein Saadeq – covered the couple's hotel expenses until they left Rome to be welcomed back home three days later. Khosravi was kidnapped and murdered in Rome shortly after the Iranian Revolution. The Iranian government's general policy had been one of empathy and assistance whenever possible. Ambassador Ahmad Tavakoli, a retired Iranian diplomat, recalls that a number of Jewish families had crossed the Iranian border from Soviet Central Asia during the Second World War without passports, possibly from areas around Bukhara, seeking passage to Israel. They were granted Iranian passports to do so. In 1948 when Mohammad Sa'ed was Iran's prime minister a group of about 500 Jewish Kurds calling themselves Israelites and tracing their lineage back to the time of the Medes arrived in Tehran to emigrate to the new State of Israel. They did not have the funds to travel on their own and Israel did not have the money to support them. Iran, itself financially crippled, somehow procured the required funds to send them off to their new country. Dr Michael L. Chyet, author of a Kurdish-English dictionary, describes meeting a group of Jewish Kurds from Iran in an Israeli kibbutz in 1980–82 who spoke neo-Aramaic, a language similar to the one spoken by Christ. It is likely that the kibbutz residents, originally from Kerend, a town known for its delicate metal-works, silverware and pocket knives, located near the city of Kermanshah, are the descendents of the Iranian Kurdish 'Israelites'. Tavakoli was himself involved in a case as Iran's deputy chief consul in Milan, Italy in 1962–63. Some 50 Iranian Jewish families allegedly from the province of Khorasan on the Afghan border and known as *Mashadees* (from Meshad), but probably from central Asia, were residents of Italy holding Iranian passports acquired in Lebanon. In Italy they had married, raised families and sunk roots. Although some authorities questioned the authenticity of the passports acquired in Lebanon, Tavakoli renewed them. Fereydoun Hoveyda recalled a visit in Tehran by one of his former pre-war Beirut classmates Maurice Helouani in 1966, then an Israeli attorney. He was seeking assistance for a Jewish group residing in Milan with Iranian passports who were not from Iran. Later in 1974 when Hoveyda was at the U.N., Mrs Rita Hauser, a New York attorney, sought his assistance. The attorney represented a number of Iranian Jewish families in Syria, wishing to immigrate to Israel. The Syrian Government had kept them under surveillance, not allowing them to leave the country or to contact the Iranian Embassy. Hoveyda prepared a confidential report for his brother the Prime Minister who in turn presented it to the King, Mohammad Reza Shah. Again, the humanitarian aspects of the cases were thought compelling enough. The Iranian Embassies in Syria and Italy were thus authorised to assist. Correspondence with Dr Michael L. Chyet, 5 September 2003; Ambassador Ahmad Tavakoli, 3 September 2003; conversation with Ambassador Fereydoun Hoveyda, 1, 5, 8 September and 10 June 2003. Iraqi Jews, probably double the number of Iranian Jews, began looking to Iran for safety after Zionism was declared a serious crime in Iraq in 1948. Iraqi refugees were allowed to enter Iran and at times were smuggled in with the assistance of Iranian security agencies in large numbers. See Sohrab Sobhani, *The Pragmatic Entente: Israeli-Iranian Relations, 1948–1988* (New York: Praeger, 1989), pp.4, 86.

372 The country's name has always been Iran, Persia only one of its provinces. When several kingdoms were united by Cyrus, the Iranian Empire was founded over 2500 years ago, regardless of what the Greeks, or the French or the English chose to call it. Iranians have always called their country Iran, ever since its founding.

373 In a note to the German Foreign Ministry dated 17 August 1936 the Iranian ambassador is shown to be claiming that Iranians are Aryan and of the same ancestry as the Germans. The ambassador had discussed the issue with the Office of the Racial

Affairs, which had promised him further investigation and a ruling within the year. Diplomatic notes and a postcard from Karl Acker to the German Foreign Ministry [Abschrift Pol.VII 1292, 'Kurze Notizen zu dem Fruehstueck am Montag den 17.8], 17 August 1936, German Foreign Ministry Archives, Serial K854, frames K182741-4; National Archives Microfilm Publication T120, roll 4558.

374 Donald N.Wilber, *Riza Shah Pahlavi* (Hicksville, NY.: Exposition Press, 1975), p.182; Richard A. Stewart, p.10. Many Jewish families in Berlin who became Holocaust victims had resided in 'Iranische Strase'. Their names and addresses are prominently listed on the Monument to the Holocaust Victims in Berlin. I am indebted to Professor Ahmad Mahrad for photographs with highlighted names and addresses accompanied by an informative letter dated 21 March 2005.

375 Habib Levy, v. III, pp.856, 950, 963.

376 Marzieh Yazdani ed., *Records on Iranian Jews Immigration to Palestine 1921–1951* (Tehran: Records Research Centre, 1996), p.68, document 86; Ministry of the Interior, National Police Department, Political Bureau, Office of Records, No. 61162/35360, 23 Bahman 1317 (1317/11/23), Confidential. The case involved an accusation against several Jewish businessmen. The Shah took a personal interest in the case and ordered the National Police Chief to assure that 'no one is inconvenienced unless proven guilty'.

377 See Rafael Medoff, 'Churchill's record on Saving Jews,' *The Washington Post*, Saturday, 17 November 2007, c.3, and Michael J. Cohen, *Churchill and the Jews* (London: Frank Cass, 1985) pp.268, 269, 271, 281. Churchill favoured the so called Philby Plan to create an independent Jewish national home in the British mandate of Palestine, in a confederation of independent Arab states led by Ibn Saud of Saudi Arabia. President Roosevelt accepted the Philby Plan and proposed it to Ibn Saud after the Yalta Conference but Ibn Saud rejected it. After his re-election for a fourth term in 1944, he considered the possibility of a population exchange. He expressed his view on Palestine to Undersecretary of State Edward Stettinnus that 'Palestine should be for the Jews, and no Arab should be in it.' By coincidence, that was probably the very day, upon the assassination of Lord Moyne, that Churchill dropped his support for creating a Jewish state in a partitioned Palestine. Gerhard L.Weinberg, *Visions of Victory: The Hopes of Eight World War II Leaders* (New York: Cambridge University Press, 2005), pp.157, 207.

378 Michael J. Cohen, *Churchill And The Jews*, pp.266–267, 263.

379 See Chapter Seven, note 308. Davood Monshizadeh, an Iranian employed by the German Ministry of Propaganda during the Second World War, returned to Iran to form a National Socialist Workers Party with the acronym SOMKA, reflecting the Persian name of the party –Socialist-e Melli-e Kaargaraan-e Iran.

380 William H. Forbis, *Fall of the Peacock Throne: The Story of Iran* (New York: McGraw-Hill, 1981), p. 249, 250; Cyrus Ghani, *Iran and the Rise of Reza Shah: From Qajar Collapse to Pahlavi Power* (London: I.B.Tauris, 2000), p.44; Vincent Sheean, *The New Persia* (New York: The Century Co., 1927), pp.27, 28. Frederic Tellier, an astute French diplomat, wrote in 2006 that 'Nationalism is, in fact, the most widespread religion in Iran, the most spontaneously accepted, and the most deeply felt.' See F. Tellier, 'The Iranian Moment,' The Washington Institute for Near Eastern Policy, Policy Focus # 52, February 2006, p.6.

381 German Propaganda in Iran November 1939–September 1941, Berlin, 10 January 1942, German Foreign Ministry Archives, Serial 4739, frames E233106-20; National Archives Microfilm Publication T120, roll 2433.

382 The founder of the Islamic Brotherhood Hassan al-Bana of Egypt, who opposed British dominance, was also an admirer of Hitler and Mussolini, created his own youth paramilitary group (Kataeb, meaning phalanxes), and was proclaimed the 'Supreme Guide' in 1938. Bana was killed in 1949, but was replaced by Seyed Muhammad Qutb

who spent 1948–51 in the United States and considered the West 'sheer damnation'. He was arrested and hanged in prison in 1965. See Fereydoun Hoveyda, *The Broken Crescent: The Threat of Militant Islamic Fundamentalism* (Westport, Connecticut: Praeger, 1998), pp. 10, 24–27; Amir Taheri, *Holy Terror: Inside the World of Islamic Terrorism* (New York: Adler & Adler, 1987), p. 50; Amir Taheri, *The Spirit of Allah*, (New York: Adler & Adler, 1986), p. 98.

383 *Mein Kampf*, Ralph Manheim trans. (Boston: Houghton Mifflin, 1943), pp. 231, 296; also quoted in Lee Cameron McDonald, *Western Political Theory* (Boston: HBJ, 1968), pp. 519, c. 2.

384 The reference to 'state intervention' clearly counters accusations that Iran's government was a pro-Nazi regime.

385 Confidential communication from Tehran to Berlin, 207/41, 2 February 1941, Secret 207/41, German Foreign Ministry Archives, Serial 4739, frames E233100-3; National Archives Microfilm Publication T120, roll 2433.

386 'Esther was taken to the King Ahasuerus, in his royal palace, in the tenth month, which is the month of Tebeth, in the seventh year of his reign. The king loved Esther more than all the other women, and she won his grace and favour more than all the virgins. So he set a royal diadem on her head and made her queen.' Esther 2:16–17.

387 Houman Sarshar ed., *Esther's Children: A Portrait of Iranian Jews* (Beverly Hills, CA: The Center for Iranian Jewish Oral History, 2005), pp. 21–29.

388 Badi Badiozamani, *Iran and America: Rekindling A Love Lost* (Santa Fe: East-West Understanding Press: 2005?), p. 92.

389 One must hasten to emphasise that all Iranians, whether Muslim, Christian, or Zoroastrian, have suffered.

390 Mayer I. Gruber, 'The Achaemenid Period,' Houman Sarshar, ed. *Esther's Children: A Portrait of Iranian Jews* (Beverly Hills, CA: Center for Iranian Jewish Oral history, 2005), p. 11.

391 Saul Shaked, ed. *Irano-Judaica: Studies Relating to Jewish Contacts with Persian Culture Throughout the Ages* (Jerusalem, 1982), p. 305; Houman Sarshar, p. xix, 52.

392 Yusuf Sharifi and Riza Gawharzad, *Dard-i Ahl-i Zimmah: Nigarishi bar Zindagi-i Ijtimai-i Aqalliyathayi Mazhabi dar Avakhir-i Asr-i Safavi* (Los Angeles, CA: Ketab, January 2009).

393 Neguin Yavari, 'Toward A History of Jewish-Muslim Interaction in Medival Iran,' in Sarshar, p. 54. Avicina is known as Pour Sina (son of Sina) in Persian and Ibn Sina in Arabic, thus 'Avicina' in the West.

394 Abu Isa Esfahani founder of Isavieh (also known as Obadieh, a blending of Judaism, Christianity and Islam), Abu Musa Omran (a Karaite leader), Anan Ben David (founder of Karaitism/Qaraism), Molla Hayim El Azar, Abu Isa Ben Ya'qub al-Esfahani, Rabbi Mosheh Levy, Molla Rabbi Isac, Molla Yehuda, Benyamin Ben Musa Nahavandi, Rab Yussef Or-Sharga (whose shrine in Yazd is a destination for both Muslim and Jewish pilgrims). Houman Sarshar, p. 417–426.

395 Babai Ben Lotf Kashani, Babai Ben Farhad, Benyamin Ben Mishael (known as Amina), Khwajeh Bukharai, Yehuda Lari, Sa'id Sarmad (Aref Sarmadi), Mowlana Shahin Shirazi and Yehuda Ben Benyamin. Sarshar, p. 417–426.

396 Ebn Kamuneh, Molla El Azar of Hamadan (known as Lalezari), Ya'qub Ben Masa al-Nikrisi, Hakham Shim'un, Molla Siman Tov Melamed, Ya'qub Ben Yusef Tavus. Sarshar, p. 417–426.

397 Hakim Haqnazar (Qajar Court physician), Hakim Nur-Mahmud (Nasser al-Din Shah's personal physician). Sarshar, p. 42.

398 Abu Sa'd Ben Samha al-Yahudi and Ya'qub Ben Phineas top the list. Sarshar. p. 420.

399 Sarshar, pp. 57–59, 417–422.

400 John Limbert, *Shiraz in the Age of Hafez: The Glory of a Medieval Persian City* (Seattle & London: University of Washington Press, 2004), p. 23. Dr Limbert has recorded

the name 'Malek al-Yahud' – king of the Jews, but accepts the likelihood that 'Malek al-Yahudi,' may have been grammatically more appropriate, and more meaningful, thus perhaps the more correct form. Communication with Ambassador John Limbert on 15 May 2006.

401 Vera B. Moreen, 'The Safavid Era,' in Houman Sarshar, ed., pp.63–74.

402 Jean During and Zia Mirabdolbaghi, *The Art of Persian Music*, (Washington, DC: Mage Publishers, 1991), pp.42.

403 Sarshar, p.xxi.

404 Janet Afary, 'From Outcastes to Citizens: Jews in Qajar Iran,' in Houman Sarshar, pp.149–154.

405 Department of State, RG 59, Decimal File 1945–49, Box 7235, 891.00/10-647 –CSA, letter, Confidential, Tehran, Oct. 6, 1947, Addressed to the Honourable Secretary of State, Washington, Signed by Ambassador George V. Allen, on Jewish Iranians.

406 David Menashri, 'The Jews of Iran: Between the Shah and Khomaini,' Sander L. Gilman and Steven T. Katz, eds. *Anti-Semitism in Times of Crisis* (New York: NYU Press, 1991), p.358. Dr Menashri teaches at Tel Aviv University and heads the Centre for Iranian Studies.

407 Richard M. Weaver, *Ideas Have Consequences* (Chicago: University of Chicago Press, 1980), p.3.

408 For anyone who doubts this, the text of a letter from the US Embassy in Tel Aviv to the US Embassy in Tehran, dated 30 April 1976 should suffice.

> Ovadia Danon will be coming to Tehran in the near future on assignment with the Jewish Agency. He told us that Israeli leaders are somewhat concerned about the Jewish community in Iran; he described the community to us as being wealthy but becoming increasingly Persian. The community has been generally supportive of Israel but not as helpful as would be desired.

See *Documents of the United States Embassy in Tehran* Volume 11, 1979, p.54. Quoted in Sohrab Sobhani, *Pragmatic Entente* (New York: Praeger, 1989), p.134.

409 Andrew Scott Cooper, 'Showdown at Doha: The Secret Oil Deal That Helped Sink the Shah of Iran,' *Middle East Journal*, volume 62, No. 4, Autumn 2008, pp.567–591. Dr Kazem Vadi'i, former cabinet minister, Tehran University professor and royal advisor has also referred to the secret deal, after the Shah turned down a request to reduce crude prices. See 'Interview,' *Iranians* (Washington, DC), Vol. 13, No. 407, Friday 26 December 2008, p.12.

410 God, pleased with King Jamshid's good governance, granted him light and grace. The kingdom prospered, but Jamshid, overcome by hubris, commanded that he be worshipped, upon which God (Ahura Mazda) removed His grace. Without God's grace, the devil (Ahriman) helped Zahak to overthrow Jamshid and institute a tyranny. People finally revolted, overthrew Zahak and put on the throne Fereydoun, a just king. Another remarkable leader, King Kaykhosrow at the height of his power and popularity, having served God and his people well, decided to give up his royal powers and retire to the seclusion of the mountains. He feared that by staying in power for too long he would – perhaps unintentionally – displease God and the people. See Fereydoun Hoveyda, *The Shah And The Ayatollah* (Westport: Praeger, 2003), pp.38–39, 104.

411 Roy Mottahedeh, *The Mantle of the Prophet: Religion and Politics in Iran* (Oxford: Oneworld, 2002), pp.134–44, 183–85, 197, 383–84.

412 Shahrokh Meskoob, *Iranian Nationality and the Persian Language*, Ali Banuazizi ed. (Washington, DC: Mage Publishers, 1992) pp.15, 34.

413 Quasicrystalline patterns on the door of 'Darb-i Immam' shrine in Isfahan built in 1453 suggest that Iranian mathematicians had been at the time some 500 years ahead

of their Western counterparts. Harvard Professor Peter J. Lu, the *Washington Post*, 23 February 2007, p.A10, c. 1: 'They made things that reflect mathematics that were so sophisticated that we did not figure out until the last 20 or 30 years.' See Peter J. Lu and Paul J. Steinhardt, 'Decagonal and Quasi-Crystalline Tilings in Medieval Islamic Architecture,' *Science* V. 315, 23 February 2007, pp.1106–1110.

414 William H. Forbis, *Fall of the Peacock Throne: The Story of Iran* (New York: McGraw-Hill, 1981), p.204. The actual quotation is 'take from what is generally called Arabian science ... the work contributed by Persians and the best part is gone.'

415 Erroneously referred to as Al-kharazmi, as is the case with Al-Farabi, and other Iranians who have written important texts in Arabic as well as Persian.

416 Flamenco is said to have been inspired by Persian music. See William H. Forbis, p.207.

417 Those concerned about Iran's territorial ambitions ought to ask themselves how many times Iran has attacked its neighbours in the past 100 years, then apply the same question to the accusers, as well as their own nations.

418 Roy Mottahedeh, p.334.

419 Abbas Milani, *Moamaye Hoveyda* (Washington DC: Mage Persian Editions, 2001), pp.196–214.

420 See Fariborz Mokhtari, 'Security in the Persian Gulf: Is a Security Framework Possible?' *American Foreign Policy Interests* Volume 26, Number 1, February 2004.

421 Joseph Campbell, *The Power of Myth* (New York: Anchor Books/Doubleday, 1991), p.26.

422 See Fariborz Mokhtari, 'Central Asia and the Natural Flow of History,' *Persian Gulf Beyond Desert Storm* (Carlisle: Strategic Studies Institute, Army War College, 1993, pp.125–139.

423 See Fariborz Mokhtari 'Iran's 1953 Coup Revisited: Internal Dynamics versus External Intrigue,' *Middle East Journal*, Volume 62, No. 3, Summer 2008, pp.457–488.

424 Suzanne Maloney, *Iran's Long Reach: Iran as a Pivotal State in the Muslim World* (Washington DC: United States Institute of Peace Press, 2008), pp.75–77; H.E. Chehabi, 'Religion and Politics in Iran: How Theocratic Is the Islamic Republic?' *Daedalus* 120 (Summer 1991): 81.

INDEX